T0308804

A SINGING ARMY

LOUANN ATKINS TEMPLE WOMEN & CULTURE SERIES
BOOKS ABOUT WOMEN AND FAMILIES,
AND THEIR CHANGING ROLE IN SOCIETY

A SINGING ARMY

*Zilphia Horton and
the Highlander Folk School*

KIM RUEHL

UNIVERSITY OF TEXAS PRESS ◆ *Austin*

The Louann Atkins Temple Women & Culture Series is supported by
Allison, Doug, Taylor, and Andy Bacon; Margaret, Lawrence, Will,
John, and Annie Temple; Larry Temple; the Temple-Inland Foundation;
and the National Endowment for the Humanities.

Requests for permission to reproduce material from this work should be
sent to:
Permissions
University of Texas Press
P.O. Box 7819
Austin, TX 78713-7819
utpress.utexas.edu/rp-form

♾ The paper used in this book meets the minimum requirements of
ANSI/NISO Z39.48-1992 (R1997) (Permanence of Paper).

LIBRARY OF CONGRESS CATALOGING-IN-PUBLICATION DATA

Names: Ruehl, Kim, author.
Title: A singing army : Zilphia Horton and the Highlander Folk School /
    Kim Ruehl.
Description: First edition. | Austin : University of Texas Press, 2021. |
    Includes bibliographical references and index.
Identifiers: LCCN 2020008828 (print) | LCCN 2020008829 (ebook)
    ISBN 978-1-4773-1825-6 (hardcover)
    ISBN 978-1-4773-2155-3 (library ebook)
    ISBN 978-1-4773-2156-0 (non-library ebook)
Subjects: LCSH: Horton, Zilphia, 1910–1956. | Highlander Folk School
    (Monteagle, Tenn.)—History. | Women civil rights workers—United
    States—Biography. | Women musicians—United States—Biography. |
    Protest songs—United States—History.
Classification: LCC E185.98.H67 R84 2021 (print) | LCC E185.98.H67
    (ebook) | DDC 323.092 [B]—dc23
LC record available at https://lccn.loc.gov/2020008828
LC ebook record available at https://lccn.loc.gov/2020008829

doi:10.7560/318256

FOR THORSTEN AND CHARIS, AND QUINN ZILPHIA

Art is not a mirror reflecting reality, but a hammer with which to shape it.
—BERTOLT BRECHT

I have learned that people will forget what you said, people will forget what you did, but people will never forget how you made them feel.
—MAYA ANGELOU

CONTENTS

PHOTOGRAPHS FOLLOW PAGE 134.

INTRODUCTION

IN FEBRUARY 1935, Zilphia Mae Johnson arrived at the Highlander Folk School in rural Monteagle, Tennessee. She came as a
student in a six-week labor organizing session and stayed for the
next twenty-one years, becoming one of the school's most influential teachers and labor and civil rights organizers. She created
a culture program whose elements continue to be employed by
people organizing for freedom around the world today. But that
February, she was twenty-four years old, a college graduate, and
an award-winning classical pianist. She was close to six feet tall,
broad-shouldered and deep-browed, with dark hair and a wide,
easy smile that put people at ease.

The daughter of a coal mine boss in Arkansas, Zilphia had
watched her father, Robert "Guy" Johnson, work his way up
from the bottommost rung, the most dangerous job in the mine,
to management. On her mother's side, she came from a strong
matriarchy—Ora Ermon Howard was one of five sisters raised
by a single mother. Zilphia was the oldest of six sisters, two of
whom died in infancy. The four who survived became known as
a collective force: the Johnson Girls.

The sisters' family life was marked by privilege, ambition, persistence, and pride. Zilphia also developed a deep intellectual and
compassionate curiosity. She loved people and was determined to
get to know them and find ways to empower them. She wanted
everyone to have the opportunity to rise the way her father had.

Zilphia loved life and the world, the arts and nature. She was decades ahead of her time in her views of sex and race equity, in her environmentalism, and in her ideas about world peace and her vision of how the arts might make those ideas a reality. She knew art amplified empathy, allowing people to work together across differences that might otherwise keep them separated. "There is only one thing people must have in common before they can sing together," she would tell her students, "that is, that they believe in something."[1]

Contrary to some of the mythology around her, Zilphia had never been an organizer when she arrived at Highlander. Yet, when she was thrust into the role of culture director there, she created songbooks for striking workers and built a radical dramatics curriculum that evolved into the kind of role-playing program that was used to train civil rights activists. She built a culture that made the school feel like the home you never knew you always wanted, where the sexes and races are equal and where everyone pitches in and then relaxes around a fire and swaps songs.

She married Highlander Folk School (HFS) founder Myles Horton three weeks after meeting him, though that was not the romantic whirlwind it might seem. The Hortons were crazy about each other, but these two strong personalities formed a natural yin-yang relationship. They were deliberate and mindful about how their marriage, if treated less like the patriarchal tradition and more like an equal partnership, might realize Myles's vision of building an adult education center that could transform people's lives. And while he gets most of the credit these days for building Highlander into the force it became, the reality is that he did not—could not—do it alone.

Although he knew Highlander's culture program was going to be vital from the beginning, Myles had no idea how to bring it to fruition. But Zilphia did.

To hear their friends explain it, Myles was the head of Highlander Folk School and Zilphia was its heart. He pushed students and she gave them somewhere to land. Myles took them apart and Zilphia put them back together. These memories create a remarkable picture of how her contributions to Highlander were inextricable from its success. Together, these two changed the lives and hearts of countless people in such a way that, as their impact rippled out, America began to evolve in large, visible ways on labor and race.

Many others came and went from Highlander in those early years, contributing in valuable ways. Some remained after Zilphia died and carried her legacy forward. Many of their stories have also been overlooked in other accounts, but I have tried to give them some life here.

Myles's story has been told many times—by him as well as others who have written about the school—but Zilphia is usually included as little more than a footnote, her innumerable contributions distilled to nameless descriptions of the school's "spirit" and "atmosphere." To hear most authors tell it, she was simply his first wife, the woman who led the singing with her accordion after dinner.

I first encountered this diminished version of her life story while researching the histories of many of the songs she contributed. I immediately became curious. It didn't make sense that someone who was a catalyst for some of the most important songs of the twentieth century, whom Woody Guthrie and Pete Seeger both considered influential in their lives, could have possibly been just some charismatic man's wife. Moreover, it was hard to imagine that Myles Horton, who dedicated his life to helping people upend power imbalances, would have been content married to a woman who simply fell in line. Certainly, she had agency and a life worth exploring.

I thought there must be enough of a story for an article at least, so I contacted Guy and Candie Carawan, the folksingers and song collectors who had assumed a version of Zilphia's role after she died. Candie had done some of her own digging and had amassed some research on the topic. So had Zilphia's friend Aleine Austin, who had considered writing a book-length biography about Zilphia but simply never got around to it.

Starting from their research and ideas, I spent hours and days—in some cases, years—interviewing Zilphia's children Thorsten and Charis, her sister Bonnie Guy Johnson Flint, her niece Shelby Flint, and various friends of the family. Charis especially endured frequent calls, texts, and Facebook messages out of nowhere and pulled from her long, clear memory, through the analytical lens her parents instilled in her, to help me characterize Zilphia's personality and approximate her thoughts and feelings. When it came to characterizing the community that gathered at Highlander, Candie Carawan, Highlander librarian Susan Williams, and Zilphia's friend Anne Lockwood Romasco all responded quickly, across several years, to my various impromptu questions.

I mined the Zilphia Horton papers at the Wisconsin Historical Society, the Zilphia Horton Folk Music Collection at the Tennessee State Library and Archives, and the Guy and Candie Carawan and Southern Folklife collections at the University of North Carolina at Chapel Hill. I poured over numerous files in the library at Highlander Research and Education Center in New Market, Tennessee, which contains interviews with dozens of people who spent time at the school during its first half-century, from famous out-of-towners like Pete Seeger and Rosa Parks to locals like May Justus and staff like Septima Clark.

Through all this, I discovered that Zilphia's contributions to Highlander, as well as to ongoing movements for fairer wages, sex and race equality, and freedom in general, have been innumerable. She was at the center of a community of activists, organizers, and educators who looked to her for comfort and support, who all played vital roles in the building of the labor and civil rights movements, and who found deep inspiration in Zilphia's artistic energy, big-picture perspective, and calm, welcoming spirit.

Many who recognize her name will recall that she was an important catalyst for some of America's most vital empowerment anthems, such as "We Shall Overcome," "This Little Light of Mine," and "We Shall Not Be Moved." But Zilphia didn't just share these songs; she impressed upon people the importance of drilling into their meaning. She conveyed the power of music and the reason it can be effective. When people who had spent time with her sang these songs, they knew exactly what kind of tool they were wielding. She emphasized that music is the lifeblood in the heart work required to change the world.

As early as the 1930s, she was designing a dramatics program meant to create empathy, implicitly instructing people how to identify and navigate systemic oppression in order to dismantle it. Some of the people who became leaders in the civil rights movement first represented their labor unions at Highlander workshops in the 1940s, immersed in Zilphia's culture program during the school's integrated resident sessions.

As I write this, almost eighty-five years after Zilphia arrived at Highlander for the first time, her role-playing curriculum remains powerful and easily adapted to movement after movement. Songs she taught labor activists have been employed by folks as far away as South Africa, Iran, and China's Tiananmen Square. These songs have been heard again during recent years of renewed activism, as people continue to organize for fairer wages; sex, gender, and racial equality; and freedom in general around the world.

So why has Zilphia's story never been told?

Well, her life and legacy are two separate things, loosely tied together. At the time of her death from accidental poisoning in 1956, she had been focused on racial justice for more than a decade, and this work was beginning to emerge on the national stage. The Montgomery bus boycott captured the news media that same spring, thanks to Myles and Zilphia's friend and former student, Rosa Parks.

Zilphia and Myles had always been far more concerned about the work than about who got the credit for the work. There was no urgency to tell Zilphia's story, but there was a real, practical urgency to press ahead with the program she had created. They wanted to change the culture of America from one of overt, widespread racial oppression to one that at least reached mindfully toward equity. Continuity was more important than credit, and with hindsight, we can see how we've all benefited from that decision. But, at the same time, something was lost in the process.

Many of the people who knew Zilphia intimately have died, taking their stories with them. A few friends—most notably, Emil Willimetz and Charis Wilson—wrote memoirs that described their experiences with her in some satisfying length. Myles tried on numerous occasions before he died to make clear that she deserved more credit for the work she did. The Highlander staff has renewed interest in her story, and, with some dedicated digging, one can find significant pieces of it in their library and archive.

Zilphia was not a journal keeper, but she and Myles maintained an almost daily correspondence when they were apart that is remarkably telling. And they were frequently apart. Further, toward the end of her life, she dabbled in writing essays and poetry. These compositions depict a woman who struggled for her entire life with the imbalance between what was expected of her and the person she believed herself to be. They show a woman committed to the causes of fairness and equality. They also reveal her love for her fellow humans, but at the same time her longing for the space to simply explore the world and be an artist.

Late in life, Zilphia discovered a passion for filming people, animals, landscapes, and various expressions of cultures. Sure, she would likely have been on the podium leading songs on the National Mall when, in August 1963, hundreds of thousands of people marched for jobs and freedom. But it's just as easy to imagine that, had she lived longer, she would have eventually delved into filmmaking.

Indeed, considering the scenes that composed it, her life would have made a fine film itself. It would have begun in the room at Highlander, where Zilphia's spirit still commands attention and where I first came face to face with her legacy.

IT WAS MAY 2012, early afternoon at the Highlander Research and Education Center. I made my way upstairs from the dining room to the workshop space to find my seat. I passed a couple of people sitting together on the floor, harmonizing wordlessly. Someone else was singing the word "freedom" over and over in a meandering gospel melody. Two of the workshop staff were discussing something on the far side of the room. Someone else was sitting in a rocking chair, writing in a journal. There were coffee cups around, water bottles, people's various things. In the center of the circular room was a giant, handwoven rug and on its perimeter, a ring of wooden rocking chairs.

Through the large, tall windows that take up almost half of

the outer wall, I could see the Blue Ridge Mountains to the east, cutting a contrast against the grayish spring sky. The landscape between here and there felt wide open, forever, untouched. But I knew there was the civilization of Knoxville, Tennessee, a dozen or so miles down the road.

Suddenly, Marquez Rhyne, one of the Highlander staff, lunged forward. His argyle socks peeked out from under his gray slacks, which were held up by purple suspenders. His whole getup was punctuated with a neat little bowtie. He was singing out a call-and-response that amounted to the word "organize!" over and over.

Everyone stopped what they were doing, came together, and joined in. Soon the room was full of bodies standing and dancing, singing, "Organize, organize, organize!" Some people had their eyes closed. It was like a call to worship, almost. There was something deeply connective and spiritual about it, though the song was secular.

We spent the afternoon thinking about nonviolence as a tool. Sitting in our rockers, we went around the room, sharing whether we thought nonviolence was a valuable and effective tactic for achieving change. We played some games that challenged us to consider what nonviolence is and isn't. We sang songs and laughed a lot. We improvised through dialogue and role-playing.

When the discussion loosened up and everyone relaxed, one of the young Black women freely admitted that, after hearing stories from her grandmother and mother and thinking of some of the experiences in her own life, she wasn't sure sometimes if nonviolence was the right way to deal with white people.

This was the moment when the work of Highlander—the whole thing about its history and what it has done throughout various American social justice movements—came crashing into my head and heart. As one of the few white people in the room, I sat still with that comment and kept my mouth shut. Though I had never had even a remotely comparable experience, I understood that it was not my job to respond, but to listen.

I have sat with that comment for years. I sit with it now.

It is what comes to mind with every news story about police

brutality and every vaguely racist joke someone tries to pass off in my presence. That little loose moment changed my worldview in a split second. It changed my understanding of systemic racism from a thought exercise in my privileged white life to something with infinite tendrils wrapped around everything American—indeed, everything human. Tendrils that can only come undone if we all lend our hands and throw our weight into dismantling these systems.

Moments like that have been happening there for the better part of a century. This one came during a six-day workshop called the "Zilphia Horton Cultural Organizing Institute." This gathering of artists and cultural organizers from across the American South—Black, white, Latinx, gay, straight, bisexual, trans, and cis—was probably the most diverse group I've ever encountered.

It came barely two years into what would ultimately be my nine-year pursuit of Zilphia Horton's story, my attempt to understand her life and work well enough to bring it into the wider world. The folks at Highlander invited me to this gathering not so I could learn any facts or collect any research, but so that Zilphia's work might seep into my bones.

I had thought about her work so much by that point that I was unsure if I could experience it authentically, but I played the games and sang the songs and showed up anyway. She was so good at what she did that, decades after she died, Zilphia's cultural legacy changed me when I wasn't looking. It loosened me up and wrested me from my assumptions, so that when the moment of confrontation came I could, as the kids say, get shook.

So there I was, shook.

Unsure of what to do with my eyes in the uncomfortable silence, I looked around the room at the quotes that we had scrawled on paper on the first day of this immersion: "Everything you need is in your bones." "The revolution is to be well." "Self-love is a revolutionary act." "Art is not a mirror reflecting reality, but a hammer with which to shape it."

If ever there was a human who understood the way art is like a hammer, it was Zilphia Horton.

CHAPTER I

A LONG LINE OF STRONG WOMEN

IT WAS A COLD WINTER DAY in Montana, 1956, and Zilphia Horton was talking to a room full of farmers. She had been doing this for twenty years by then: Coming into rooms crowded with strangers, people tired of working hard for little pay and seeing their life savings dwindling. These people felt understandably powerless in the face of things over which they had little to no control: tariffs, wholesale prices, weather patterns. Zilphia would tell some stories, sing some songs. And somehow, when she left, they all felt braver, stronger, better connected.

It had been a decade at least since she had felt a kinship with the labor movement. She had long since moved her attention to Black civil rights and what others might consider the impossibility of world peace. But Zilphia knew from experience that, where people could find a modicum of hope, she could help them sit up just a little straighter and see just a little farther down the long road in front of them by teaching them some songs and reacquainting them with the gumption they had inherited from previous generations.

As she told those who were gathered now:

I think one of the most important songs that workers sing all over the United States is "We Shall Not Be Moved." I think we take it for granted and forget what it stands for and where it came from. If you would think of the simple words: Just like a tree that's planted by the water, we shall not be moved. Of course, it means that a tree that has its roots where there is water to nourish it, is so strong the wind can't move it. That's a spiritual [song], of course, as you know, and it means that our faith will not be taken away, nobody can shake it.[1]

And who doesn't like to be told that? By now she had their ears and she carried them through more stories. She told them about the time in 1935, a matter of months after she had started doing this work, when she led the singing after someone opened fire on a strike parade near Chattanooga. She recounted how the singing had made the workers feel brave in the wake of the machine-gun bullets and how "We Shall Not Be Moved" had cemented their organization.

The room grew still, so she kept talking. She told them about the Washington miner, Ralph Chaplin, who wrote a song called "Solidarity Forever" around 1920, when working people were starving and desperate. She sang a little for them:

It is we who plowed the prairies
built the cities where they trade
dug the mines, built the workshops
endless miles of road we laid
Now we stand outcast and starving
'midst the wonders we have made
but the union makes us strong.

She pointed out that workers were no longer starving and desperate, so singing the song can be a reminder of how much progress had been made. Recognizing the progress, she said, can help people believe that they can make even more. Zilphia had opened the minds and hearts of the union farmers, so she made her point—one of her last opportunities to get through to a room full of people before her life came to a sudden, shocking end: "Know your strength and how important you are, that by working together and voting together you can do all these things that you stand for and you believe in. You don't need guns. You have *ideas* and you need to stick together."

And then she told them to stand up, and they stood. She started singing, and so did they.

"Solidarity forever, the union makes us strong."

FORTY-FIVE YEARS EARLIER, on April 14, 1910, she was born Zilphia Mae Johnson, the latest girl child in a long line of strong women. Her maternal grandmother, Floribell Pyles, saw her childhood home pillaged by the Union army during the Civil War when she was barely more than a toddler. As a small child, Floribell watched President Lincoln's funeral train make its way through Tennessee to Illinois.

After her marriage to Thomas Howard, Floribell gave birth to five girls: Ora, Roxie, Zilphia, Elsie, and Millie. With such a large brood, the Howards moved from Tennessee to Arkansas to be close to one of her cousins.

Floribell raised her girls to be well versed in music and various other creative endeavors. Thomas died from influenza in 1893, "when [the eldest, Ora] was eleven years old, and Grandmother Howard was left to bring up her five daughters on a dirt-poor farm. They worked in the fields, but she would never let them work in anyone's home. It wasn't decent. They were brought up God fearing and independent."[2]

Despite the hardship and trials of raising five daughters by herself in a time when women simply weren't breadwinners, Floribell once told her granddaughter, Bonnie, that she never remarried simply because "[n]obody I'd have would have me with those five girls."[3]

Ora grew up working on the farm with her sisters.[4] Alongside her mother, she delved into creative projects with a passion that seems to have been passed down through the Howard bloodline. She gained enough education to become a teacher and left the farm after marrying Lewis Willett.

Ora and Lewis had a son, Tom, named for her late father. But the marriage was unhappy, and Lewis was a jealous man.[5] It was probably an easy marriage to quit, despite the times and despite what was expected of a young Arkansan lady just after the turn of the century. There weren't many avenues for a woman like Ora to assert her personal power. She wasn't yet granted the right to vote, but she could walk away from a bad marriage.

Through mutual friends, she met Robert "Guy" Johnson. Five years younger than Ora, he had also grown up farming and had a work ethic that wouldn't let him stay still for long. The courtship was quick. Guy married her, adopted the boy, and got to work on starting his own family.

Ora had six daughters with Guy, and she relished having so many little girls with whom to do big projects. She was especially formidable with a needle and thread. At the age of ninety-nine, Bonnie Guy Johnson Flint, Ora's second daughter, was still bragging that her mother could spot a photo in a fashion magazine, disappear into a room with some fabric, and emerge with the entire outfit as if she had plucked it directly from the pages of *Harper's Bazaar*, to which she, incidentally, subscribed.

Ora named her firstborn daughter after her sister, Zilphia Mae, and handed the others who survived infancy an array of plucky family names: Bonnie Guy, Elsie Newell, and Ermon Fay.[6] Indeed, the early loss of two of her daughters was simply one of many things Ora would endure. From the Civil War to the Great Depression, generations of Howard women had raised a parade of girls, confronting violence, poverty, uncertainty, and even the heartbreaking loss of newborn children along the way. Each impressed upon her daughters the imperatives of strength and persistence, faith and optimism. The women from whom Zilphia and her sisters came did not get worried; they got busy. They were problem solvers, creative souls, survivors.

GUY, BORN IN 1888 to Harris and Ida Johnson, was the second of three brothers. He grew up to be a tall and proud-looking man with dark hair, soft eyes, and a kind, playful smile. A master marksman and a skilled hunter, he brought home enough deer and elk each season to feed his family all year. He spent most of his career working in coal mines in Arkansas and Idaho before moving to Wyoming, where he ran a small lodge and took tourists out for hunts.

By then, Guy had left Ora for his secretary. His open-minded daughters encouraged this change, but, according to Zilphia's sister, Bonnie, it sent Ora into a spiral from which she never recovered. She spent the final years of her life traveling from daughter to daughter and demanding respect she didn't always receive from her grandchildren. Stories from Zilphia's children, Thorsten and Charis, and her niece Shelby recall Ora as a racist, judgmental, harsh woman. After the too-soon death of her father, the loss of two infant daughters, and two failed marriages, she was probably also heartbroken and lost.

DESPITE THE WAY THEIR MARRIAGE TURNED OUT, Ora and Guy provided a happy, comfortable home for the Johnson Girls' childhood. "Mother and Dad taught us to shoot a rifle, to fish, and to recognize all the trees, flowers, and animals in the woods," Ermon Fay wrote. "We would go camping—we would move into an old abandoned house by [the] river. . . . We explored the woods to find flowers and mushrooms. We always checked around the steps of the old house to make sure that there were no copperheads."

With all his ambition, in another place and time, Guy might have climbed the corporate ladder, but in northwest Arkansas in the first third of the twentieth century, the only climbing to be done was up the tipple to survey the workers loading and unloading coal at the mine entrance.

The year Zilphia was born, he was working as fireman. Dressed in wet wool, he would crawl into the mine ahead of the miners and "fire" the built-up methane by using a candle attached to a long pole. It was dangerous grunt work, and within a decade, he had earned his way out of the position.[7] Then, in just a couple more years, he had clawed his way up to management. Guy believed the best way to get ahead was to ignore other people's expectations and pour his whole self into his work—a lesson he learned from his mother Ida and no doubt occasionally regretted passing on to his eldest daughter, Zilphia Mae.

Zilphia would look back on her childhood, guessing she was about six years old when she began to notice things about the world around her:

A stock company had come to town. You know the kind, always had a Toby with a red wig, as a comedian, always had one play with a storm in it, lightning, rain coming in splashes, curtains flapping. . . . It was understood that I could never go to the show but once a week and that on the week-end. Next night, I approached my father about going again. He hesitated long, then said, "Why do you ask that?"

"All the other little girls go."

"Remember this—no matter if every single person in this town goes to the show, if that's your reason then you have no reason. You'll never amount to anything if you do things because other people do them."

This is the answer I always received if I had no real reason for what I asked. I think this was one of the things that made me a "doubter" as a child. If a person said a thing is true, I said, "How do you know it's true and can you prove it?"[8]

The coal industry had been booming in Arkansas since the end of the nineteenth century when coal was so prevalent you could grab some for heating your home by just running your fingers through the dirt. Especially in the years leading up to the Depression, mining in the area was seasonal work: The mines were alive with workers in the winter when coal was in high demand. Though some miners spent the off-seasons farming, hunting, or pursuing other jobs, many followed the mining jobs.[9] Guy also moved with the mining jobs, bringing his family along. The result was that his eldest daughter developed an early interest in the people and cultures that churned in the outside world.

Zilphia again:

I never tired of the stories he told at the supper table when he came home from work. They were about the miners he worked with—he called them Finns, Swedes, Dagos, and Poles. They were romantic to me for I had never known any foreigners. . . . The story that impressed me most was one he told about a Swede. He was sitting at the table and when he was about through with supper and we all knew it was about time for him to begin telling the story of the day, he straightened up, puffed out his cheeks, banged his fist on the table, shouted, "Man is yoost an animal. All he wants is something to fill his belly and nothing in his head. When will the workers preach the brother-hood of man?" Then he doubled over in laughter. I said, "Who is he?"

"He's an IWW."

"What's an IWW?"

The smile vanished from his face and he looked straight at me as though I were treading on forbidden ground. Then he said very seriously, "They are people who are never satisfied with anything."

I knew I was never to ask about it again. But the thing that I remembered most, was that, although he might represent something unknown to me, he was a warm and colorful person, and that I'd like to know another IWW.[10]

This story, about Zilphia's first awareness of labor unions—in this case, the Industrial Workers of the World, or the Wobblies—made her daughter Charis cluck, "I'm suspicious of any story that ends like that."[11] Yet, it lines up with the family dynamic reflected elsewhere in her papers, as well as with the history of that union. Regardless, the story of the IWW worker offers important context to the work Zilphia took on later in life.

THE IWW, FOUNDED IN CHICAGO IN 1905, was particularly successful in organizing variously skilled migrant workers who were chasing jobs out West.[12] No doubt Guy encountered countless Wobblies in the mines in both Idaho and Arkansas.

Union membership peaked when Zilphia was about five years old. It was one of the most radical labor unions in American history, welcoming anyone who wished to join—Black, white, foreign, female, and otherwise. It was also one of the most successful in employing culture as a means of organizing. One of its most famous members was Joe Hill, a Swedish immigrant and the creator of the *The Little Red Songbook*, which Wobblies carried in their pockets from jungle camp to work site to bunkhouse and picket line.

Hill had a knack for changing the words in church hymns to

reflect Wobbly ideals and singing them at work and on strike. One of his best-known songs was "The Preacher and the Slave," which he wrote in 1911, the year Zilphia turned one. It was sung to the tune of "In the Sweet By-and-By." Like many hymns, the lyrics of the original song focused on the promise of sweetness and beauty in the afterlife:

> There's a land that is fairer than day,
> And by faith we can see it afar;
> For the Father waits over the way
> To prepare us a dwelling place there.
>
> In the sweet by-and-by,
> We shall meet on that beautiful shore . . .

However, for so many immigrants who did the back-breaking, mortally dangerous labor of building railroads and streets, mining coal, picking fruit, and blasting out hillsides to make way for future transit, the IWW was committed to creating some semblance of sweetness and beauty in this earthly life. So Hill rewrote the song, frequently repeating the chorus in the kind of call-and-response method that made it easy to sing and learn, even for those who had never heard it before. Further, the repetition of the chorus ensured that those were the words that might come to mind during a long day when fieldworkers or miners might start to wonder if all that work was going to get them anywhere at all:

> Long-haired preachers come out every night,
> Trying to tell you what's wrong and what's right;
> But when asked about something to eat
> They will answer in voices so sweet.
>
> You will eat (you will eat) by-and-by (by-and-by),
> In that glorious land in the sky (way up high!);
> Work and pray (work and pray), live on hay (live on hay),
> You'll get pie in the sky when you die (that's a lie!).[13]

Hill was eventually charged with murder—many believe he was framed—and executed in Utah in 1915. Shortly before he was led in front of the firing squad, he wrote a final letter to his comrades in the union. The last words of that letter—"Don't mourn; organize!"—have been repeated often as a rallying cry for generations of labor activists and other participants in the long history of US social justice movements.

Zilphia wouldn't discover the *The Little Red Songbook* and Hill's impact on the American labor movement for another twenty years. But when she did, his work influenced the way she approached the new collections of labor songs she began publishing in the 1930s.[14]

THE JOHNSONS STAYED IN IDAHO for a year or two then moved briefly to Clarksville, Arkansas, where Floribell, whom the girls called Grandmother Howard, could help with the children. Never one to sit still for long, Guy moved the family a few more times before landing in Paris, about thirty-eight miles from Clarksville, when Zilphia was a sophomore in high school.

She later wrote that her family moved a total of nineteen times during her childhood, though she lived most of the time with Grandmother Howard in order to attend the public school in Clarksville and study piano.[15] She excelled at the piano, and by the time the family settled in Paris, she was able to make money playing in a small community orchestra that performed at local events.

Her time with Grandmother Howard strikes an interesting contrast to the lives of her sisters and parents as they moved around from mining town to mining town, often living in tents or finding homes on the fly as Guy worked his way toward a better life.

Grandmother Howard was always cooking and had an innate sense of what to do with food—after tasting something, she almost instinctively knew how to make it. Music was always playing, and there were supplies around for projects. Zilphia had plenty of time to sit and play the piano without having to compete with her sisters. So much of the hostess she became, the radical caretaker whose presence was vital to the well-being of Highlander staff and students, can be traced back to her grandmother's kitchen and all the creative avenues Grandmother Howard embarked upon with her granddaughter.

Nonetheless, Zilphia was happy when, in high school, she moved back into her parents' home. She and Guy had a special bond. He treated her the way he would have treated a son, and she relished the opportunity to draw his attention.

Guy's job as a mine manager in Paris was hard work with good pay, enough for him to afford to, once and for all, plant roots and build a house on a hill, at 1816 Klan Road, for his wife and children. Ora designed the lovely, spacious brick home with the Doric columns. She gave it a porch on the side and tall front windows that faced downhill. The six stairs leading to the main entrance fanned out from the door so friends coming for a visit might feel as though the home was spreading its arms to embrace them. The amount of care and passion Ora poured into imagining the home's design rubbed off on Zilphia, who was, like her mother and grandmother, always inspired and ready for a project. With all its modern conveniences, including indoor plumbing, and the amount of space it provided the family, the home stood out against the shacks downhill, where many of Guy's employees lived.[16]

As Bonnie recalled, the Johnson Girls would sit outside on the grass in summer, watching fireflies light up the dusk until the stars and moon took over. They went swimming in the town's reservoir, and in the winter, they donned costumes and made puppets with supplies kept in the cupboards under the window seats. They jockeyed for time in the phone booth that was installed by the stairs, with a door that closed, allowing a teenage girl the perfect illusion of privacy from her many sisters. They hosted teas and birthday parties for friends and were well known enough in the small town that every gathering was reported in the local paper, including the names of all those present.[17]

Zilphia especially captured the attention of the town with the awards she won in statewide contests for classical piano and singing. Her high school didn't have a glee club, so she started one, then took it to competitions and won. She also worked on the school paper and student council and was a member of the Long Hair Club, though it's not clear what the club did, exactly, at its meetings. The Long Hair Club yearbook photo shows a handful of young women with their long hair drawn up to look short, which was the style of the day.

When the City of Paris raised enough money to pave the main thoroughfare in 1928, the year Zilphia graduated high school, a lively six-day festival celebrated the new road.[18] It included a parade, a curious event simply listed as an "airplane circus," several band concerts, and events running daily from ten in the morning until seven thirty at night, with dance parties every night on the newly paved street. Presiding over it all was the lucky girl crowned Paving Jubilee Queen. The whole town cast votes for this honor and, though her sister Bonnie suspects Guy "greased the wheels" for her a bit, Zilphia was chosen to receive the crown and a beautiful, rose-cut diamond ring.[19]

In a large photograph portrait that remained in its ornate frame for some seventy-five years, Paving Jubilee Queen Zilphia sat on her throne in the Johnson family kitchen, posing in front of a backdrop that she painted. In her hand is a scepter, on her head a crown, and draped around her shoulders is a floor-length velvet and ermine cape designed and sewed by her mother.

The Paving Jubilee was a notable event, but the way Zilphia dressed and decorated for it wasn't necessarily atypical in the youth of a girl who would become a master of the big picture. After all, no matter what she was doing, it was never enough for Zilphia to simply dress the part; she believed in the power and utility of set design, developing not just the backdrop for the Paving Jubilee portrait, but also for a piano concerto she took to a competition. She labored for days, designing and painting the set to match the mood of the piece. Ora designed a dress to match the backdrop, ensuring that Zilphia's five minutes onstage would provide a complete, momentarily transformative experience for the audience.

When Zilphia and her sisters weren't romping in the woods, camping, or playing piano, cards, or dress-up, they would wander down the block on Klan Road to the "klavern," a large building constructed for meetings of the local Ku Klux Klan. According to Bonnie, the Johnson Girls liked the ledge that wrapped the building. They would climb up and walk it like a balance beam.

There was a piano inside, and now and then, they would sneak in to play it. None of the Johnson Girls were sympathetic to the Klan, but there's reason to believe that Ora was the seamstress responsible for their white robes.[20]

In the small mountain town, many of the men were involved in the Klan, particularly during the Depression years when work was scarce.[21] Most of the still-living family doubt that Guy was ever involved, but the KKK was so pervasive in the social life of Paris, Arkansas, that it was not a clandestine group nor was its meeting place secret.

When I asked Zilphia's sister Bonnie what the Johnson Girls thought of the Klan, considering how ubiquitous it was in their town, she was visibly uncomfortable. At ninety-nine, Bonnie was all elbows and limbs. She lived independently in an apartment where her baby grand piano took up most of the space. Remembering stories of Zilphia's house at Highlander, I recognized this as somewhat of a family design trend. Bonnie's small face was covered in the wrinkles of time, but her eyes were still wide and full of joy and her memory was clear. When she laughed, it was almost silent, not the full-breasted musical laugh of her sister Zilphia. Bonnie would giggle before opening her mouth wide in a silent guffaw, her lively eyes seeming to convey the Johnson Girl spirit and an unspoken question: *Isn't life just absurd?* She remembered wandering over to the klavern with some fondness, but she tensed when I asked what she had known about the Klan as a child.

In the South, well-meaning white folks have to reckon with the possibility that their grandfathers or beloved uncles were Klansmen. I've met some of these people and recognize the internal conflict that shows on their faces when they wrestle with how to love their family and yet hate things in which their family may have been involved. But there was none of that in Bonnie's sudden change of energy when I brought up the Klan and her memories of exploring the klavern.

Still, the proximity of the Johnson home to this klavern raises some interesting questions about how Zilphia became aware of race issues and what kinds of memories she carried with her into her work. Did she witness Klan activity during her teen years?

Bonnie didn't know for sure when her big sister became aware of racial disparity, which was probably impossible to miss, considering the size of the town and the well-connectedness of the Johnson family.

The Klan wasn't the only vehicle of injustice Zilphia encountered during these first few years in Paris. It was during the end of high school (1925–1928) that her curiosity about the imbalance of power took root. Her earliest memories of labor disputes were inextricable from the prejudices she witnessed from adults toward anyone who didn't have white skin or speak English. The way she experienced these things as interrelated tells us much about how she would later hop seamlessly from labor to civil rights, organizing as though they were two parts of the same whole. She wrote:

I remember . . . seeing a train load of Mexicans come into town—the first Mexicans I had ever seen. I was told they had been brought in to work in the mines because the men in town had decided they didn't want to work. Then when I went out to the mine before work time, I saw tents pitched around the slack [sic] heap. Instead of seeing the men I was accustomed to seeing, I saw Mexicans coming out of the tents dressed in pit clothes. I started climbing up the tipple as I always did and was shouted at. I came down knowing there was something mysterious about the tipple. I later saw a machine gun taken to the top. I heard Jack Pettijohn, top boss, cursing about what poor workmen the Mexicans were—saying that some had never worked in a mine before. I looked up and said, innocently, "If they're so bad, why did you go to so much trouble to bring them here?" They looked at me in amazement and I was told to go back to the truck and wait.

Then I remember being told one night that there was trouble at the mines. Then of hearing my father walking back and forth in the house after the lights had been turned off. Of hearing a car drive up the hill, crawling out of bed and tip-toeing in bare feet until I could see in my father's room—seeing him standing in front of the window with his pistol in his hand. Then as the car passed on, seeing him sit in the chair.

This night after night until it seemed like we never slept.

Then one afternoon at dusk, my father had fallen asleep in a chair. On the opposite side of the house, I heard a car drive up and stop in the pine thicket. I recognized two of the miners whom I knew and liked—who always smiled and had something pleasant to say when I was at the mine. I knew there was nothing for me to be afraid of, but I knew without knowing why, that they had come for something very mysterious concerning my father. I thought, "If I pretend they have come just for a visit, maybe it will smooth things over."

I opened the door and ran out to the car. They weren't smiling and they looked off in the distance. I ignored this and said, "Hello." Gomer Owens, sitting in the front, said "Howdy."

Finally, I said, "Did you want to see someone?"

There was a dead silence. Then Gomer said, "No, I guess we don't want to see anybody." And pushed his car in reverse and drove off down the hill.[22]

Though these memories were possibly embellished, their basic thrust is nonetheless believable.[23] She shared them in a way that eschewed judgment and told the story from the point of view of a teenager who was only just beginning to pay attention to the complex dynamics of the adult world. Zilphia was discovering how she could relate to people across severe tensions. Over time, she found a way to wield her femininity with intention and irony. She had an unconsciously genial nature that simultaneously put people at ease and shed light on the absurdity of their actions.

She also had an intuition that these men had come to harm her father and felt a responsibility to smooth things over. Though a bit naïve, her impulse in that moment would become a skill that she would sharpen with great mindfulness in the years to come.

ZILPHIA WATCHED THE WAY her father advanced toward a more comfortable life, privileged by his skin color, sex, and ability to work. She knew the amount of sweat and exhaustion that went into his profession. But she also saw how hard people like Gomer Owens worked—the men under her father's charge—and yet how little they had to show for it.

Her curiosity about how to improve those men's circumstances would cause much grief in her relationship with Guy
later. It would be the point at which his influence over her di-
verged from her own perspective. During childhood, though, Zilphia simply paid attention.

If there was trouble at work, Guy preferred to absorb it. He
would not have been happy to know that any of his daughters,
especially his beloved Zilphia, was witness to any of his stresses.
Nonetheless, she was perceptive and empathic, unable to rest until she knew not only what was bothering her father, but also
whether she could do anything to help.

She later recalled this period as being one of the most influential in her life. "As I think of it," she wrote, "it has been incidents
like these that have done more to shape my way of thinking than
anything else."[24]

CHAPTER 2

GROWTH AND EXPLORATION

IN FALL 1928, after her tenure as Queen of the Paving Jubilee and fresh out of high school, Zilphia moved back in with Grandmother Howard, choosing not to pursue the path of becoming a secretary, standard for an educated girl of her generation, but rather to matriculate in "piano and public school music." As her sister Ermon Fay wrote, "Our parents were ambitious for us, although they didn't push. But Zilphia, being the first born, probably was expected to achieve the greater heights."[1]

Besides, Guy's mother, Ida, had always wanted to go to college but was not afforded the opportunity. She drilled that fact so far into her son's head that he knew there was no acceptable route for his daughters other than that they complete a higher education. Guy never resented Zilphia's determination to expand her mind. He viewed the education of his daughters as one of the most important things he could provide for them, right alongside food and shelter. It helped that there was a respectable college mere blocks from Grandmother Howard's house.

The University of the Ozarks (it was the College of the Ozarks then) sits atop a hill in Clarksville, with dormitories on the outskirts, surrounded by tall pines. There's a rustic, summer camp feeling about the housing area, but the quad is wide open with paths crisscrossing the grass. Academic buildings line the perimeter, and as I walked past them in 2018, it was easy to picture a young Zilphia: tall and strong-bodied with a head of thick, long, dark hair, a book of music in her hand, strolling past the fountain, heading to practice on the piano in the chapel, a large, gorgeous stone structure situated on the west side of the perimeter. The day I visited, someone was rehearsing on the chapel organ, and the music piped across the campus, offering some semblance of human warmth to what was otherwise a quiet, frozen winter afternoon.

At college, Zilphia poured herself into every opportunity, excelling in academics, playing field hockey, and acting in plays. ("She sang in an outdoor performance as Orpheus and carried Eurydice across the grass to backstage," wrote Ermon Fay.) Through her classes and unbridled practice time, she developed an understanding of and affection for music history and musical forms around the world that would accompany her through the rest of her life.

She could spend hours at a piano—something she had always done for fun, but now there was a chance to perfect her approach to the instrument. She loved the dynamic nature of classical music and was equally as entertained by show tunes. But it wasn't enough for her to just play the notes. Zilphia always wanted to know where the music came from and why. Her intellectual curiosity was insatiable, and as she became enthralled with the work of composers like Franz Liszt and Johann Sebastian Bach, she learned about the men behind the music and gleaned from their stories how she might use music to move her own story.

She was enamored of their experimental compositions—Bach's forty-eight fugues, for example—and was intrigued by their creative employment of simple, traditional folk melodies in these grandiose works of art. She had yet to truly embrace the music of the common folk, so these compositions made a lasting impression on her.

Later, when she led songs for the labor movement, her notes about the reason for focusing on folk music emphasized this fact:

Music has been too generally thought of as an art for leisure
time—performed and enjoyed "by" and "for" the "chosen few."

Yet why has the simple folk song, though crude in form and sometimes breaking all formal rules of music, lived through the centuries?

Why has it had so great an appeal that it has been handed down from generation to generation by the singing voice? Why have composers such as Bach and Liszt spent months and years collecting folk tunes which they later used in their great compositions?

The folk song grows out of reality—out of the every day lives and experiences of people. It is this stark reality and genuineness which gives the folk song vitality and strength—which gives it real musical merit, enabling it to overshadow its imperfection of form. Where can more be found to sing about than in the joys and sufferings of people in their struggles for existence?[2]

Beyond the compositions of these artists, Zilphia was drawn to the worldviews of the Romantic composers—especially Franz Liszt and his contemporaries. Liszt published essays about the role and responsibility of an artist.[3] In their music, the Romantics tended to pour their hearts through their hands in a way that was not widely done until Liszt, Frederic Chopin, and Robert Schumann—among Zilphia's favorites—came along.

Though the piano was not to be her life's pursuit, it was one of her greatest passions. As the years passed, her career in music would see her spending many more hours on folk instruments, but on her own time, Zilphia would indulge in her uniquely passionate, emotive piano playing for hours on end.

The memories of her friends and family often begin with the way Zilphia seemed to enter a different world when she sat down at her piano. This was also recognized by her good friend Roy Harris, who became a fairly well-known American composer in the 1930s and '40s. Harris regularly sent Zilphia new compositions to play to get her feedback and then occasionally called upon her to premiere them in public.[4] On those occasions, Zilphia performed classical music in concert halls, taking a break from her rural, radical life and getting a small taste of what her life might have been like had she never landed at Highlander.

Her niece Shelby Flint, who became a professional musician herself, met Zilphia only a few times, but remembers the way her aunt's piano playing affected her at a young age:

> I remember going [to Highlander] and being outside, somewhere kind of near the living room, and hearing a piano piece being played. One I can't tell you the name of but that was familiar to me because we all grew up playing the same pieces. I'd heard my mom play this piece, too. I heard it like I'd never heard it before. First I thought, *Could that be my mom playing?* Then I thought, *It can't be her because she doesn't play like that.* Then I realized it was Zilphia. I was a kid, so I didn't have language for it. I know what I heard was authority and skill and interpretation and musicality like I'd never heard that piece played by anybody that I knew of.[5]

Having played with some of the finest musicians of the past half-century, Shelby notes, "I can still remember that feeling of being outside the house, hearing the music come floating out, and having it stop me in my tracks. She wasn't just playing notes."[6]

Zilphia was channeling Liszt, Chopin, and Schumann, whose musical ideas did more for her than simply provide artistic inspiration. Their lives and work, and their worldviews, planted seeds in her mind as to the role of an artist in society, what music was capable of doing for those who play it as well as for those who listen.

DURING ZILPHIA'S SOPHOMORE YEAR at college, thirteen hundred miles away in New York City, the stock market crashed, crippling the economy in a way that had not seemed possible since the previous crash decades earlier. Zilphia's later speeches and writing would remark on the stress the economy placed on local farmers and others in Paris. But when I asked her sister Bonnie about the Johnson Girls' experience of the Great Depression, in Arkansas, she shook it off.

In Bonnie's memory, people in large cities—whose way of life relied on things like grocery stores and shipping lines, landlords and whatnot—saw their lives upended. But out in the middle of the country, in communities that had always been poor and self-reliant, where people grew and hunted most of their own food anyway, the earliest years of the Great Depression barely registered as a blip—at least in the Johnson household.[7]

Local historians in Paris contradict this. For many of the coal miners who made up the labor force in Logan County, Arkansas, the Depression was plenty devastating. The Johnsons were simply better placed than many in their community because Guy was, by this time, a boss and mine owner.

That Guy was such a skilled hunter, and that both sides of the family had farms producing fresh food, meant that the Johnson Girls never went hungry. The only dip in their privilege that Zilphia's youngest sister Ermon Fay remembered was their father rushing home on Christmas Eve with a paycheck, sending Ora out to do the Christmas shopping they had been putting off. This was a minor inconvenience.

All four of the Johnson Girls were still afforded a college education because their father had done well for himself in the mining industry. The privilege was not lost on Zilphia—nor was the opportunity.

Still, Zilphia had no option after graduation other than to head back to Paris. There she took her music degree to the town square, where she played piano for the silent movies. And, while that may have been fun for her, it's easy to imagine Zilphia feeling as though her talent was wasted in such a context.[8]

Talent could be both a blessing and a curse when one is female and the boss's daughter in a small Arkansas town in the 1930s. It wasn't enough for Zilphia to be a big fish in a small pond; she wanted to *do* something. Many women of her generation went to college primarily to find a husband, but Zilphia wasn't satisfied with the typical way of things, much to her parents' dismay.

Unsure of her next move, she developed a habit of creating work for herself, treading water until she could think of a way out of town. For example, she started dance classes for children and exercise classes for adults. Though she had almost no knowledge of or experience with teaching dance, she started a ballet class for children anyway. It "finished with a recital in the local movie house." Ermon Fay remembered this well because Zilphia had dressed her littlest sister "in a red tutu."

Zilphia was restless. She was discovering that, in the eyes of society, it was now fine for a girl to get an education and even vote, but then she was expected to go home, marry a local boy, and raise his children. She had her boyfriends through the years, though none with whom she developed any real relationship. Probably her unconventional ideas made her too challenging for most of the boys in Paris. She had a certain élan that attracted men, but, Bonnie noted, "Zilphia was pretty pick-and-choosey about whom she went with. She didn't go out with a lot of people. There was one person she really was crazy about. His name was Robert Brown. I think she thought a lot about him, but she didn't think he would go very far. So she kind of broke it off, as I recall."

Going far was, for Zilphia, already an important prospect. When a cousin in Sallisaw, Oklahoma, informed her of an opening for a high school music teacher, she jumped at it. It was an exciting exit ramp for Zilphia, then twenty-two, and gave her the opportunity to do something that felt meaningful. Ermon Fay recalled, "The football team took one look at the new teacher and signed up for the class. That year—with her determination—the football team learned counterpoint."

But then during a lesson one day, Zilphia referenced the Biblical story of Jonah and the whale, making a flip comment to the effect, *You know that's not a true story, just a metaphor.* Parents were livid that a teacher would even suggest the Bible isn't factual history. She wasn't exactly fired, but it was suggested she go home.

In 1933, after just one year away, Zilphia moved back into the house on Klan Road. She got a job at the high school she had attended, but that wouldn't start until the fall. She formed a vocal trio with her sisters Elsie Newell and Ermon Fay. But Guy noticed his daughter's mind drifting, saw how she was hungry for some purpose in her life, and suggested she check out the free-spirited youth Bible study gatherings called "philosophy clubs" at the home of the new Presbyterian minister, Claude Clossey Williams.[9] Ermon Fay remembered philosophy club as being rather informal, "just to be sociable and talk about ideas . . . to talk about what kind of a world we live in." Zilphia had never been much of a churchgoer—her parents could never agree on a denomination—but, according to her sisters Bonnie and Ermon Fay, their father urged her to go and the suggestion piqued her curiosity.

CLAUDE WILLIAMS WAS TALL with dark hair, a neat little goatee, and a thick Tennessee accent. When he arrived in Paris in 1931, he had somewhat recently experienced an epiphany that the Bible was intended to teach the common person about empathy and freedom. Contrary to the fire and brimstone on which he was raised, Williams now saw the holy text as a tale of economic strife, with marginalized and oppressed people as the "chosen."

As he explained, those in positions of power—the Pilates and Herods of the stories—were always being shown the way by the fishermen, farmers, and penniless travelers of the Bible. Williams saw Jesus's teachings of love as the only way forward, and he believed this was a universal message that he was called to share. He liked to paraphrase the Bible: "If any man—white, black, or polka dot—says I love God and hates his brother, he's a liar."

He and Zilphia shared a ready, good humor and love for singing. They hit it off immediately. Letters indicate that Williams fell in love with her, but the feelings were not mutual.[10] He wasn't much younger than her father, he was married, and all Zilphia wanted from him was his intellect.

Still, when she entered Williams's house for the first time that spring, Zilphia couldn't possibly have known to what extent he would change her life.

Williams seemed somewhat unconventional in the context of Paris, Arkansas, but he was part of a well-connected network of Presbyterian theologians who had awakened to the notion that the Bible's lessons could empower individuals. He had been born and raised just north of Jackson, Tennessee, quite close to his friend, Myles Horton. Both men considered the other among the greatest minds of their generation.

Like many Southerners whose parents had been traumatized in childhood by their witnessing of Civil War carnage, Williams grew up deeply suspicious of "Yankees, Republicans, and blacks."[11] His family were sharecroppers and devoted churchgoers, and the path to righteousness was of deep, early interest to Williams.

He served in the army for five years in his twenties, then attended seminary at Bethel College in Tennessee. There, he met and married his wife Joyce and the pair headed off to his first assignment in a church in Auburntown, Tennessee, where he led services from 1924 to 1930.

During this time, Williams picked up a copy of Henry Emerson Fosdick's book *The Modern Use of the Bible*, which introduced him to the notion that the ancient text could be viewed as more of a philosophical and spiritual guidebook than a word-for-word documentation of actual history. This, together with lectures by social activist Alva W. Taylor at the Vanderbilt School of Religion, changed Williams's mind about the utility of Christianity. He began to see the teachings of the Bible as tools for social change and cultural awakening. These epiphanies led him to work with Black communities, something that no doubt scandalized his Auburntown congregation and opened his own eyes wide. He often said his mission was to "save [people's] never-dying, ever-precious souls from the devil's hell eternal."

By the time Williams arrived in Paris and encountered Zilphia Johnson, he was bent on social justice. He believed civil equality was an innate right bestowed upon humanity by its Creator. In letters, he discussed setting up an independent labor church in Paris with his friends Myles Horton and Jim Dombrowski, a Methodist minister and early staff member of the Highlander School.[12] They believed that joining religious theology with a man's pursuit of meaningful labor seemed only natural. They hoped to install labor temples not only in Paris, but also throughout the South.

They never quite pulled it off. Williams was not exactly met with open arms in Paris. He had been born and raised just the other side of the Mississippi River, but in the eyes of Paris teenagers, he may as well have come straight from the moon.

Zilphia was enthralled.

"Claude did things that our little town hadn't done before," Bonnie told me. "He was very attractive to all the young people."

The teenagers giggled and gossiped, sharing rumors that he sunbathed nude in his backyard. This rumor persists and was possibly true.[13] Perhaps he thought such exposure could help with his somewhat sickly constitution, despite the fact that this strip-mining town on the edge of the Ozark range couldn't exactly be trumpeted at the time for its clean mountain air.

Williams believed the path to righteousness was through experience and exposure, so he encouraged the Paris teenagers to take over church services, thinking that leading the services might help them worship more deeply themselves. This act of thrusting people into the spotlight who might not otherwise be taken seriously, expecting them to rise to the occasion, made a lasting impression on Zilphia.

Williams also wasted no time in engaging teenagers from the segregated Black community on the other side of the Paris railroad tracks for integrated Bible studies. This angered local Klansmen and made all the adults woefully uncomfortable, even as it excited the town youth, including Zilphia and her sisters. These integrated philosophy clubs focused as much on labor issues and the unlikely pursuit of desegregation as they did on the verbatim teachings of Christ.

According to Ermon Fay, they "attracted a small circle of young people who tended toward the left. It was a very exciting time and Dad didn't object to anything until Claude Williams started talking to the miners in Dad's mine."

Guy Johnson owned shares in a few mines around Logan County at the time, and Williams was interested in re-organizing the Paris Purity Mine specifically, which had been affiliated with the United Mine Workers since 1899.[14] Unimpressed with the leadership of UMW president John L. Lewis, who was anti-Communist, Williams was hoping to sway the miners into organizing instead with the Progressive Miners of America (PMA), a union that promoted local autonomy—something Lewis would not have granted the UMW Paris local.[15]

In 1934, roughly a third of the town's adult population worked for Paris Purity. The company's coal was sold as far away as Missouri, Minnesota, and Nebraska. Local coal historians maintain that "it burned clean and practically smoke free."[16]

The mining of coal has never been the safest job, but Paris Purity had a decent safety record. The mine had only been open a few years, and the men were paid a daily wage of one dollar, which was standard union pay at the time.

While Williams was talking up the Progressive Miners of America among Paris Purity miners, he was also organizing a meeting in town, the Church and Labor Conference, for that August.[17] In the end, Paris Purity didn't organize with the PMA, and the Presbytery of Arkansas transferred Williams out of Paris soon after his conference. His organizing efforts and scandalous philosophy clubs had caused local parishioners to petition for his transfer. By the end of 1934, he had been installed as minister at a church forty miles away in Fort Smith.

In January 1935, Williams was in New York planning a relief workers' strike, and he was arrested during the strike. However one looks at it, Williams wasn't even in town when a growing rift between Zilphia and her father hit its apex, which throws into question one of the few prevailing narratives that has been passed down about her life. This common and likely fiction posits that Zilphia tried to organize a union at her father's mine sometime in late 1934 or early 1935, though there's ample evidence to the contrary. In addition to the whereabouts of Claude Williams, the fact that Zilphia's family didn't recall her participating in any organizing effort before she arrived at Highlander brings the story's legitimacy into question.[18]

If there is any truth to the rumor, it probably amounts merely to Zilphia gauging the interest of her father's subordinates. Guy would have been annoyed if his daughter was prying into his professional affairs. Considering her personality and the strength of their family ties, however, she more likely learned of her father's frustration and told Claude what he already knew—it wasn't going to work.

Though the mythology of Zilphia, then twenty-four years

old, undermining her father's authority in such a public way to take her first bold step toward the labor movement is attractive, there's no indication beyond the memories of a few people outside the family that this actually happened. To hear Bonnie tell it, "she wouldn't have crossed father like that. She didn't have any reason to hold anything against him."

"I don't think Zilphia was actually a part of the organizing," Ermon Fay wrote, echoing her sister. "But [the organizing] upset our father."

The mythology holds that Guy learned of Zilphia's supposed organizing effort from whispers on the job and he lost his temper. He went home and upstairs to her bedroom, gathered all her belongings, and threw them out the window into the front yard.

Yet, there was no upstairs in the Johnson home at the top of Klan Road, much less any upstairs window through which to dramatically throw anything. If Guy wanted to make such a scene, he would have had to crawl up into the attic and force open the small attic window, then shove her things through one at a time.

If the mine organizing story is to be believed, it would have been made infinitely less dramatic by the tossing of Zilphia's belongings out of a ground-floor window that faced into the backyard, away from the street and the curious eyes of small-town neighbors. Guy had a temper, but this story makes him out to be a caricature of himself.

The true story is a little more complicated. It involves honest mistakes, youthful idealism, and the distinct likelihood that Guy Johnson never thought his daughter would actually leave.

CHAPTER 3

A RIFT

THE WAY ZILPHIA LEFT her parents' home and the reasons she did so are so consequential in the story of her life that it is worth backing up a bit to explore what is reasonably certain about the account.

It's clear that the lore about her organizing a union at Guy's mine and him throwing her things out the window is categorically false. At that time, young people didn't regularly engage in rebellion without good reason, and it certainly wasn't part of Zilphia's character. She eventually wound up in radical circles, but she was drawn to them more by her overwhelming sense of empathy and her desire to do good in the world rather than by some deep-seated disdain toward authority figures.

The mythology was passed down by activists who discovered her story in the 1960s, when youthful rebellion became the mark of an entire generation. What we would now call Zilphia's "rebellion" was far more nuanced and complex than the drama of the prevailing narrative.

It helps to consider the years 1933 and 1934 in her life. Piecing together the memories of her sisters, the stories the family passed down, and her personal letters, it becomes clear that Zilphia was simply following a path that those around her seemed not to notice at the time. Perhaps she didn't even realize she was on it.

IN SUMMER 1933, soon after she returned from the short-lived teaching job in Oklahoma, Zilphia started socializing with men,

but not in the sense that other girls her age did. She wasn't looking for a husband; she was looking for peers. She could shoot and
gamble as well as any of them, and she found their conversations
more stimulating, their questions more intellectually provocative
than those of the girls from her childhood.

At twenty-three, Zilphia was one of the few among her female
peers who had yet to marry and start a family. Even her sisters,
who shared her unconventional streak to a degree, were more
and more interested in finding a mate. But Zilphia sensed that
there was more to being young, comparatively well-off, talented,
and smart than prioritizing the location of a husband. Like the
young men in her town, she wanted to explore what she could *do*
in the world. And, like them, she developed an appreciation for
whiskey and cigarettes.

"At that time, nobody smoked. I mean, girls didn't, not in
public," Bonnie told me, making clear one of several ways her sister was beginning to stand out. "But Zilphia did."[1]

Zilphia was restless. She had traveled beyond the confines of
Paris and Clarksville, if only for a short time, and had tasted life
beyond what her father and mother could imagine for her. She
began looking around for another avenue, somewhere she could
go where the options were more expansive than "teacher" or
"secretary." But young women didn't just pack up and wander
away from their hometowns without a job or university to attend
or without a husband to take them.

Somehow she learned of seasonal job openings for young people at Yellowstone National Park.[2] Yellowstone is about fourteen
hundred miles from Paris, Arkansas—an overwhelming distance
in the days before Eisenhower's highways, when heavy American
cars topped off at forty-five miles per hour. Perhaps that was half
the allure. Zilphia applied and was hired for the 1933 summer.

Early that June, she and Guy tossed her suitcases in the car
and he drove her from Paris to Kansas City. The drive alone took
more than a day. In Kansas City, she boarded a train for Wyoming.[3] It was the farthest from home that Zilphia had ever gone
by herself.

She was hired to work as a waitress near the Grand Canyon of the Yellowstone. But she learned that the hotel's pianist had become ill. The search for his replacement was made short when Zilphia took to the hotel's instrument. She was hired as the summer pianist for the hotel orchestra and waited tables when the orchestra wasn't needed. The ensemble toured the park now and then but mostly performed in the hotel for the most distinguished and wealthy guests visiting the park in the thick of the Depression. It was the first time Zilphia's piano prowess would be required at a moment's notice, but certainly not the last. For starters, she was invited back the following year to fill the piano bench for another season.

According to Bonnie, the dorms that housed the workers were run as if Yellowstone was a boarding school. Women stayed in their dorm and men in theirs. Visitors were signed in at the desk, and a curfew was maintained. Seasonal workers who held managerial positions had access to golf carts, and though her work kept her busy, Zilphia hitched a ride on one as often as she could to explore the vast attractions in America's first national park.[4]

We can surmise that, because of the extent to which she was mesmerized by the scenery and culture in later travels, Zilphia was enchanted by the alien landscape of Yellowstone with its gurgling geysers and sulphur pools. The brilliant colors of dormant volcanic activity. The strange moonscape of Mammoth Hot Springs. The omnipresent wildlife and peaceful placidity of Yellowstone Lake. If she wrote letters home during this time, none were preserved. But the artist in Zilphia must have been inspired by the infinite expressions of nature in that park, so different from anything she had ever seen or imagined. And the park's visitors, traveling from far-off cities and countries, would have intrigued her.

"At the end of the summer," Ermon Fay recalled, "Dad would go back to Kansas City to pick her up. In the evening of her return, we would sit on the front porch, overlooking the town, watching for car lights coming from the West, hoping they would turn off the highway and come toward the house. Great excitement. She brought Navajo rugs, tourist trinkets from the outside world."

Having held Zilphia's treasures collected from afar, hearing her stories of late nights with her coworkers and of vistas in the beautiful canyon, all the breathtaking sights of Yellowstone, her younger sisters yearned even more to apply for their own summers at the park, and only Ermon Fay would miss out.

Guy Johnson was by then aware of the influence Zilphia had over her sisters. She was able to tell a story so well, any listener wanted to follow right along with her. It was a trait Guy knew well, since she had picked it up from him. She wasn't trying to lead anyone astray. She just wanted everyone around her to experience life's most dazzling possibilities.

That fall and winter, and the following spring, she taught music at the high school and went through the motions of being back home in Paris, as much as Zilphia ever went through the motions of anything. But as another summer came around, Zilphia was excited that her sister Elsie got a job at Yellowstone, too. In June 1934, the pair set off for Elsie Newell's first summer away from home—doing a maid's work, mostly, but also, when called upon, singing harmony.

By the end of the summer, when Zilphia and Elsie returned home, they had become bosom buddies. Guy noticed his eldest daughter was hardly growing into the young marriageable woman he had hoped would emerge. Rather than agreeable and delicate, she was daring and blunt. Still warm and entertaining, still easy to love. But, Ermon Fay wrote, "she was becoming mature, outspoken, and was as stubborn as her dad." There was a brooding determination behind Zilphia's brow that worried Guy. One adventurous daughter was tolerable, but he couldn't stand to see it rubbing off on Elsie. He hadn't worked his way up to middle class just to see his daughters become a bunch of tub-thumpers.

Zilphia, meanwhile, was fearless. She returned to Claude's philosophy club and stayed out late nights congregating with the men from the church, gambling at poker games, and shooting bottles in the woods. The ability to shoot was not unusual for Arkansan girls of her generation who came up hunting with their fathers, but Zilphia's gun skills set her apart. She was handy with a rifle, to be sure, but her pistol shot became very precise. As she once bragged to Myles, employing her sarcastic, self-deprecating humor, she had shot a cigarette on the ground: "Sort of restored my self-respect."[5]

Guy was beginning to worry that Elsie's marriage prospects—and those of Bonnie and Ermon Fay—could narrow if their sister continued on this path, influencing them with her worldview. When he heard that she had been smoking in public, that was the final straw. "He didn't want her influencing Elsie Newell," Ermon Fay recalled. "Dad and Zilphia were equally stubborn and independent, and the conflict became unbearable. She left, or 'was thrown out.'"

Even more than a half-century later, Bonnie remembered the tension with remarkable clarity:

> It was more than Dad could take. So he spoke to her about it. He didn't have enough courage to tell her that he didn't want her around the girls. He was afraid we'd all start smoking, so he wrote her a note, with words to that effect. . . .
>
> He wrote her a note and . . . put it under her plate where we all had our meals in the breakfast room. She read it, of course, but I don't even think he stuck around for her to read it. He mentioned that she was a bad influence on the girls, but he didn't make any suggestions about where she was going to go. I understand that he tried to get her to change her mind and she didn't want to change her mind.

Imagine Zilphia sitting down to breakfast, dressed for the day, hair piled atop her head, a gap-toothed smile across her face, and that characteristic giggle of hers reacting to some sisterly teasing. Then the smile slowly fades as she reads the words her beloved father wrote to her, telling her to either change her behavior or leave.

The one thing every version of this story has in common is that it was Guy who told Zilphia to go, and Zilphia who didn't even try to make amends. Guy expected her to argue, put up a fight, make her case, but Zilphia was happy to have a reason to leave. Ermon Fay remembered the incident as being "really a matter of one will against another."

Guy retreated in shock.

"And so then he wanted to take it all back, you know," Bonnie said. "It was almost as though she had died. Everyone was so heartbroken."

After a year in Oklahoma and two summers at Yellowstone, Zilphia was convinced the world outside of Paris, Arkansas, held opportunities she would never find at her parents' house, much less through marrying some Paris boy. Happy to have a reason to leave, she ran toward the only person she knew who had ties far beyond Arkansas, whose worldview paralleled hers, and who may have had some idea of where she could go next: Claude Williams.

She moved in with the Williams family, who had just relocated to Fort Smith after the Arkansas Presbytery changed his assignment to a church there.[6] Though Fort Smith was familiar, it was still a good hour away from Paris—far enough for Zilphia's anger to fall away as she settled into a new reality.

With Claude away, the daily rhythms of his wife Joyce and the children provided welcome reprieve from the tension that had long been gathering back home in Paris. Ever the kind hostess, Joyce set up a cot for Zilphia in the living room, expecting the family feud to blow over. Zilphia expected no such thing.

Williams had talked to her about the labor schools she could attend, tossing around some of the options that awaited a woman like her. One place he had emphasized, Brookwood Labor College, was a residential academy in Westchester County, New York. He believed that, with a little extra guidance and encouragement, she perhaps could become a teacher there. However, his connections—Howard "Buck" Kester and Ralph Tefferteller—thought she might have a better first experience closer to home at the Highlander Folk School in Monteagle, Tennessee.

Founded by Williams's old friend, Myles Horton, Highlander had opened its doors only a couple of years earlier in 1932. Williams thought Zilphia could find somewhere worthwhile to be and something productive to do at Highlander. According to letters, he was also interested in finding her a place to go where she could be with kindred spirits whose ideas could reassure her that she was not alone in her thirst for new ways of thinking and being in the world.

She received two letters, two days in a row, at the Williams home. The first was from Tefferteller, whom she came to call "Teffie," a classmate of Myles from Union Theological Seminary in New York City:

This is undoubtedly a time of crisis, a time when those who possess honest convictions should voice them and stand by ready to defend the rights of the great masses of our American people. One is able to delve below the realm of the superficial in human relations to find the strong bonds of mass strength that are so evident among the working masses. And you must realize that the very thing which has happened to you is taking place in the lives of countless individuals over the country during these days when the lines are tightening, forcing one either to the right or the left. I am hoping you will be getting into the social struggle in as effective a manner as possible.[7]

The second letter came from Kester, the executive secretary of the Committee on Economic and Racial Justice in Nashville. "You are a very courageous soul for taking the stand you are," he wrote, "and I am certain that you will never regret having done so."

Both Kester and Tefferteller suggested Zilphia attend the winter session at Highlander Folk School in Tennessee, and Kester added that it would provide her with a good foundation to continue on to Brookwood Labor College in New York or "some other more advanced labor school."

At Highlander, he told her, "You would also be able to make a genuine contribution to the school yourself. You will find a pleasant, genial group with which to work. The life is simple but exhilarating and stimulating."[8] Kester closed his letter by suggesting that she travel to Nashville and let him drive her the rest of the way.

The roaring '20s and the swinging '60s are well known for their bohemian generations. But these men were familiar with a burgeoning trend among progressives in the '30s, who were defying tradition and striking out in the name of justice and equality.

The deep explorations of Timothy Egan, William G. Roy,

Glenda Gilmore, and others reveal the 1930s as a decade when young people responded to incredible strife with an eye toward exploration and discovery—one of those historical moments when the collective consciousness begins to shift.[9] This is almost always eventually met with equal and opposite backlash.

The same year that Zilphia Johnson refused to bow to her father's wishes, Mickey Mouse was cementing his celebrity with *The Band Concert*, dust storms churning in Oklahoma would soon drive an opinionated young man named Woody Guthrie out of the Dust Bowl and into California, and Amelia Earhart was soaring in the skies.

Adolf Hitler was also, meanwhile, consolidating power in Europe. America and the world were shifting in large and lasting ways. There was something about being young and determined that compelled a generation to buck convention and grab hold of history's steering wheel. Whether or not Zilphia was conscious of the trend in her generation—maybe she met some like-minded folks while at Yellowstone—she certainly was interested in exploring the possibilities.

IN THE WINTER THAT BEGAN 1935, the biggest drought of a generation swept across the plains. But, on the Cumberland Plateau in central Tennessee, where Zilphia was headed to the Highlander Folk School, the weather was mild with frequent rain showers.

On a Sunday morning that February, she left Fort Smith. Her bags were packed for six weeks. She planned to return after the winter session and then travel on to Brookwood.

Central Tennessee was no farther from Paris than Sallisaw, Oklahoma. But Zilphia was going somewhere on her own, and for the first time, there was no turning back. She didn't know anybody in Monteagle. She had only heard stories about Myles and the others from the Williamses. She was going to see what she could learn, to get away, and to open her mind, her heart, and life to possibility.

"There is so much more to know than I am accustomed to knowing," she wrote soon thereafter. "So much more to love than I am accustomed to loving."[10]

Considering how much her worldview opened up once she planted roots at Highlander, one can surmise that she didn't have an inkling, when she arrived, about her future: the decades of countless names and faces, hundreds of songs, the births of two children, trips to big cities and foreign countries, meals and discussions with the First Lady of the United States, and cooking tips from foreign dignitaries. It was a parade of private moments that, when taken in full, would lead to a mainstream American cultural revolution. That kind of uncharted territory was simply not afforded coal miners' daughters from small towns in northwest Arkansas in 1935. Yet, there she was, once again gazing out the window of a train.

The country rolled by, past the wide-open farmland of eastern Arkansas, over the rushing muddy water of the Mississippi River, finally toward the foothills of a new range of mountains. I'm sure she shed a tear that day. But then she probably sat up a little bit taller as she watched the miles roll by, stretching the distance from the girl she had been in Arkansas to the woman she might become in Tennessee.

CHAPTER 4

EVERYTHING NEW

NASHVILLE'S UNION STATION IS a luxury hotel now, but in 1935, it was a remnant of the late Gilded Age, a glorious architectural achievement where everyday folks sat around, just waiting for a train. It was one of the great depots of its time. Its soaring tower housed the first digital clock in the United States and was topped by a statue of the Roman god Mercury. On the February afternoon when Zilphia arrived, a couple of pools in the station's lobby housed live alligators for gawking travelers. Why not?

For Zilphia, rolling into that building after leaving behind a long-escalating rift with her father must have felt like entering a new universe, a fresh start. She probably didn't know what to think.

Buck Kester was there, waiting, in the dark slacks and light shirt he typically wore, a hat on his head, a vest, and a necktie. He was a serious fellow with dark hair that was long on top, tight and clean around his neck and ears, but the sight of Zilphia would have spread a smile across his face. She had that effect on people.

By then, the place where she was headed—Highlander Folk School—had been open for barely more than two years, but its vision was just beginning to spin into high gear.

THE DRIVE FROM NASHVILLE to Monteagle took about an hour and a half as Buck and Zilphia followed long, winding country roads through undeveloped hills and small rural com-

munities. Eventually, they rounded the curve off the Dixie Highway onto Monteagle's Main Street, taking a left on Fairmont Avenue, then following as it became Tracy Road toward Tracy City.
There, between the two incorporated towns, a dirt road stretched
off to the north toward the community of Summerfield and the
Highlander Folk School.

Today, it's all historical territory with roads renamed for the
school and its friends and a plaque near the turn, distilling the
history of the school down to two short paragraphs. There's Marlowe Lane, named for Bill Marlowe, one of Highlander's first students from the community. His son J. D. was a hunter and miner,
a "real Daniel Boone type," with whom Zilphia became incredibly close.[1] There's also Justus Street and Monteagle's May Justus Memorial Library, both named for May Justus, the children's
book author and nursery school teacher. When the school opened
its doors, Justus had already been living for years on the edge of
the Highlander property with her life partner, Vera McCampbell,
and their impressive collection of hats.[2]

Across the street was a small graveyard and behind it, in coming years, Unitarian work campers would dig a lake. Students
would frequently hike there for a swim during hot days on the
plateau. Today, of course, it's called Highlander Lake, but in
1935, these landmarks bore no names. Everything was new in a
way; nothing was known. Territory was uncharted in more ways
than one.

These days, Highlander workshops take place entirely in the
large circular meeting space at the top of the hill in New Market,
but in those early days in Monteagle, staff led residential sessions
in the main house, between stints organizing "coal miners and
bugwood cutters" throughout the South.[3] Workshop attendees
were occasionally called upon to pitch in on site or on a picket or
to help lead recreations for a union that was trying to strengthen
its organization. The education Zilphia was in for was experiential, immersive, and profoundly intense by design.

Founder Myles Horton was passionate about the possibilities
inherent in a holistic education—one that continued whether a
student was having an intellectual discussion during a workshop,

sitting down for a meal, gathering around a campfire, or playing a game of volleyball to blow off steam. His vision was as experimental as it was radical, although it was also incredibly simple.

At its heart, the Highlander idea was to get people together to talk about their problems and solve them. That's pretty much it. Where students didn't have the knowledge, the staff could step in and provide information. This straightforward "popular education" approach was, like so many things, made infinitely more complex by the personalities in any given room.

Myles liked to tell people how the Highlander staff was able to get white folks and Black folks to ignore the Jim Crow laws and sit down for a meal together: "First, the food is prepared. Second, it's put on the table. Third, we ring a bell."[4] Much like Zilphia, Myles was a student of human behavior, a keen observer with skills so astute, he was able to simplify what seemed complicated to others. This encouraged his students to observe themselves and change their minds about what was possible.

Indeed, in order to appreciate the breadth of the other world into which Buck Kester drove Zilphia from Union Station, it's important to first consider the story of Highlander's founder.

MYLES FALLS HORTON WAS BORN in Paulk's Mill, Tennessee, on July 9, 1905, the eldest of Perry and Elsie Horton's four children.

In *We Make the Road by Walking*, Myles recalled that Paulk's Mill was "right outside of Savannah, Tennessee, down the Tennessee River in a misplaced part of Appalachia," but there's no official record of an incorporated town by that name.[5] Once, an FBI agent tasked with verifying Myles's citizenship informed him that he had found the cabin where Myles was born in that tiny, unincorporated community.

Elsie and Perry were both teachers, each with only a grammar school education. They became qualified to teach after a three-week summer course made them two of the most learned people in their community. In those days, in the Tennessee hills, it was standard that the teachers needed only a little more education than the people they were teaching. A college education wasn't synonymous with the ability to challenge and awaken a child's intellectual curiosity. That was viewed as an innate skill, and the elder Hortons possessed it in abundance.

They taught for years before the federal requirements increased so that teachers had to have some high school education—something the Hortons could not afford with their paltry income and a budding family to consider. Thus, one of the first events Myles witnessed in his life was his parents becoming disqualified in a profession at which they excelled because the rules for that profession had changed.

Now desperate for income, Perry floated through different professions for a time, including serving as a county clerk and landing on a sharecropper's farm. As Myles wrote in his memoir, *The Long Haul*, "We didn't think of ourselves as working-class, or poor, we just thought of ourselves as being conventional people who didn't have any money."[6] The family background of farming—in Myles's case, tenant farming—was something he had in common with Zilphia. The pair of them would later embark on a farmers' union effort that was as personal as it was political.

For Myles, the civil rights work was also personal. His grandfather, Mordecai Pinckney Horton, had grown up alongside a slave girl named Donnie, who, after the war, having few other options, stayed on with the family as a domestic servant and eventually Myles's nanny. She was one of Myles's most important early influences. "She always called us her children," he wrote. "It never made much difference to us whether Aunt Donnie or mother was taking care of us."[7]

Myles was part of a generation of Southern white children who were raised in whole or in part by older Black women. But where many of those white children were not able to reconcile their love for their nannies with the prevailing systems of racial oppression that they perpetuated, consciously or not, Myles recognized early on that Donnie's presence in his family was part of a dubious reality. She was as important to him as his mother, but to the world she was just another Black woman. He recognized the nonsensical disparity and determined early in his life to be part of an effort to correct it.

In 1927, when he was twenty-two and working as a student coordinator for the YMCA, he attended an integrated conference in Nashville. There, free to discuss ideas with the diverse array of attendees, he discovered that taking a Black friend to the library crossed a line. Another evening, he wanted to take a Chinese girl from the conference on a date and discovered she wasn't welcome in the restaurant he had chosen.

The following year, Myles held an integrated YMCA banquet at a hotel in Knoxville. The law allowed integrated meetings, as long as Black attendees stayed on one side of the room and whites stayed on the other. They could eat together, at separate tables. But Myles wondered what would happen if a room full of people was invited to break that convention. He set up the room so that there wasn't a clear "whites" side or "colored" side, and he simply welcomed all the guests to figure it out for themselves. He wrote:

> Now if you confront people with a reality that is different from the one they are used to and they don't know how not to do what they're supposed to in a given situation, they won't know how to act. When we entered the dining room the black kids started looking around and the white kids started looking around. They were all the same age, they were all Y members. They did what they were used to doing in a dining room—they sat down to eat. They did the familiar in an unfamiliar situation. I'm not sure they even gave it much thought at that moment.[8]

The Black waiters were nervous about serving this integrated banquet but ultimately went along with it. Nobody was hurt or arrested, and young Myles, seven years before the next integrated meeting he would host, was tickled that more than one hundred people in Knoxville, Tennessee, got to experience how actually unremarkable, and yet how radical, it would feel in 1928 to eat with someone of another race.

This was one of the first times Myles tested his hypothesis about how love and acceptance take over when someone is nonviolently placed in an uncomfortable situation. But it most certainly would not be the last time. Just as those who attended could not un-know what desegregation would actually feel like, so too could Myles Horton not un-know how good it would feel to effect real change.

His focus on love and acceptance was not accidental, but rather a key part of how he was raised and what was emphasized in his family. Aside from Donnie, his mother Elsie and his grandfather Mordecai were strong influences on the way he centered unconditional love in both his personal life and his vision for Highlander.

Myles remembered his grandfather as "an illiterate mountain man who was born before the Civil War."

> He said the only reason he didn't learn to read and write was that at the time he was supposed to go to school, there weren't any schools, and it never occurred to him, after he was grown, to go to school. The idea of lifelong learning just wasn't there. He wasn't embarrassed about the fact that he couldn't read or write. . . . Because of him I've always understood there is a difference between being able to read and being intelligent.[9]

Myles had a studious face framed by short, wavy brown hair. More intellectual than many of his peers, he also had a biting wit and no hesitation about using it. While he defied his teachers by reading the "wrong" books at school, he defied his pastor at Cumberland Presbyterian by challenging the notion of saving souls.

At one meeting with a famous evangelical preacher, who had earned his renown by "saving souls" in Africa even as he said the souls he didn't save were going straight to hell, a teenage Myles stood up and asked something to the effect of, *How many souls did you not save? How many of those people are going to hell?*

He could almost hear the church elders blinking in shock, but he sensed that there were some holes in the man's argument, so he continued. *You said that for every soul you saved there were a number of others who were destined for hell. But they would have gone to heaven if you'd never shown up and placed upon them the responsibility of choice, right? Wouldn't it have been better off for more souls if you had just stayed home?*

This theological challenge was the first of many Myles would deliver. By the time he started Highlander, intellectual provocation had become habit.

Though the Horton family regularly attended Cumberland Presbyterian Church, their membership there was less about strictly following the church's theology than it was about the family having something to do, a place to connect with friends and role models for their children. Myles's parents, especially Elsie, instilled in him an understanding that the most important thing in life was to love your neighbor as yourself. The only thing one needed to know about the Bible was this Golden Rule.

"She had a very simple belief: God is love," he wrote. "And therefore you love your neighbors. Love was a religion to her, that's what she practiced. It was a good nondoctrinaire background, and it gave me a sense of what was right and what was wrong."[10]

This fundamental allegiance to love became deeply ingrained in Myles's worldview. His strong, internal moral compass came from his mother, and he often ruminated on how it influenced him. "For several years I have been aware of the influence of my mother," he wrote in a personal essay. "I am aware of the connection of my social passion with my mother's interest in social work."[11]

Much later in life, looking back on how Highlander had evolved, he wrote, as if picking up where he had left off with that essay in his pre-Highlander days:

> I've taken this belief of my mother's and put it on another level, but it's the same idea. It's the principle of trying to serve people and building a loving world. If you believe that people are of worth, you can't treat anybody inhumanely, and that means you not only have to love and respect people, but you have to think in terms of building a society that people can profit most from, and that kind of society has to work on the principle of equality. Otherwise, somebody's going to be left out.[12]

Trying to serve people and build a loving world was the entire motivation for Myles Horton's life, and it was to be the glue that connected him with Zilphia, who shared this mission. The educational and organizing culture they built together would be viewed as radical, or partisan at least, by the outside world, but their motivation was always from a place of love and service. Often, they would disagree about tactics, but they were able to complement each other's divergent personalities and priorities so fully because they shared this core belief and because they were well aware, from the beginning, of their different set of priorities.

For Myles, in these early years, love and service, paired with what he viewed as the family business of education, swirled around in his mind. He knew he was motivated to do something more and bigger than may have been expected of him, but he had yet to find a way to make all his interests connect.

He earned his bachelor's degree from Cumberland Presbyterian College in 1928, then he spent some time working with the YMCA all over the state before hitchhiking his way up to Union Theological Seminary in New York in 1929. There he found the person who would provide his greatest intellectual challenge. Just as Zilphia's mind had been opened by her relationship with Claude C. Williams, Myles's thinking was to be deeply influenced by his professor, Reinhold Niebuhr.

Like Williams, Niebuhr—Myles called him "Reinie"—saw an intersection between theological discussion and political discourse. The inequity among social classes in America at the time ran parallel to the inequity portrayed in biblical stories.

Niebuhr believed Christ's life was focused on social justice, love, and equality for all. He viewed advocacy for the poor, the disenfranchised, and otherwise marginalized people to be the mandate of the modern preacher. "Nothing that is worth doing can be achieved in our lifetime," Niebuhr wrote in *The Irony of American History*. "Therefore we must be saved by hope."[13]

If any collection of ideas from history spoke toward the urgency of things like labor unions, women's rights, and Black civil rights, to Niebuhr's mind, it was the text of the Bible. "He was interested in human problems as well as the theological and philosophical ones," wrote Myles. "He also had a brilliant mind that gave off sparks. He was young and radical and full of enthusiasm, in addition to being a stimulating teacher, speaker and explorer."[14]

Myles agreed with his teacher's underlying philosophy but was averse to dedicating his own life to the pursuit and proliferation of any particular theology because he believed anything so debatable couldn't possibly hold universal truth. He was at Union because he felt there were things he needed to learn from the people who were teaching there. Things that would help him better understand his own path forward and the best use of his skills.

"I went to Union because I had problems reconciling my religious background with the economic conditions I saw in society," he wrote. "Reinie later wrote a book called *Moral Man and Immoral Society*, in which he talked about society being immoral, and about people being moral and how they can live in an immoral society, exactly my problem. I was moral and society was immoral. I wanted to see if I could get help on my ethical ideas."[15]

Many in Myles's generation, especially in New York at that time, gravitated toward the Communist Party USA (CPUSA) for satisfying these decidedly progressive ideas. But Myles was interested in universal truths, holistic thinking, ideas that dug deeper than any answers a single political party or religious denomination could provide. As such, for the rest of his life, despite the lengths to which many people would go to try to pin him as a member of the Communist Party, Myles steered clear and never became a member.

"My strong mountain background of independence," he said of his aversion to joining the CPUSA, "prevents me from pledging in advance to do what someone else decides for me. I could never do it."[16]

As Myles contemplated the teachings of Reinhold Niebuhr, mere blocks away were Paul Robeson, Bessie Smith, and Langston Hughes, thick in the throes of the Harlem Renaissance. Their poetry and music gave voice and energy to the cause of Black freedom, justice, and social and civil equity. Whether or not Myles spent any time in Harlem while at Union is impossible to know, but his future wife was certainly a consumer of that neighborhood's creative ideas. Over the next few years, the pair would clip poems by Langston Hughes from the newspaper to mail to one another, as they fired ideas back and forth about how to employ love and service to make the world a better place for working people everywhere.

Indeed, like the young woman from Arkansas whom he hadn't yet met, but who would soon enough thoroughly influence his life, Myles was part of a generation that witnessed the dawn of women's suffrage and the peak of the labor movement and saw the earliest seeds of a Black civil rights movement taking root on the fringes. He bore witness to the excesses of the Jazz Age. Given his intellect and almost intuitive understanding of economics, he was likely unsurprised when capitalism came crashing down just before his second year in New York.

He felt the desperate urgency of his generation, and he knew the time was ripe for moving in brave new directions. After all, what did absolutely anybody have to lose anymore?

IN 1930, AFTER ONE YEAR AT UNION, Myles enrolled in a master's program at the University of Chicago to study sociology.[17] He left the following year to pursue an idea: He had begun to envision an adult education center back home in Tennessee. He had read about Danish folk high schools and believed the philosophy behind them could hold promise for the people of lower Appalachia. Never satisfied by simply reading about something, he thought it was important for him to go to Denmark and see for himself. So off he went to Europe to immerse himself in Danish culture and to study the Danes' approach to collective learning.

There, people learned in communities from each other in a popular, populist manner. From Copenhagen, on Christmas night 1931, he wrote a little pep talk to himself:

What you must do is go back, get a simple place, move in and you are there. The situation is there. You start with this and let it grow. You know your goal. It will build its own structure and take its own form. You can go to school all your life, you'll never figure it out because you are trying to get an answer that can only come from the people and the life situation.[18]

Myles's charm, deep intellectualism, and musical mountain man accent endeared him to struggling mountaineers as well as to wealthy metropolitan liberals. It was the perfect combination for someone seeking to raise funds in the Northeast to start an education-based nonprofit in the South focused on giving people a space to teach each other how to change their own situation.

Though the school Myles envisioned would eventually prove markedly different from any number of other folk and labor schools scattered around the United States, it's important to note that there was an existing context for such a creation. For at least a decade, radical thinkers—the Claude Williamses and Reinhold Niebuhrs of the education world—had believed that adult education was one vital avenue toward empowering individuals and creating a "new social order." Groundbreaking educators had focused their efforts on schools like Commonwealth College in Mena, Arkansas, and Brookwood Labor College in Katonah, New York. The latter, opened in 1919, was the first labor school in the country. Another folk school aimed at getting Appalachian people back in touch with their own traditions in the name of social change, the John C. Campbell Folk School, had opened in Brasstown, North Carolina, in 1925.

Thus, by the time Highlander's first fundraising letter was sent in May 1932, it was to a pool of supporters who already had a baseline of knowledge about the utility of such a place. To add some extra muscle to his request, Myles enlisted his mentor to author the letter. Niebuhr held great influence in certain circles, and he sat on an advisory board for what Myles was then calling the Southern Mountains School.

Without a location settled, fundraising was taking place via The World Tomorrow, an organization that operated out of an office on Vanderbilt Avenue in New York City.

To potential donors, Niebuhr wrote:

> The southern mountaineers who are being drawn in to the coal and textile industries are completely lacking in understanding of the problems of industry and the necessities of labor organization. We believe that neither the AF of L nor the Communist

leadership is adequate to their needs. Our hope is to train *radical* labor leaders who will understand the need of both political and union strategy. Without local leadership a labor movement in the South is impossible. . . .

A small group of workers, above 18 years of age, will live with the teachers on a small farm where all will work, study and discuss together. Personal relations will play an important part. . . .

No one is to receive a salary. With the help of the community, in the form of labor and food, $3000 will launch the project and support it for the first year. An effort will be made to make the school more and more self supporting from year to year.

We are proposing to use education as one of the instruments for bringing about a new social order. Assuming that an individual can be integrated by having his interests aroused in a great cause in which he can lose himself, our problems—individual integration, relation of the individual to a new situation, and education for a socialistic society—become one.[19]

Meanwhile, Myles was talking up his plans among friends and one suggested he get in touch with Don West, a student of Alva Taylor at the Vanderbilt Divinity School. West was a poet and theologian who shared Myles's Niebuhrite appetite for building a better way forward for common people. He had also spent time in Denmark and had his own interest in starting an adult education center in the South.[20]

Myles and West started poking around Lower Appalachia for a space. They looked in the vicinity of Asheville, North Carolina, hoping to find a spot in Boone or Black Mountain. They appreciated the area's deeply rooted mountain culture and stunning vistas. So apparently did like-minded folks who opened Black Mountain College near Asheville in 1933.

Friends soon connected Myles and Don with a retired Bryn Mawr professor named Lilian Johnson, who had 250 acres and fourteen buildings in Grundy County in central Tennessee for which she was seeking a meaningful use.[21] Dr. Johnson—Highlander staff would take to calling her "Aunt Lilian"—was a radical with a strong allegiance to her social justice interpretation of Christianity. She also had a great interest in social equity and environmentalism.

She had moved to the land in question in 1915, after spending much of her career in New England. She planned to develop a community farm as a means of empowerment for the locals, as well as "a community center for the depressed mountain community where children could come for games and social gatherings and their parents could attend meetings and hear speakers."[22]

Her land had two homes and several small log cabins, plus a large, three-story central building. The downstairs of that building included a kitchen and meeting area; upstairs were enough bedrooms to house twenty-five people. There was a badminton court and a field for playing baseball.

Dr. Johnson knew that the people of Summerfield and neighboring communities had been left impoverished by history. Many had been born on land their predecessors had successfully farmed. But after Reconstruction, Northern industrial magnates had seized it to exploit the region and its people and to profit from mining its coal and logging its forests. Having stripped the land of its natural resources, most of the industries had bailed on the people by the 1910s, leaving behind rotten, sandy soil and no jobs.

The poverty was profound. By the time the Depression set in, Grundy County was the eleventh poorest in the nation. A few men could still find patchy work in the mines, and a couple of local craftspeople sold their handmade furniture and other wares in Chattanooga. But most families in and around Summerfield subsisted on what little crops they could grow, plus biscuits and gravy.

During the 1920s, Dr. Johnson created a county fair and recruited teachers for the underfunded and understaffed community school. The teachers she enlisted also provided literacy education for the adults in the community—a program upon which Highlander would build.

Despite all she did and tried to do in the area, locals developed a deep suspicion of Dr. Johnson's motives. As was true in so many parts of the South since Reconstruction, there was a seething resentment toward Northerners who came down to "save" the poor Southerners only to wind up exploiting them, their land, and their labor. Dr. Johnson had only good intentions, but she remained an outsider and that fact hindered her ability to effect real change in the conditions of the community. By 1930, she was looking to "turn the job of community betterment over to someone else."[23]

So when Myles Horton, who had grown up just over the way, came looking for some land on which to build an experiment in popular education, Dr. Johnson's ears perked up. She was so interested in her property being put to "good use," she told Myles and West that they could have it, including her home, for one year. If she was happy with the way Highlander was using the land, she would grant it to them for free. If not, she would reclaim it, and nothing would be lost.

Myles and West had been hoping for just such a break. They moved in that autumn 1932 and, with the help of friends from Union and Chicago, got to work. They changed the name of the school so that it might better speak to the people of the area, who referred to themselves as "Highlanders."

After a few months of settling in and meeting the neighbors, "put[ting] in a late garden, cut[ting] a little wood and [trying] to get acquainted,"[24] they began to hold community meetings that turned into impromptu sing-alongs and games. When problems arose between neighbors, or even within families, Highlander staff helped folks to organize and come up with solutions. Bible studies and poetry readings organically emerged. But it was months before the first residential session was organized, and it had exactly one student—"a coal miner's son who, after a few months in a conservative southern college, had come to us hoping that we would help him in facing some of the vital problems of life."[25]

DON WEST PROVIDED ideas and support, but it was clear from the beginning that Highlander's holistic, immersive experience was Myles's vision. There was much that he hadn't yet figured out, but he had a sense that education was best tackled with a "two-eyed" approach: Keep one eye on where the student is and another on where they would like to go. The mission, then, as educator is to help them find their way from Point A to Point B.

There would be workshops, but by keeping students together in a bunkhouse (and tents, in some cases) for weeks at a time, learning would naturally occur through their extracurricular conversations and activities—what Zilphia would codify as the culture program.[26]

In the 1930s, Highlander's early staff spent their free time trying to recruit students and raise money. In workshops, they led discussions that tackled broad, often intimidating questions like "What's wrong with the way things are?" and "How could your situation be improved?"

In a 1981 interview with journalist Bill Moyers, Myles said, "Adults come out of the past with their experiences. [We] run a program at Highlander based on their experiential learning, from which they may not have learned very much because they haven't learned how to analyze it, but it's there. The grist for the mill is there. Our job is to help them understand they can analyze their experiences and build on their experiences, maybe transform those experiences."[27]

The staff also explored and revitalized the old ways of the area—square dancing, food preservation, basket making, quilting, carpentry. As neighbors started to use the school as a gathering place, they began to see the benefits of forming cooperatives, and the Highlander staff was happy to help them organize in that way.[28]

In those first couple of years, Summerfield residents organized cooperatives around farming, canning, furniture making, and other marketable skills. In 1934, the Highlander staff helped them apply for $19,000 in Federal Emergency Relief Administration grants.[29] In the end, the funding was not approved and the only cooperatives that survived were a sewing co-op, which connected and thus empowered the local women, and a cooperative community nursery school led by Claudia Lewis, whom Myles had recruited from the Bank Street School for Teachers in New York.

When neighbors came to the school for cooperative meetings or Bible studies, Myles's sister Elsie Pearl offered childcare, freeing up the time and hands of the neighborhood adults. Indeed, Myles's entire family became beloved in the community around the school. His parents, Perry and Elsie—neighbors, students, and staff alike took to calling them Mom and Dad Horton—moved onto the edge of the property. Mom Horton was particularly focused on offering canning classes and evangelizing about birth control, both efforts in which Zilphia would eventually join.

Thanks to Franklin Roosevelt's New Deal, new labor laws started rolling out within Highlander's first two years and thus came new incentive for workers to learn about those laws and demand they be enforced. This gave the labor movement, which had taken a hit with the Depression, some new swagger. Highlander staff started training representatives from union locals on topics including *Robert's Rules of Order*, practical economics, and how to effectively file a grievance.

Though he was certain about the intellectual mission of the school and the involvement of work within the workshops, Myles wasn't clear about how to incorporate arts and culture—only that they were vital to the holistic education he wanted to offer. He had some kind of gut sense that he wanted to reconnect the community of Summerfield with the fighting spirit that had helped their ancestors survive much more challenging times. So even though tall tale-telling and square dancing had fallen out of vogue with the young people, he found storytellers and square dance callers to reintroduce Highlander's neighbors to their own traditions.

He also found people to make music. One, Rupert "Hamp" Hampton, offered piano lessons to local children. Myles also found good cooks to make food. But all these different people doing small pieces of culture work seemed to him a too-fractured approach. He wanted to find someone who could tie it all together with concrete ideas and a clear vision.

In February 1935, that person rolled up the street in Buck Kester's car.

CHAPTER 5

NEW IN TOWN

IF ZILPHIA WAS NERVOUS, she never let on. Every comment recorded about her in those first few weeks at Highlander mentioned her calmness.

She was one of a handful of folks from rather different backgrounds, pulled together for a residential session about labor organizing. "An Arkansas college graduate [Zilphia] with a degree in music who was seeking to find her role in the movement; a member of a Clothing Workers' local from Knoxville, Tennessee; a young textile worker from Atlanta and a transport worker from Finland, active in unions and cooperatives in his country, along with four men and women from the community."[1]

Zilphia was somewhat of a society girl by habit, inasmuch as Paris, Arkansas, had "society." She was accustomed to parties and gatherings and knew how to conduct herself with strangers. Her innate warmth drew people to her, and she knew how to direct their attention once she had their eyes and ears. All this helped her find her place in the workshops and ease into the hard work and hard play atmosphere.

During the second week of the workshop, the students were called upon to travel to the twin towns of Daisy and Soddy, Tennessee, to assist with organizing efforts. In keeping with the spur-of-the-moment nature of union organizing, the workshop attendees pitched in next to Highlander staff. There, Zilphia finally had a chance to spend some time with Highlander's founder.

Myles recalled, "I was always so busy while at Highlander that I barely saw Zilphia when she first came. . . . We stayed in the homes of strikers [in Daisy] for a week, and she and I saw more of each other there than at Highlander. I had a chance to take a new look at her, and I really just fell in love."[2]

Both were young idealists with commanding personalities, and with what we know of them now, it's easy to see that both had met their match. With an athletic build to complement his strong and nimble mind, Myles was often attractive to young women, but none had yet been able to ignite in him the kind of fire he possessed within himself and sought in a partner.

She was tall and striking, but it was Zilphia's intellectual wit that most people found disarming. She often giggled, not in an airheaded way so much as in the spirit of someone who recognized the absurdity of life and was thoroughly amused by it. Her sister Ermon Fay called it Zilphia's "we're all just people" giggle.[3] She had plenty of insight and knowledge and was able to retain a certain optimism about the world despite it all.

Once they connected, Zilphia and Myles dove into intimate discussions about cooperative living, sharing their personal histories and devising a plan for an equitable marriage based on mutual respect—one where each of them would remain in the relationship only inasmuch as it served them both. They also discussed, in depth, their aversion to conventional marriage.

Later that year, as she studied theater for several months in New York, Zilphia wrote to Myles:

> Human relationships are so delicate, one realizes love is in a constant process of evolution, constantly changing and taking new forms, increasing or decreasing as the personalities involved develop or vice versa. . . . It seems to me that we are striving for an independence balanced by a certain degree of dependence— the freedom of two personalities made richer by the blending of their complements and supplements. As incoherent and muddled as this may sound, I have earnestly attempted to put into words at least something of what I feel. I think that I can quote with

greater feeling than when I wrote them, "Our love is like the autumn leaves, apart from their branches, yet a more complete part of the whole."[4]

In his typical, more cerebral way, Myles would echo this in his autobiographical writing:

> In applying for admission as a student, February 12, 1935, in answer to the question, "What is your trade?" she had written, "Music." My trade was education. We were both interested in radical social change but realized that neither of us would give up our own way of working although at times there might be overlap. Could there be a marriage of equals? We didn't know the answer but decided to give it a try with the understanding that the marriage would last as long as it was mutually workable, as long as we had no children. That, we agreed, would require a different and possible permanent commitment. The current commitment was to try to make it work because both of us could see advantages in trying to enrich our lives through being and working together.[5]

Following the breadcrumbs in their letters, we can see that Myles and Zilphia didn't even cross paths much until they were in Daisy, their courtship amounting to about a week and a half.

The school's staff had formed somewhat of a bohemian culture, where affairs and open relationships were commonplace and acceptable. Thus, it's interesting to wonder why Zilphia and Myles didn't simply indulge in their attraction and then move on with their lives. But if Zilphia was ever going to marry anyone, here was the man. Why shouldn't now also be the time?

It would be tempting to guess that she was willing to leap into this marriage because her family ties seemed to be severed, but there's nothing in her character leading up to this moment to indicate that she felt she needed a man in order to feel grounded. Quite the opposite. She had developed a habit of exploration and independence, of not wanting to be tethered to anything or anyone. At the same time, she was drawn to unconventional people and radical thinking—two characteristics that Myles embodied.

"You have great feeling and express it through creative ideas," she told him at one point, "while mine is a jumbled mess of emotions. I think we are very good for each other."[6]

A marriage to Myles meant an emancipation rather than an entrapment, as marriage would have been back in Paris. Most of the men back home would have expected deference from her in a marriage, but Myles was interested in Zilphia both as she was and as she might yet become.

"I'm glad you had the opportunity to hear the Town Hall concert even though it does start old fires burning," he wrote to her in early 1936, referring to her innate pull toward classical music, which he recognized as incongruous with life in Monteagle. "Well, you know how I feel about you doing what you want to do but you also know how much I want to be with you all the time. I wish we could both live a thousand years—together."[7]

Myles appreciated Zilphia's desire to balance her varying interests. Thus, a marriage to him would grant her the opportunity to wander off into the wider world during an era when most people never even thought about leaving their hometown. And she could do this without worrying how her exploration might look to others. After all, making sure people could achieve their true potential was Myles's entire mission in life, and his wife wouldn't be an exception. He probably would not have even fallen for her if he had felt that she was after a more conventional arrangement.

Aside from the physical and emotional attraction, Myles also saw in Zilphia the potential to fill the conspicuously empty position of culture director—a position he still didn't entirely understand.

She exuded creative energy and had a magnetic personality. She had the knowledge and artistic instinct to transform what at that point was a vital, if disorganized, program, into something more like a vision with a corresponding curriculum. This was her opportunity to tie her music degree together with her experience as a teacher in the public schools of Sallisaw, Oklahoma, and Paris, Arkansas, even as she explored a long-percolating idea that music is best delivered within a context and that the arts have a purpose in the world beyond just providing entertainment. What was abstract to Myles was concrete to Zilphia, and she leapt at the invitation to explore what she could do with music and the arts in the context of this experimental atmosphere.

If she was going to be living and working at the school, she and Myles were going to have to reckon with their attraction to one another. Both recognized it as more than simply a physical magnetism.

Though she wrote gushy love letter after gushy love letter about wanting to pour herself into Myles, to become something new with him physically or emotionally, she had never wanted to tether herself to anyone else's intellect—neither to their ideas nor to their ideals. She would not line up behind a husband. She would agree with Myles when and where she agreed with him. When she disagreed, she vowed to make it known.

"Good by and I love you," she signed one brief letter a year or two after their marriage, "but don't keep on treating me this way."[8]

There was a sweetness to this intentional marriage as well. In their letters, the Hortons regularly fawned over one another, expressing great longing, as well as concern for each other's well-being. Zilphia once closed a letter: "Are you working in the afternoon? Are you drinking milk between meals, and are you going to bed soon enough? Answer these truthfully young man."[9] Their commitment to an egalitarian bond and her ability to call him out in a loving and effective way was just one way in which their marriage was atypical for the times.

The wedding ceremony, too, was unconventional. To officiate, they enlisted Reverend A. J. DeJarnette, who had led the strike march in Soddy-Daisy, carrying an American flag. A "sweet and gentle man,"[10] the Reverend was a firm believer in the cause of justice, and his involvement in the Daisy strike would cost him his ministerial job, but not before he officiated the wedding of Myles Falls Horton and Zilphia Mae Johnson. First, though, they had to wait for him to arrive at Highlander from Soddy.

Thus, with twelve hours to prepare, the couple got to work planning the wedding. Zilphia organized some people to help her pick fresh flowers to decorate the room. It was early March, before the colors and abundance of full spring, but she was able to find enough daffodils and other early blossoms to suit her.

In a letter dated March 7, 1935, someone named Hilda wrote at length to their friend Dorothy:[11]

Yesterday Myles got married to Zelphia [*sic*] Mae Johnson, the daughter of a Paris Arkansas mine owner, who came just a month ago this coming Monday!

They were as surprised as anybody else and maybe more so! But those of us who were with them during the days at the strike, were not surprised at the fundamental issue . . . only at the suddenness of the wedding. Zelphia is a very capable, calm, determined girl . . . full of poise and guts, and at the same time lots of charm. She doesn't show her feelings very much, but is capable of carrying through big decisions with security. . . . If she was calm, Myles was emphatically not. I never saw anyone so excited inwardly. The rest of us all accepted the marriage as naturally as we did the strike occurrences . . . all a part of radical living! I think they were sensible, for there is a chance for a honeymoon in a cabin in Florida, out of the blue . . . and it's vacation time for everybody.

The wedding . . . was very simple. We had a big dinner with the tables down the middle of the room and daffodils, which had just come out. Franz, the two organizers whose strike we helped to win, Doc Holder and Hunkie, and Bill, the DeJarnettes, with their beautiful young daughter . . . made up the party. Mr. Lutman walked in during the feast and walked out again none the wiser. That great big boy (name?) came in just before the ceremony and stayed a little surprised, but not showing it. Hamp played softly during, and kept everybody happy before and after, running around pretending to take pictures on a camera that had no film. They all left about four. The sun came out and pictures were taken on the lawn. Zelphia was the most collected member of the party. I can just imagine what it would be like to get married among almost complete strangers to a man you had known three weeks! . . . When she really gets into work here and sees its importance, I think she will be very much liked by the community.[12]

Zilphia had never been predisposed to journaling, but she also recorded her experience of the wedding, though in sparer terms:

Mar. 6, 1935

Weds morn—raining and Myles' suit reeking of gasoline couldn't be aired—so spent the entire morning steaming odor out and assembling shirt, socks, et cetera for wedding. . . .

About twenty people (staff and neighbors) were present for Wedding dinner at which last of "Rose Petal" was sewed.

Shortly after dinner, ceremony was performed by Rev. DeJarnette. Hamp played "MacDowell" music softly throughout the ceremony.

Pictures of wedding party were taken by musician Hampton and organizer Ward.

At 4:o'clock, Franz, Zilla, Walt, Myles and I left for Chattanooga where we registered at Key Hotel—Wedding party held in Walt's room. John, Bart, Harold Cash, Stan and Bobby Reese, Franz, Zilla, Hamp, Jane, Hap, and two textile workers. A lively party continued long after we "escaped" about 11:30 P.M.

N.B. the only melancholy note—Jim [Dombrowski] was not present at wedding or party, due to New York Trip.

PS Walt kept a picket line around our door all night and hourly attempts were made to break in.

Mar. 7th & 8th

Had fun finding new eating places. Myles bought a nice looking top-coat, shoes et cetera!

A "news" reporter called Myles for an interview concerning our marriage but he told them merely what he thought they needed to know and "hung. up."[13]

The couple hopped into the one car that Highlander staff had been sharing and drove off for their weeks-long honeymoon in

Florida, with a brief detour to Paris, Arkansas. As much as Myles appreciated the idea of his new wife's willingness to defy her family for some greater purpose, he didn't like taking any part in a rift between Zilphia and her father. He insisted they start their honeymoon in Paris, making nice with Guy Johnson. Perhaps Myles knew he would have enough enemies in the life of Highlander; he could use a father-in-law on his side. Probably Mom Horton encouraged him to at least try. As Myles wrote:

> I was determined that she reunite with her family because to me, someone without a family is bound to have problems. Mine was loving, and I was terribly disturbed about hers. I said, "We're going to go out there and see if we can work this thing out." And Zilphia said, "Guy said if you ever show up, he'll kill you." I said, "Well, I've been killed before." So we went to Arkansas. It was an awkward situation, but we finally achieved a little reconciliation. . . .
>
> Guy was a very creative person, and very strong. Zilphia was his pride and joy, and very much like him. One time he said to me, "Zilphia's so opinionated." I said, "Guy, you're opinionated too." And he said, "No, I'm just determined." They were two of a kind.[14]

Guy wasn't thrilled about the direction Zilphia had chosen for her life, and he was flat-out opposed to Myles's social perspective, but he regretted taking such a hard line with his eldest, beloved daughter.[15]

Ermon Fay was there when Myles and Zilphia came to visit and remembered the reunion. "Dad was glad to rebuild the relationship with Zilphia," she wrote, "which remained good for the rest of their lives, although he could never condone what she and Myles were doing. After all—he was a self-made man, and why couldn't the rest of those men [in the labor movement] do the same?"

After that visit, it wasn't long until Guy was writing to invite Zilphia and Myles for fishing trips on Lake Dardanelle.

AFTER A FEW DAYS IN PARIS, Myles and Zilphia hit the road for Florida. They landed on the Gulf Coast, "practically out of the water at Sarasota, Florida . . . where they have pitched their tent on the beach."[16] During the days, they visited with friends of the school and spent their evenings enjoying the food Zilphia cooked over the fire, basking in the dwindling glow of the warm Florida sun, gazing across the placid, shallow water of the Gulf of Mexico.

A month later, Myles and Zilphia returned just in time to prepare for summer sessions. Zilphia ran smack into the reality of Highlander life, becoming acutely aware that the school was not only in need of a good musician, but also of someone who could help them effectively bridge the gap between Myles's love-and-service-centered mission and the omnipresent, polarized suspicions that flew around the community.

While the Hortons had been away, the staff began hearing new concerns from the folks in Monteagle and Tracy City. Long-held suspicion of Dr. Johnson's motives had rubbed off on the folks who had since taken residency on her land. Baseless rumors came in waves that would crash over the school periodically as long as it was in operation. Rumors continue even now, but in 1935, area newspapers ran editorials accusing Highlander's founder and staff of being Godless Communists. These public accusations would be matched by private inquiries to the FBI, which opened a file in April 1936 on Myles, the staff, and anyone else associated with the school. The file opens by echoing local conspiracy theories, calling the school "a hot-bed of communism and anarchy."[17]

At one point while the newlyweds were away, a reporter came in search of dirt and found none. He walked in on this unprovocative scene: "Paul and Bill were in the front room reading. [Hamp] was talking to a boy in the library."[18] Unimpressed, the reporter drove to Tracy City and started asking questions about what people had heard about Highlander, then wrote his article based on the gossip and judgment of the rumor mill.

Back from her honeymoon, Zilphia immediately seized upon the already well-attended Community Nights. Summerfield neighbors were by now used to gathering at Highlander for square dances, picking parties, and other cultural activities. Zilphia steered those events from a benign opportunity to blow off steam toward the mission of collective empowerment and connection. She especially encouraged the music and dancing. She considered it a way to connect people with the traditions of the area while at the same time teaching them how to enjoy and appreciate one another at the school.

Further, she recognized, in a way that Myles did not, the extent to which the arts could be a major tool for organizing people around a common goal. She was emphatic about the notion that the arts were not what she called "trimming," but rather existed in the very fabric of any movement. By connecting people through creative expression, the arts allow people to open to one another in a way they would never dream of doing in a partisan debate.

Zilphia didn't immediately instruct people on this but rather let them experience it for themselves. She reserved her lessons for later, once folks were feeling relaxed and enjoying the company of the others, about whom they may have initially made prejudiced assumptions.

After they had been square dancing together for a while, for example, she might point out that people cannot enjoy each other unless there is trust. Square dancing requires partners to hold hands, take off together around a square, not bump into anyone or step on any feet. There must be eye contact, and mouths must stay closed. Eyes watch from smiling faces, working together with the other couples in a square to interpret the folksy instructions that are called and complete the song together. The callers at Highlander would often add something silly and subversive into their calls. One recorded square dancing call went like this:

Meet your partner, promenade
Join the union—don't be afraid
Second couple, balance and swing
Down the center and divide the ring
Gent to the left, lady to the right
The tenant union's gonna put up a fight[19]

Further, square dancing—like folk songs, weaving, and handicraft—is an intrinsic lesson in how previous generations confronted the darkest difficulties of their times and celebrated

despite those troubles. It's a lesson in collaboration across differences. Zilphia knew that if she could get the neighbors who
thought Highlander was threatening together with the staff for a
square, barriers would start to break down in a way they would
not through confrontational discussion and debate.

Dancing, like all the arts, amplifies empathy—something for
which there is always more room.

EVEN AS SHE SHIFTED THE FOCUS of the Community Nights,
Zilphia settled into the one-room log cabin where Myles had
been living. He had built the cabin during the early days of setting up the school.[20] The distance from the workshop goings-on
afforded the newlyweds the privacy necessary to unwind after a
long day—and to become better acquainted. Both appreciated
the hike. It helped them collect their thoughts on their way to or
from a long day full of people, activities, and ideas.[21]

The cabin was similar to the domiciles of so many poor people in the area, who slept mere feet from where they ate. The
Hortons obtained water from a well between their cabin and the
workshop space and shared the duty of hauling it to their home.
When it was time for the school's dishes or linens to be washed,
staff gathered near the well with buckets and rags, forming a
work party that helped them bond even as they did mind-numb-
ing-but-necessary labor. Photographs of dishwashing and laundry time show Zilphia and other staff standing over wash basins,
surrounded by the tall evergreens of the plateau.[22] Occasionally,
they took a break against the fence for a cigarette.

When students were present, the Hortons rose before the sun,
dressed, and prepared for the day. Zilphia walked through the
woods to the workshop center, her feet crunching against dry
twigs and leaves as she went, humming a tune to herself or simply gazing about, her mind full of thoughts. She headed for the
kitchen, preparing breakfast for the students. She or another staff
member would harvest eggs from the hens they kept and vegetables from Myles's own garden. Zilphia especially enjoyed preparing salads for breakfast because they were quick to make and
easy to stretch.[23] She or someone else would ring a bell to let stu-

dents in their dorm rooms know it was time to wake and dress for breakfast.

With her work in the kitchen and the readiness with which she prepared food for the students, Zilphia began to blur the lines between her personal life and the life of the school in a way that would become foundational to the trust relationship the Hortons would have with their students, as well as with the people of the wider Summerfield community, for the rest of her life. This began with the way they decided to marry—as much for the school as for themselves. But for Zilphia, the blurring of boundaries was an important aspect of her cultural curriculum. It created a certain seamlessness that students and other visitors experienced as simply the joy of seeing her and Myles around, socializing with them, appreciating their attention and approval.

Zilphia's friend Charis Wilson recalled from her visit to the school: "Myles admitted it was difficult for the two of them to sequester themselves long enough to plan curriculum or work on fundraising, because the students needed to see them on the front lines: in the garden, at the washtub, or on the KP [kitchen patrol]."[24]

Indeed, student-written articles and letters home always included some personal notes about Zilphia and Myles, as if they were part of the physical structure of the school. In an undated, unsigned letter from the 1940s, one student sandwiched a report on the patriarch and matriarch of the school between reports about the academic experience: "M and Z are back from vacation. Zilphia has a nice, brown tan, and Myles looks fine, and he is much more pleasant to people than before he left." Another unnamed student, around the same time, reported on union issues before noting, "Most of the group left after a while and there was just me, Jean [Casson], Zylphia [sic], Myles and myself left. For the first time, Myles indicated approval of my work." These sidenotes are typical of the letters one might find in Highlander's archive. Students told the folks back home about the beautiful grounds, the challenging workshops, and personal details about the founder and his wife, often focusing on the way they provided approval or emotional support.[25]

And emotional support was vital in this isolated plateau where students were challenged to imagine how different the world could be if working people were more empowered. Thus, a word should be said for the women of Highlander. In some ways, the staff in the early years was particularly progressive in its gender dynamics, especially during the 1930s, a decade before World War II drove many women into the workplace, empowering them in new ways through industrial employment.

But at Highlander, women were part of the decision-making process from 1932 forward, though Myles always had the final word. They were instructors and active in every debate. As Ermon Fay recalled, they did the work of the school, but they were also responsible for the "traditional roles" of cooking, cleaning, and maintaining house. Though this may seem like an unfair imbalance to some twenty-first-century feminist minds, for Zilphia, whose mother had to abandon her career entirely when she got married, this must have seemed like a balanced opportunity for empowerment and self-fulfillment.

IT WOULD BE NICE to paint a picture of a woman who showed up and knew just what to do, but Zilphia experienced a period of adjustment that summer and fall in 1935, as she found her way in her strange new context. She was likely relieved to find an upright piano at the school, which Hamp used to teach lessons to the children of the surrounding community. But from the moment she arrived, it was obvious to her that her partiality for classical music had no place in Highlander workshops.

So Zilphia began asking folks what songs they knew. There was a canon of hymns and folk songs that most Southerners shared, but she wanted to dig deeper to both engage and inspire the people atop the plateau. So, in an effort to relate to them, she dug into the traditional music and instruments of the area, learning as she went from neighbors and students alike. She picked up the mountain dulcimer and recorder during this time. Both were more portable than her beloved piano and neither created a barrier between her and the people with whom she was singing.

Music was central to the lives of churchgoing Southerners,

who found refuge, hope, and promise in their hymnals, if no-where else. Most didn't read music. Instead, they were accustomed to the deep tradition of Sacred Harp (also known as shape note) singing. Rather than using the sheet music with treble and bass clefs used by Western composers, Sacred Harp is notated with shapes like circles, squares, and triangles that tell the singer what note to sing. This was the primary method of group singing across the region at the time. (Zilphia always relished the opportunity to travel out of town for an occasional Sacred Harp gathering.) But cajoling everyday people into singing outside of church or Sacred Harp events required a motivation that was akin to promising the saving of their souls.

As Aleine Austin, who was on Highlander staff in the 1940s and became good friends with Zilphia, noted, "The singing in the labor movement was a religious experience. . . . The labor movement had qualities that were like a religious movement to people; a fulfillment of a dream."[26]

In the tradition of Joe Hill's *Little Red Songbook*, Zilphia started rewriting the hymns that people in the area already knew and loved. She called it "parody songwriting." New lyrics were exaggerated to make light of the original words and to draw greater attention to the new. Life was dramatized in parody songwriting, wrought with lyrical gesticulations that made the conditions of the workers out to be patently absurd and inhumane—which, with hindsight, we can see that they were.

One of the finest examples of this was the late 1930s composition "You've Got to Go Down and Join the Union" by Woody Guthrie and Pete Seeger. Zilphia collected the piece in a songbook, and Guthrie and Seeger recorded it with the Almanac Singers. Based on the melody of "You've Got to Walk That Lonesome Valley" ("You've got to walk that lonesome valley / You've got to walk it by yourself. . ."), the new song riffed on the original lyrics, carrying forward the theme of personal responsibility within one's mortality.

Similar to the original verses, but with more comic aplomb, Guthrie and Seeger's parody pins the loneliness of mortality onto a question of whether or not to join the union:

You've got to go down and join the union
You've got to join it by yourself
Ain't nobody here can join it for you
You've got to go down and join the union by yourself.[27]

The pair recorded that tune after they spent some time at Highlander talking about the utility of folk music with one Zilphia Horton. But that visit and her influence on them—and by extension her influence on decades of the development of folk music in the popular arena, in general—was years off. For now, young Zilphia had to come up with a curriculum and determine how best to be of use.

Most working-class Southerners were accustomed to a went-without-saying folk process. People added turns of phrase or a new word here and there to the old songs in order to put their own signature on the tradition that had been passed on to them. The concept of writing parodies was merely a natural extension of this habit.

As Teffie, who worked closely with Zilphia in the early years, later recalled:

We encouraged the people in the community to recall the old songs. . . . I remember when [Highlander neighbor] Vera Kilgore began to recall the verses to "The Farmer's Cursed Wife." Well, in Child's collection, this probably has more variations than any number of songs and here is Vera Kilgore, there on top of the mountain, coming up with a recall of one of the versions, which had been handed down to her. Doubtless as she recalled earlier remembrances of the song, she may have been changing it a bit and adding some of her own [words], but isn't this very true of the . . . folk artforms that are placed on the oral transmission belt, moving on down through the generations? . . .

Of course people, as we know so well, in poor, rural areas came together for singings in the rural churches. So this was a familiar artform for them and it made it possible for them to use it effectively when it came to the need to carry new and strong messages to each other and to the outside world.[28]

THOUGH ZILPHIA WAS INSPIRED by this process of music making and the potential she saw for the arts in general at Highlander, the school's mission was still a new concept to her. She had barely begun to adjust before she came face-to-face with the occasionally dangerous activities inherent in resisting oppressive systems.

Zilphia arrived at the school with the intention of delving into labor union organizing and its related challenges, but 1935 also saw Highlander veering for the first time into work related to the simmering movement for Black civil rights. According to Myles's second wife, Aimee Horton:

> The most dramatic and unforgettable of these early [integrated] meetings, at least for its more than fifty Negro and white delegates . . . was the All-Southern Civil and Trade Union Rights Conference held at the Highlander Folk School in 1935. The broadly conceived interracial conference which announced as its objective "a higher standard of life in the South" had to struggle for the right to meet before it could consider its agenda.
>
>   . . . When a second floor hall was finally secured from a Negro proprietor, the delegates were forced to flee as a mob gathered and threatened to dynamite the building. Faced by the mob, the delegates managed to escape to Highlander, some fifty miles away, where the sessions proceeded. Zilphia Horton, in writing about the harried conference some years later, noted that a group of loyal mountain neighbors who attended the sessions, "sat at the edge of the conference group and kept a watchful eye toward the road in front of the School. They were," she explained, "defending the right of the mixed group to meet at the Highlander Folk School."[29]

This experience helped Zilphia internalize how important it was for her to maintain close friendships within the Summerfield and Monteagle communities. Though there is no telling the story of Highlander without exploring the suspicions and adversaries that plagued the school from the moment it opened its doors, its history is also equally peppered with stories such as this, about how some of Highlander's neighbors pitched in to stand up for their own.

The people of Monteagle who most frequently attended the Community Nights, or sat in on discussions during workshops, knew that there was nothing threatening about the Highlander staff. Zilphia's outreach, though it had only just begun, was already strengthening the relationship between the school and its surrounding community.

It wasn't lost on her that the people with whom she had a personal relationship lacked the suspicious ideas held by those who kept their distance. Her habit of visiting neighbors and inviting them to the school was simply a reflection of her belief in the value and power of human connection. Still, as friends of the school would testify during the 1959 trial that would lead to the end of the school's era in Monteagle, "Highlander's reputation was 'mixed' in the . . . area because some residents 'radically disapproved of integration of any sort,' . . . and these 'social and political' considerations made the folk school controversial."[30]

If twenty-five-year-old Zilphia Johnson Horton still harbored any romantic ideas about how the labor movement could be exciting and glamorous, her first summer on the plateau scratched that record, bringing the reality and the size of her task into sharp perspective.

In so many ways, she was well equipped for the job. In so many others, she had some learning to do.

CHAPTER 6

CLASS AND PRIVILEGE

AT AGE TWENTY-FIVE, as a white woman from a fairly well-off Southern family, Zilphia had already experienced a great deal of privilege. It's worth pausing her life story to consider the way she came to both understand and wield this privilege.

Claude C. Williams's integrated philosophy clubs had introduced Zilphia to the concept of racial disparity and the notion of walking through the world with an open mind and heart. But it was something quite different for her to do the work of actively dismantling oppressive systems in order to empower poor people toward a better life for themselves and for generations to come. Then, as now, there was a gulf between valuing freedom and being truly free, a space between loving thy neighbor in thought and doing so in deed, which was foundational to Myles's mission. Zilphia knew that if she was going to dedicate every day to these lofty concepts in order to build the world as it should be, she first would need to reckon with the ways she had benefited from the world as it was.

Zilphia had aunts, uncles, and cousins who were poor farmers. Her mother had been poor as a girl, but Zilphia had spent many years with Grandmother Howard in a nice home inside the city limits, next to a college, attending the public school. Many of the children of her time and place were torn away from the classroom early in life to assist the family on the farm or to go to work for a wage in the mines. Those who attended school often walked a great distance to a country school, where all grades sat together in one room and were taught by a teacher who had little more education than they had.

On one level, assimilating into life at Highlander meant Zilphia had to stretch herself a bit to not only begin to believe in the qualities that would make her effective as she built her culture program, but also to embody them. She had to confront her privilege and amplify her empathy so she could meet people where they were. Only then could she encourage them to stretch toward their own empowerment. At times this meant just being herself, getting people to come over and have some fun.

The loose atmosphere she helped to create at Highlander, paired with the radical ideas that flowed in its workshops, attracted college-educated liberals to Highlander's staff, but the students and community were certainly not highly educated when Zilphia arrived in 1935.[1]

Where Myles had grown up poor with poor neighbors, life experience that influenced his path to Highlander, Zilphia had mostly led a privileged life, separate from the poverty she now had to help people navigate. She had to listen to those around her to both learn and embrace their culture if she was going to be part of empowering the locals, or at least helping them to understand that Highlander was not, as its FBI file would assert in early 1936, "honeycomb[ing]" the South in Communism and anarchy.[2] She was going to need to learn how to relate to people on a level that was not implicitly, if unintentionally, condescending. She had to be mindful about not only acknowledging her privilege but also regularly checking it.

In one rare, undated bit of autobiographical writing, she shared some insight into the way she was coming to know and understand her neighbors:

> Humming a mountain ballad as I was washing dishes one morning, I was interrupted by a weary and monotonous voice that can come only from a life of drudgery and disappointment.
>
> "The Bishop over the way died yesterday."
>
> "That's too bad. I had heard that he was ill but I don't know him," I answered half sympathetically and indifferently.

"Hit always seems that the people that wants to live, dies, and them that wants to die, lives," she said musingly, looking me straight in the eye.

Thinking she was merely asking for sympathy, but not wanting to appear disinterested, I paused a few moments from washing dishes to answer, "There are millions who might feel like you but the only thing for us to do is to stick together and work together, so that our lives can have some happiness instead of drudgery."

Looking down at the floor, half timid but with a stubborn note as though she were determined to get it out, she said, "Sometimes I reckon I oughta live to see my children brought up, but with a body has seven n'two dead n'no chance ter quit havin em', n'nothin to feed what you got, then I reckon ye git to wher ye don't care much."

"What does your husband do?" I asked.

"He works in the mine when the's work, but he's sick to where he can't work half the time," she answered.

Realizing she was groping for something, I began, "A few years ago, people didn't know these things but now if people have all the children they want and can take care of, they don't have to worry anymore."

Raising her eyes, she blurted out in a quivering voice, "If one is careful without the other n carin' then hit don't help none. Why I've gone out at night when the snow was on the ground an' with cold after too. I tell you, men ought be strung up: my husband ain't nothin but a brute an' I tell him so."

With these words, she lost all trace of self-consciousness and she held nothing back.

Aroused by the pitiable plight of this young woman whose best years were gone, I suggested, "There is an appliance which women can use without the aid of the husband so it doesn't matter whether he's careful or not."

Her eyes lighted up and she pleaded, "Well for Gods sake, tell me what it is!"

"Haven't you ever asked anybody about these things?" I asked.

"I've asked different women in this here neighborhood but none of 'em tells me nothin'. I asked Alf Kilgore's wife. She aint got but one an' she told me she don't use nothin', but she lied."

"Have you ever said anything to 'Mom' Horton about this? She thinks that all women should know this—that they should not have to have children until they can take care of them and want them," I said, thinking that it would be better for "Mom" to talk to her about it as I am a young woman and my judgment might not be valued so much as hers.

With the thought that I might give her something to read about it, [I] started to ask her if she wanted a pamphlet, when the thought occurred to me that perhaps she could not read.[3]

It's likely that Zilphia's intention in writing this was to keep the interaction as true to reality as possible. She kept the woman's vernacular intact as a means of respecting it, the same way she would respect a folk song or folktale that she picked up from a neighbor.

Yet, implicit in the telling is the sense that Zilphia felt apart from the woman, recognized that distance, and struggled with how to navigate that reality. This separation between who she needed to be in order to excel at her work and who she actually was became a theme in her life that would run through from its beginning until its end.

"I think there was a very sophisticated side to her that she had to suppress," her daughter Charis says, "because it was out of place there and it would have been off-putting, and she cared about not being off-putting. It was important to not have that persona."[4]

With that in mind, we can recognize Zilphia's story about the woman as a glimpse into the way Zilphia struggled to close the gap between her privileged experiences and the poverty of Highlander's neighbors.

In fact, a handful of observational writings among the papers that have not previously been culled reveal Zilphia's thoughts about the classes and races interacting. In them we see how she

set herself on a journey with her own privilege, seeking to understand and unpack it.

In another essay, she was on a train from Montreal to New
York, seated next to a Black woman.

The wheels were already turning as I landed on the bottom step
of the New York bound train at Montreal. I paused to get my
breath at the entrance of the coach. Each two seats had one oc-
cupant. No chance to stretch out and rest so I might as well pick
what appeared to be the most interesting seat mate. There was
one Negro in the coach—a woman sitting next to the window
a few feet down and to the right of the aisle. I had seen surpris-
ingly few Negroes in my three weeks stay in and around Montreal and Quebec City. This might be a chance to find out what
kind of work Negroes do here.

I used the polite formality of asking her whether the seat next
to her were occupied or not to begin the conversation.

"No, it isn't," she said. Her voice was soft and she left her
words half suspended in mid-air as though something else might
follow. But nothing else did.

As I settled down in the seat beside her, I was struck by her
heavy expensive perfume. At closer range what had appeared to
be expensive clothes were almost cheap, although excellent in
style and color.

She was dressed in a tailored suit of deep green wool. Her short
grey hair curled softly under a felt beret which matched her suit. A
small silver faun fastened to the collar of her white silk shirt.

We rode in silence for a few minutes. I tried without success
to see the title of the book in her hands. Then in a typical tourist
manner, I said, "Do you live in Canada or are you an American
tourist like most of us?"

"I live in New York," she answered. "I've just been up to
Montreal for my vacation."

We talked about nothing for about ten minutes—the sti-
fling hot New York weather we had been missing, traveling difficulties. By now, her voice had lost most of its reserve. And just

as I was thinking she must be a public school teacher or social worker, she came out with, "I'm a personal maid for a woman on—Park Avenue."

I smiled inanely and said, "Oh, is that so?" I'm sure it was my voice this time which hung suspended. Sure for two reasons: first, amusement at my ridiculous attempt to pigeon-hole her work, and second, at the possibility of getting first hand information about what are the actual duties of a personal maid.

I thought a few minutes and decided that at this stage, rather than beat around the bush, it would be better to be frank.

"See here," I said, "All my life I've wondered and tried to imagine what a personal maid would do."

She didn't seem at all shocked at this blunt statement—just faintly amused.

As the train plodded along, Zilphia and her seatmate discussed a maid's duties, exchanged pleasantries about their husbands and families, and watched as various well-off women boarded the car with their fancy clothes and pets, drawing attention to themselves as if they deserved it. After some time, the woman spoke again:

"The South is not your home, is it?" she said in an artificial "and-now-incidentally" manner.

"Yes—I was born there."

Her comment was a warm smile.

They rode the rest of the way in silence, until the conductor announced the 125th Street Station, where Zilphia's seatmate was to depart.

I stood in the aisle to give more room. As the train pulled to a stop, she extended her hand and as we shook hands, said, "I have enjoyed riding with you and I hope your husband meets you and that your son is fine when you get back to Tennessee."

As she started down the aisle, she bumped into the bird cage which extended out over the top of the seat. "I'm very sorry," she

said in a low voice, looking straight ahead. I saw a faint smile
reach back to her left ear and she disappeared through the door.[5]

Here again, Zilphia juxtaposes her observations with what
she could only imagine this other woman was thinking and feeling about the scene. It's important to note that she could only
imagine, and, to an extent, she was projecting. But Zilphia had,
by 1944, come to recognize her privilege and her prejudices. She
wanted to connect with a stranger, however awkwardly, despite
it all.

BEYOND ZILPHIA'S OWN WRITINGS, other early portrayals
of Highlander consider the juxtaposition of class and privilege.
In the 1937 short propaganda film *People of the Cumberland*,
a smiling, jovial Zilphia stands outside a shop door, handing
broadsides to everyone who exits. The film was written by Er-
skine Caldwell, directed by Elia Kazan, and was widely circu-
lated in the 1930s and '40s. In 1938, First Lady Eleanor Roosevelt
invited guests to the White House for a private screening.[6]

People of the Cumberland featured the melodramatic narra-
tion of actor Richard Blaine. ("Men of strong backs and weak
minds!") It won awards and swayed audiences, as it was meant to
illustrate how the labor movement was turning around the lives
of countless impoverished people in the South. It also spotlighted
the forces of oppression—the violence and threats of violence—
that Southern industrial workers faced when they started to organize into unions. The film cast Highlander as a force for good, an
example of what working people could do by banding together.

People of the Cumberland certainly tugged at heartstrings,
though hindsight affords us the opportunity to see it as cross-
ing a line in its almost fetishized depictions of poverty: filthy, be-
leaguered mothers with starving babies at their breasts, staring
hopelessly into the camera.

We can't know what Zilphia thought of the finished film,
but we do have her written thoughts about people less fortunate
than herself. Her natural inclination was to empathize with anyone seeking help, but her writing reveals the work she had to do

within herself on her awareness of others and that she was highly conscious of the journey she was on. She knew she had to un-learn many things in the process of learning her role at High-lander. And she was aware of the difference between intellectu-ally and emotionally embracing an idea and doing the practical, daily work of bringing it into existence.

This made her a bit heartsick. In the late 1930s, Myles recog-nized how this transition was weighing on her:

> Sweetheart, you will have to be selfish at times and protect your-self for the emotional upheavals that come from having people lay their souls bare to you. You are too sensitive a person to have to carry too many people's problems, you see too deeply and feel too keenly to be able to stand such exposure. Don't worry about making me unhappy by telling me your feelings. Of course I dis-like to know that you are upset but I am happy in the knowledge that such experiences make our love grow and gives it finality.[7]

Only with practice and empathy, then, could Zilphia grow into her role. And when she needed to blow off steam, she either turned to her piano—it wasn't unusual for her to sit and play for four or five hours at a time—or created projects and then poured herself into them. There wasn't much physical space in her one-room cabin for the kinds of immersive projects she most relished, and the spacious workshop center was reserved for lectures and debates, so she had to find creative space elsewhere.

Once during summer 1935, while Myles was away, she got to thinking. "Do you remember the little house where the Stars kept their car—the one with the cement floor? What do you think of making a work shop out there for you, Dillard, and me?"[8] Myles was keen on the idea, and Zilphia dove into a slew of projects—painting, block printing, and whittling jewelry, among them—in the little shop she took to calling the "Star Cabin."

One of her most beloved, long-standing projects was develop-ing plans for a new house that would provide more space for the Hortons—and maybe a couple of children—than their one-room cabin in the woods. It would be 1943 before the house was ready, but she couldn't help but develop intricate plans for the space in the meantime. Zilphia gushed about her plans to her husband in letters, across a couple of years. "The more I think about our moving plan and what we'll do with this and that," she wrote, "the more enthusiastic I get."[9]

As a teenager, she had watched her mother methodically plan for the Klan Road home, and soon she would have a chance to build one for herself. Zilphia's house would exemplify her personality. She employed local stonemasons and woodworkers, running her plans by them and paying them all a living wage. The way she managed the project and the creativity of the design illustrated how far ahead of her time she was—and how out of place.

The structure Zilphia had her eye on was a small, square-hewn log cabin that had been part of Dr. Johnson's property. The cabin had already been expanded from its original size, and Zilphia more than doubled its floorplan. As her daughter, Charis, described it:

> It had a cantilevered roof and decks . . . it was a very clever idea. There was a huge fireplace with metal doors which went into wood stock, which was stored from the outside, so you could open a door on the inside and pull the logs in. And the whole entire wall was a flagstone walkway. . . . Next to the fireplace she had these copper pots into the flagstone in front of this floor-to-ceiling window, and planted elephant ears and geraniums, with spigots that just drained right to the outside. She was totally out there.[10]

The wide-open living room featured a window along the entirety of the south-facing wall. The copper pots Charis mentioned, along with the indoor/outdoor log storage, allowed Zilphia to blur the line between inside and outside—an extension of the malleable boundaries that characterized every part of her life at the school. To tie it all together, a hand-carved mantlepiece framed the giant fireplace. Zilphia had whittled it over the course of many months, often gathering a work party of staff and neighbors around her.

"Now-a-days," she wrote to Myles in the late '30s, "the living room [in the main building] at night is a delight. Looks like the busiest workshop you ever saw. For example, tonight, Maria sat at the big table drilling holes in some cedar, Eva was at the machine, sewing her dress to take home, Juny sat over in the corner picking the guitar, Carolyn sat knitting socks and I sat over at the window working on the mantle, stretched out across some chairs."[11]

In other parts of the house, local workers installed radiant heating, alternately in the floor and ceiling. The bedrooms were downstairs. Upstairs, Zilphia had "one long space with large windows and the deck wrapping around it."[12] Thus, the room was heated by the sun in winter, with the unfortunate side effect that it felt like a dry sauna for the other two-thirds of the year. The cinder block walls protected against both wild summer storms and cold winters.

The living room was furnished with what her children would come to recognize as "patio furniture." Charis explains: "It was white, corrugated plastic, with ripples in it, [and] wrought iron. It was very expensive patio furniture . . . along with two salmon-colored Saarinen tulip chairs."

"It was quite a big house," Charis adds. "Not huge, but for that place really huge, and very sort of modern. . . . There was a big terrace that looked out at the lake. There was a huge grill out there."[13]

The largest and probably most expensive piece of furniture in the house was Zilphia's piano, for which the couple spent $85 (equivalent to $1,544 today, adjusted for inflation). It was a centerpiece in more ways than one. She stacked large cushions in the corner for guests who wanted to sit around the room or who needed to crash on its floor overnight. When Zilphia felt like playing, anyone who was around could grab a cushion, recline on the floor, and listen to a casual but intimate concert of classical piano music.

An aerial view of the Summerfield community at the time would reveal Zilphia's large, imaginative new home sticking out like a sore thumb in the eleventh poorest county in the United States—a physical embodiment of the difference in class and vision between her and her neighbors. Yet, there was something about her personality that helped it make some kind of sense in this context—her openness, her warmth, the way she was present with people that made them look past their assumptions and reach for what they had in common.

Part of Zilphia's role in building the culture of Highlander was to make everyone feel at home. And she knew that home was more of a feeling than it was the appearance of the structure in which you stood. In a way, that is what allowed her to create structures that didn't make sense in their surroundings. And fun was a fast route toward connection.

"We went on a fun binge Saturday night," she wrote to Myles during their first year together. ". . . Dillard and Juny came over and the entire house-hold played poker until two o'clock in the morning when I fried potatoes and scrambled eggs and we had breakfast at two-thirty Sunday morning. Poker stakes were a quarter cent a match. Juny named the group the Harp Singing Club. We promptly elected Leon secretary and passed a motion that all losers had to donate their losses to the club and the winners had to dig down in their pockets and donate the same amount to the club. It's the first co-op poker club I ever heard of."[14]

CHAPTER 7

NEW YORK CITY

ONCE AGAIN, IN NOVEMBER 1935, Zilphia boarded a train that would take her away from home. This time from middle-of-nowhere Monteagle, through Baltimore, to the other universe that was Manhattan.

On the first leg of the trip the train was full of "smelly children," but Zilphia's spirits lifted in the Baltimore bus station, where she became fascinated with what appeared to be a large crowd of openly gay men. We can picture her with a large purse in her hand, and her hair rolled up on top of her head, as was the style of the day for women who paid attention to the style. Her tall stature balanced on two large feet. The pause of reflection as she wonders if she's really seeing what she thinks she's seeing.

"The depot," she wrote, "was crowded with 'homosexuals,' female impersonators making up a floor show—they were going to New York for the week end [sic]. One boy was nothing short of beautiful—had golden blonde hair, cupid lips, sky blue eyes and artistic eye-brows. . . . Street corners were covered with them—friends to tell them goodbye."[1]

Zilphia had likely never knowingly encountered even a few open "homosexuals" at any time in her life, much less a crowd of them in a public space. She enjoyed their flamboyance and chatter, their affection for one another, their style. Taking a seat on a bench, she couldn't help but stare out of the corners of her eyes, the edges of her mouth upturned. She was certainly far from Paris, Arkansas.

After the twenty-minute break was over, Zilphia boarded the bus yet again and found that one of the men was also boarding. However, he was sent away when the driver saw he was traveling with a small dog—as Zilphia described it, "a lovely little snow white 'fluff.'" She continued:

> As it so happened through no forethought of mine, I drew a ticket on the front seat just behind the driver and you will be pleased to know that he had taken my welfare in hand, seeing after my comfort in general and seeing that I always got back on the bus. Ha! Thinking that I was in the average opinion concerning the homosexuals he turned and told me that about one month ago, while he was driving, a small boy of about fourteen, came rushing up to the front of the bus, frightened to death, and told him about a "funny" boy in the back seat, who wouldn't keep his hands off him. Whereupon, the bus driver manfully stopped the bus and threw the "funny" man with one hundred and fifty pounds of baggage out into the highway, miles away from any town. I asked him what he expected him to do. "Hell I told him he could take his 150 lbs. and walk right down the highway." Enough of this morose story.[2]

As the bus wended its way toward Manhattan, Zilphia watched the world go by, stewing over what she could have said or done differently to prevent any of these discriminatory episodes and worried for the young man who had been humiliated and put out. Certainly, she knew that homosexuality wasn't widely acknowledged in 1935, and surely she had absorbed the cultural norms around its unacceptable status, but her forward-thinking mind couldn't grasp why, exactly, this meant someone should be so rude to a stranger.

ABOARD THAT BUS, Zilphia was traveling farther afield from her family's home than had most young women of her generation, but there was a wide chasm between her life experiences and the kind of experiential knowledge required for her new role. She had a certain instinct about the utility of music and the arts in society, but no broader context for labor activism or how to build "a new social order"—the vision into which she had married.

Despite all this, and considering her brand-new marriage, it's curious that Zilphia enrolled in the New Theatre School so far from her new home that autumn, and there's no clear evidence to explain. Myles would have wanted his New York donors to meet his new wife, but the school was likely Zilphia's idea, as she became acquainted with the piecemeal program—if it could be called a program—that Highlander had been running around the arts and culture.

In his book about Highlander's early days, John Glen noted that the first two or so years of HFS, before Zilphia arrived, "offer[ed] a glaring example of the weaknesses in Highlander's early residence program. . . . Its overwhelmingly academic orientation was painfully evident in the extensive use of textbooks as the basis for class discussions."[3]

Glen lists dramatics and music among the subjects that early students studied from textbooks, indicating an intention to include the arts in Highlander's holistic education, however the staff seemed to be shoehorning it into the curriculum. This was the structure of the program she encountered when she moved to Highlander, and her creative mind undoubtedly would have been brimming with ideas about how to improve upon it before she even knew that could be her role.

Meanwhile, she had only a little experience with theater, having played Orpheus in a college production. But it was fast becoming a force in the labor movement, wielded as much by the Communist Party as by other entities.

Clifford Odets's landmark play *Waiting for Lefty* premiered at New York's Group Theatre in 1935, a few weeks before Zilphia arrived at Highlander, and it's likely that several of Myles's friends from Union had gone to see it during its inaugural run there. No doubt, if Zilphia brought up the idea, Myles would have been supportive of what his new wife and culture director would be capable of doing with a dramatics program, if she got a little more education in the form. She asked him to recommend her for a scholarship and he agreed.

Regardless, in fall 1935, Zilphia enrolled in a dramatics program at the New Theatre School in midtown Manhattan, and off she went.

AS THE BUS WENDED ITS WAY from Baltimore to New York, she watched the world go by. Then came the rising skyline of lower Manhattan, more and more visible as the bus rolled over the bridge from New Jersey. The buildings jutted into the sky like typewriter keys at the ready to rewrite the stories of immigrants, businessmen, and young women traveling alone from far away. Until now, the only glimpse Zilphia had had of New York City was in the pages of her mother's subscriptions to *Harper's Bazaar* and *Vogue*, both of which had seemed out of place in her hometown and would prove even more so when she started having those magazines delivered to Highlander.

The subway had been in use since 1904, but a more recent building boom had added bridges and towers, including the Empire State Building, which opened in spring 1931. It was all beeping horns and bustle where Zilphia was set to take up residence, two blocks northeast of Union Square.

Though President Herbert Hoover's administration had struggled to get ahead of a plummeting economy, it was his successor Franklin D. Roosevelt who had slowed its descent. Unemployment, still staggeringly high, had dropped from its peak of 25 percent in 1933. It would be years before most people would experience any recovery but, as has always been true in the city of New York, there was reason to feel optimistic if one was twenty-something, creative, and fresh off the bus.

After landing at the home of accordion-wielding folksinger and friend of Highlander Agnes "Sis" Cunningham and her roommate Dorothy, Zilphia moved into a boarding house at 151 E. Eighteenth St., run by the Women's Friendly Service League, a religious organization meant to cater to young women as they tried to find their way in the city. Though such homes frequently offered a new way forward for troubled women, Zilphia's cohorts were mostly students and hard-working immigrants.

Each of the residents earned her keep. Most of the women

took on chores such as cooking or cleaning, but the lead woman in the house, Bell Holloway, asked Zilphia if she wouldn't mind managing the other girls instead. Zilphia declined. She didn't like that she was automatically qualified for a position of power based on her economic background, and the suggestion was enough to sour her on the place. "I told [Holloway] I hadn't the slightest feeling of apology," she wrote to Myles, "but I did have a distinct feeling toward anyone who had that attitude."[4]

Yet, when Holloway showed Zilphia to her room—a small, shared room with no windows—Zilphia bumped up against her privilege and politely requested to be relocated. She joked to Myles that her original room was "gangrenous," adding, "I'd rather move once a week than to be shut up in a 'chicken coop.'"[5]

Instead, Holloway showed her to a private room on the top floor. The room had a window in the ceiling and four beds, but no other residents, and Zilphia grew to appreciate the space, which she took to affectionately calling "The Skylight."

Zilphia fetched her bags from Sis's apartment one taxi ride at a time, unpacking her belongings—clothing, art supplies, a framed photograph of her new husband—and settling into The Skylight. To pitch in, Zilphia earned her keep by mopping the floor.

She began exploring the city. Zilphia was invigorated by the way the classes and races interacted so freely—the starkest difference between New York and back home. She never had much patience for people who looked down their noses at the poor. And though she viewed herself as separate from her family's history of poverty, Zilphia knew that poverty was ensnaring for some. She knew many people would spend their lives working just as hard as her father and not getting anywhere despite it all. In her letters back to Myles, she commented on the way that the juxtaposition of the classes was helping her pinpoint what she was thinking and feeling as she reckoned with her own privilege.

On a few occasions, she went out for no reason other than to sit and watch other classes behave as they do—a sort of ethnographic study of disparity. "Last eve," she wrote to Myles, "Teffie and I went up to the Waldorf Astoria as I told you. It was very amusing to watch the 'debs' walk in with such ultra sophisticated manner and then when falling into the quadrille, assume or rather reveal their true girlishness by absurd giggling and gum-chewing. They weren't capable of forgetting themselves long enough to concentrate on the directions given them—was quite interesting."[6]

One episode from the beginning of her stay with the Women's Friendly Service League digs deeper into her fascination with and disdain for the upper classes and their displays of wealth and philanthropy as performance art.

> This afternoon is one I shall never forget.
>
> When we all came down to lunch, . . . we were introduced to a white-haired, "furred" dowager and her henpecked husband who was wearing a swallow-tailed coat etc. They of course stayed for lunch. I knew what we were in for—she literally took charge of the meal and preached all through it until we hardly got a bite. You know the usual line—Girls' Service League to stimulate *faith* in living et cetera et cetera et cetera. She raved on at length about how she started it twenty-five years ago—how it had brought thousands of girls in off the streets, gutters, saloons and now some of them have jobs paying as much as seventy dollars. Can you imagine that? Wonderful. As a matter of fact, the girls on this side of the house whom she was talking to, are not "problem" girls. They are attending college working as "stenogs"—one is working on her masters at Columbia.
>
> Then the prize stunt, I must tell you about—just before they left, the henpecked imbecile took the enormous rose off his wife's furs and after telling or giving instructions how to smell it, passed it around the room for us unfortunates who had never smelled a hot-house rose. We were told to smell three times. (And now Johnny you may breathe again.) You can imagine how I took it. The only thought I had was, "What a pity to desecrate your beauty by having been bought by such a fool."[7]

Zilphia's encounter with class in New York was made more complex by how she consumed the arts while there, and that is, almost constantly. Myles at one point asked how she was finding the money to go to all the musical performances, plays, and museums she was frequenting. Probably friends paid her way. In an unconscious outcropping of her privilege, people were always just giving Zilphia things.[8]

However she managed to afford it, Zilphia soaked up all the culture New York had to offer, and there was plenty. Artists were experimenting with forms, marrying the old with the new in exciting ways. George Gershwin had just debuted his latest masterpiece, the folk opera *Porgy and Bess*, a composition that was right up her alley. The classically trained, folk-inclined Zilphia would spend more than a couple of letters gushing to her young husband over its music. So much so that when Myles received a gift of five dollars from his friend, he spent a small portion of it to purchase the Gershwin composition on record.

"Have I told you that the 'Porgy and Bess' records came and are excellent. I am anxious for you to hear them," he wrote before twirling into a dream of what it would be like to hear her play the music on piano. "Darling I miss hearing you play. With no Zilphia to play the piano the place is not the same."[9]

At the New Theatre School, she signed up for a robust collection of classes that kept her busy from three o'clock in the afternoon until ten o'clock at night most days: acting, stage technique, play analysis, history of the theater as a social factor, stage make-up, playwriting, and directing.[10] It was a busy schedule, though it afforded her an hour break in the middle to unwind and wander the city. November 1935 was mild, with temperatures reaching into the sixties, allowing her a smooth and comfortable transition before the winter wind started howling down the city blocks.

Zilphia often stayed up until midnight working on projects for her theater program. She painted "a modern stage set for Hamlet" for her stage design class, and she was especially enthralled with her stage design instructor, M. Solotaroff.[11]

When her late nights left her tired in the middle of a school day, she would duck into a restaurant across the street and grab a strong cup of tea. "I get 'sort of' hungry," she wrote of her long school days, "but they are kind enough to save my supper for me at the Service League, so I can afford to be hungry a little while—besides it wouldn't hurt me to lose a little avoirdupois, you know."[12]

Though Zilphia didn't report on the content of her classes, she was studying stage technique during a time when the ideas of Russian actor and director Konstantin Stanislavski were spreading throughout the New York theater world. As dramatic production progressed away from the absurdity of vaudeville and silent film, with their over-the-top performances, Stanislavski introduced the notion that dramatic performance could be workaday and reflective of the average person's life experience. At the time when Zilphia was studying theater, his "system" would have been a radical new idea, challenging actors and directors alike to envision the stage as an opportunity not to exaggerate society, but rather to hold a mirror up to it. More than entertainment, Stanislavski sought to turn the theater into an engine for empathy. There are echoes of his system in Zilphia's early approach to a theater program at Highlander. It's safe to assume she learned at least something about it while at the New Theatre School.

Though radical theater was far from mainstream in New York, the Communist Party and other groups had theater troupes scattered around the city that operated as part of neighborhood organizations. Yiddish theater, especially, had a significant presence in the cultural zeitgeist.

Zilphia was never a member of the Communist Party. Like Myles, she never joined any political party. Still, parts of the CPUSA philosophy—specifically its use of dramatics and puppetry—appealed to her.

She was disappointed that no class in puppetry was available at the New Theatre School, so she asked around and found her way to a woman named Helen Fishlander, who was a professional puppeteer and friend of Highlander. Energized by Zilphia's interest and encouraging others who had expressed curiosity about the form, Fishlander decided to offer a six-week puppet workshop. Of course, Zilphia was an enthusiastic participant. Thanks to Fishlander, she learned how to construct a puppet theater, write a puppet play, and build her own puppets. In one cheeky postscript in a letter to Myles, she hinted at the kinds of satirical puppet theater she and her fellow Fishlander students were exploring: "In puppet class tonight, I started making Herr Hitler."[13]

ZILPHIA'S LIFE IN NEW YORK CITY wasn't all studious time spent on radical political arts. She made time for the creative sort as well. She frequented the Whitney Museum, where she marveled at Georgia O'Keeffe's *The Mountain* and *White Calico Flower* and was particularly charmed by an exhibit on Shaker handicraft there.

At the urging of her professors, she attended a theatrical adaptation of Maxim Gorky's *Mother*, a 1906 novel about the plight of factory workers in Russia. She also attended Broadway plays for fun and went to see Paul Robeson as Othello.

"Paul Robeson had everyone tense or in tears," she reported. "It was wonderful and fast. No play has ever seemed so powerful to me."[14]

She also participated in New York's music world, as she was called upon to play piano for various social gatherings and Highlander fundraisers, and she relished any opportunity to do so.

She discovered early on how to get affordable tickets to the symphony and went frequently, just as she also attended big band concerts at nightclubs with a friend from the Service League. Without men to accompany them on the dance floor, the pair would hang back at a table, ordering rounds of Manhattans and enjoying the show. "The concert was wonderful," she wrote after one such night out. "Made me wish I were studying [piano] again. I realize that I do it better than anything else."[15]

There was always so much going on in New York, the arts and so many ways of life swirling in every direction, and Zilphia spent those months focusing on learning from other cultures, experiencing and observing social contexts she would never encounter back home. She wrote to Myles about a party she attended at the home of radical writer Alfred Sinks: "There were two girls there who have lived in India for seventeen years. Quite interesting but the type of people whom I like to watch and observe as though they were in a cage. My reaction to them and their reaction to me are very interesting."[16]

She filled her mind with texts like Friedrich Engels's *The Origin of the Family, Private Property and the State* from the library and filled her heart by sitting in on French classes just to listen to people speak. "I love the sound and rhythm of it," she told her husband.[17] Indeed, foreign languages were akin to music for her—their different rhythmic cadences, their melodic variations. For this reason, she was a quick study of foreign slang.[18]

She spent a lot of time in New York with the person who had recommended her to Highlander in the first place, Ralph Tefferteller. He was Myles's old classmate from Union and a friend of Claude C. Williams. A Highlander newsletter from 1936 described Teffie as "the outstanding authority of American folk dancing."[19] Indeed, with his command of, and passion for, the folk arts, he was quite a companion, almost like a male version of herself.

Born and raised in East Tennessee, Teffie wasn't a musician so much as he was enamored of the arts and accustomed to the calling of square dances.[20] In New York, he was frequently hired to call a square. When he eventually made his way onto the Highlander staff, he worked with Zilphia to do community outreach through music and dance. Like her, he had the kind of ebullient personality to which people were naturally drawn. It's easy to imagine the pair finishing each other's sentences.

Rumors persist, still, that they were more than friends. It was accepted within the Highlander community that Myles and Zilphia had an open marriage, and they both had their dalliances, though most people agree hers were less frequent than his. (His relationship with Zilla Hawes, a Highlander teacher and board member, was of particular note.[21]) Myles's letters to Zilphia indicate he was well aware of her special connection with Teffie. Whether he was poking fun at it or expressing some mild jealousy, he did so with his tongue firmly planted in his cheek: "Tell dat man you're my gal," he wrote.[22]

Such comments didn't stop her from sharing with Myles her feelings about other men:

"Harold Cash is an old sugar foot. . . . I like him awful much."

"I haven't changed my mind about Mac—he's simply wonderful to me. If I weren't so full of love for you and hadn't known you I might even have fallen in love with him. As it is, I appreciate him as a sensitive and creative individual—he needs to have some one who's capable of it to fall in love with him."

"I have grown to love the spirit of John Thompson enough to fervently desire to be around him more."[23]

Maybe she was teasing him, maybe flaunting her harmless crushes, or maybe she was just full of love and had more than enough to go around.[24] Regardless, Zilphia was enjoying her freedom, far from her father's home and the life he would have rather seen her lead. (Did Guy Johnson ever really expect Zilphia to stay in one place for long?) And anyway, whatever was going on between her and these men, her husband never stopped loving her for a minute, and she never stopped loving him. If they set out to have a marriage of equals, they were so far succeeding.

WITH NO AVAILABLE RIDES to Tennessee and plenty of schoolwork to keep her busy, Zilphia was stuck in New York for Thanksgiving. Back at Highlander, Myles and the others cooked two hens and dressed them with all the usual fixings. He started the morning with a rabbit hunt, scaring a mess of birds out of a cave and choosing to watch them fly instead of shooting them down. He spent the holiday hiking to Bridal Veil Falls, collecting arbutus flowers along the way, which he replanted on a hill he had cleared at the school. He also transplanted a holly tree, dogwood, and rhododendron for Zilphia, planting them near the site where they planned to build the new, larger home. Careful to please his new wife, Myles, the latent romantic, drew up a map of the garden and included it in one of his letters for her feedback.

"Working back there is one of the most pleasant parts of my day," he wrote. "You are there with me as in no other place. . . . I don't want to plant anything unless I am certain you will like it."[25] Myles loved planting rows of squash, tomatoes, peas, lettuce, and peppers. One of his favorite hobbies was collecting pepper seeds on his travels, planting them, and later taking a bite to check the level of spice.

Once she returned to the school, Zilphia was happy to cook anything her husband could grow, but when it came to the garden, she was more interested in creating beauty. She planted a thriving philodendron and numerous hyacinths and put out pots of elephant ears and various flowering plants in front of the workshop hall.

In New York, Zilphia was pleasantly surprised when Zilla and her beau and fellow staff member, Franz Daniel, showed up at her door, unexpected, and she welcomed them in for Thanksgiving with the Girls Friendly Service League. After dinner, they visited some friends' apartments and then the crowd went "to a beer parlor where we sat and drank beer until 8:30."[26]

She made it home for Christmas, catching a ride with a friend, Dr. Lazare Teper, from the Brookwood Labor College. The trip afforded her only three full days—she arrived Christmas night and was gone by the twenty-ninth—but she got to see Myles and hear stories about coal mine organizing in Harlan County, Kentucky, from Myles's old friend, Don West.

She relished seeing her husband in the flesh and gave him a sweater she had spent the autumn knitting for him. Still, the trip was barely long enough to catch up and settle down. She spent her time cooking, reading, and playing games of poker and Sardines with Highlander staff and visitors. She reunited with her piano and the books of music by Bach, Brahms, and Liszt that she had brought with her from Paris.

She also led singing for the staff during the holidays but was now convinced that the piano wasn't the ideal instrument for such a task. No matter how the instrument is situated, the pianist is either gazing over the length of the instrument at the audience or is forced to sit in profile, twisting at the waist to make eye contact with anyone. She thought of her friend Sis Cunningham in New York, with her loud and lively accordion—an instrument that could afford not only eye contact but also movement. Zilphia didn't particularly like the sound of the instrument, but what the accordion lacked in nuance, it possessed in charisma, and the latter was sorely needed in the movement.[27]

Over the years, she would use the accordion for folk songs, hymns, and popular songs (she especially liked Bing Crosby's

"Ac-Cent-Tchu-Ate the Positive"), and anything else that could stir the spirits of the people for whom she was playing. Teffie recalled:

> She knew, and would use, anything that seemed to suit the oc-casion—popular music of the late twenties and early thirties, Broadway tunes, old tunes. I'll never forget how effectively she used the song "Brother Can You Spare a Dime" in little play-lets, to arouse the emotions of either working people or people to whom she was trying to give some appreciation of what the life of the unemployed worker was like. It was just a joy to be a part of it with her. . . . She had an infectious type of presenta-tion that enveloped you and drew you in. You weren't on the out-side as a spectator, you became whole-heartedly involved with the moment.[28]

Indeed, by all accounts, Zilphia was a remarkable accordi-onist, as she was proficient with any instrument she picked up. Her friend Lois Timmins, a fellow accordionist who encouraged Zilphia on the instrument, recalled, "She was such a good musi-cian. She could play it even if the keyboard was upside down."[29]

The piano, she would keep for her own artistic expression, a personal outlet, and a way to connect with her true self that she would need more and more as the years passed.

BACK AT THE WOMEN'S FRIENDLY SERVICE LEAGUE, after Christmas, Zilphia was starting to feel trapped in The Skylight. The novelty was wearing off and she was becoming annoyed with the drama perpetrated by so many very different women living so very close together. As she wrote:

> Catherine expects to have to move out because of her having a job. She "informed" me today that I was going to live with her the last month I'm here. She makes $150 or more a month and she's the type to whom money means only one thing—spending it for the things one really wants. Of course it will be fun if she does move but Miss Holloway will have ten million fits—she has

simply capped me with her own personal problems and her little world. It's like keeping a balloon blown up which has a leak in it. I envy your bobsled rides and wish I could do them with you.[30]

Catherine did move out, along with a friend named Eleanor, and they welcomed Zilphia for the final month of her New Theatre School term, January 1936.

During that month, Zilphia spent a lot of time with Teffie, went to a lecture by Eleanor Roosevelt in Greenwich Village, savored plenty of tea and Chinese food downtown, and looked forward to heading home. Closing one of her daily letters to Myles during those final weeks in New York that winter, she wrote: "Goodnight darling—I need the thrilling sweetness and calmness of you."[31]

CHAPTER 8

DIGGING ROOTS

BACK IN MONTEAGLE, fresh from her theater education and energized, Zilphia got to work trying to fashion a curriculum. She had some elements to work with, as the staff had at least set a precedent with their early, if unclear, intentions. But, by marrying her education together with her own experience and ideas, Zilphia was able to coalesce it all into a clear vision. Teffie later recalled about the beginning of Zilphia's tenure, "The direction of the cultural activity while I was there [in the mid- to late 1930s] largely got its impetus from Zilphia and myself . . . but Zilphia stood out head and shoulders above us all."[1]

For the long-oppressed mountaineers and others in the Southern working class, filing a grievance against one's boss was incredibly intimidating. That spring of 1936, during a workshop about this issue, Zilphia suggested that the workers break into groups and come up with scenarios that might, in their real life, make them feel crippled with fear. Then she had them cast the roles, write the lines, and perform the scene in front of the other students. According to John Glen:

> Zilphia Horton's dramatics class was one of the high points of the [May 1936] term. . . . She was ready not only to continue the Chautauqua style of the dramatics program but also to teach the students the rationale behind workers' theater. The dramatics class prepared a play about a strike, held a mock AFL convention, worked on mass recitations and songs, and presented a program to union audiences in Chattanooga, Knoxville, and Atlanta

and to TVA workers at Norris in June 1936. Under Zilphia's direction, the emphasis of the dramatics program shifted away from educating those who observed the plays to educating those who participated in them.[2]

The written lines helped actors avoid stumbling over what they might say to a boss. And once they had played through all the possible outcomes in front of a supportive audience, they felt more empowered around filing grievances. This program was so successful that Zilphia started the Highlander Players. The troupe began with that tour in 1936 and, for a time, brought original plays by Highlander staff and students to union locals across the South.

She focused at first on original compositions, writing a couple of cheeky musicals herself, including one called *Lolli-Pop Poppa*, which used a *Little Shop of Horrors*–style trio of woman singers to narrate the tale of a workplace in need of organizing. By 1939, the program had morphed into improvisation, and that in turn gave rise to Highlander's remarkably influential role-playing curriculum. In those early months, though, she used Stanislavski's method and her New Theatre School education for teaching empathy through dramatization.

Zilphia's notes about the theater program, which accompanied the text of plays that she sent to union locals, explain how the Highlander Players developed their repertoire and how and why they decided to write down the plays, the main reason being that they found the scenes they acted out to be both instructional and cathartic.

Each [play] was made up in about eight hours for an audience before it was written down. The actors, therefore, didn't have exact lines to memorize. They simply knew the situation and what sort of person they were playing and talked accordingly. So the lines of the script should not be taken word-for-word. No busy worker could be expected to learn some of the long speeches by heart. But if he understood what they contained he should be able to say them in his own words.

We hope that names and, in fact, any details that may bring

the play closer to the particular group that performs it, will be changed to suit each new situation. A personnel manager could be called a foreman, for instance, a textile setting changed to a hosiery mill.

You don't have to have a stage to put on these plays. They can be done in a room, or out-of-doors. If you don't have a curtain, the actors simply walk on and off stage at the beginning and end of each scene. . . . If you want any advice about producing these plays, apply to the Highlander Folk School. We'll be very happy to help in any way we can, and we should appreciate hearing if and when and how you use them.[3]

Plays, like songs, were plucked directly from the life experiences of the workshop attendees. To dramatize harassment on the job, one student would play a worker, one would play a boss, others would play bystanders, and so on. Not only did this require the playwrights to analyze a painful experience from all angles, but it also placed the actors in the roles of vilified individuals, forcing them to understand how everyone involved could have been doing the best they knew how. One staff member, Mary Lawrence Elkus, remembered:

The students turn up their nose in disdain when they first come. They all have preconceived opinions of dramatics and they aren't very flattering. But when they find that no learning of lines or putting on a dull play is involved, just living out their own experiences, they fall for it like a ton of bricks.

One of the most amazing experiences we have in the class is watching the suspicious expression on their faces turn to one of hilarity and excitement as they let off steam acting out a picket line. They just outsmart each other in a hurry trying to improve that improvisation of a picket line. Yet they soon learn that a bunch of heads is a whole lot better than one. . . . The result is that the class is putting on full length plays, completely improvised, on some vital problem of the day before the month is over.[4]

As we can see in Zilphia's culture curriculum, movement work was heart work. The point wasn't to "win" by outdoing the bosses, but rather to appeal to their common humanity. Anyone could see that these workers deserved a fairer wage and better conditions, but profit, power, and greed had gotten in the way of fairness. Without appealing to the heart, power systems might re-arrange themselves, but not necessarily with everyone's humanity in common. Zilphia knew from experience that the arts—singing, theater, even puppetry—could appeal to the bosses' innate sense of empathy in a way that discussion and negotiation could not.

She often told a story about a textile strike during her first year or two at Highlander:

> A group of clothing workers had organized and had asked for recognition. This in a place near Chattanooga. They asked us to come down and help them; make leaflets for their organization, to teach some songs, to do recreation. And we went down.
>
> It so happened that Washington's birthday came along about that time, so they decided to have a Washington's Birthday Parade and combine it with the things that they were fighting for, because to them they were fighting for freedom, economic freedom. So they made banners like that and the children of the workers in the mill were in this parade. The school band was in it. The ministers in the town, who were sympathetic to the strik-ers, were also in the parade. They were completely unarmed. We were marching two-by-two with the children in the band.
>
> They marched past the mill and 400 machine gun bullets were fired into the midst of the group. A woman was shot in the leg on the right and the ankle on the left of me. I looked around and the police were all disappeared. There had been about 10 of them there. I looked down and there was a cop lying in the ditch, and I said, "What are you doing down there?" And he said, "Hell, lady, I got a wife and three kids!"
>
> Well, in about five minutes a few of us stood up at the mill gates and sang "We shall not be moved, just like a tree that's planted by the water. . ." And in 10 minutes, they began to come out again from behind barns and garages and little stores that were around through the small town. And they stood there and were not moved and sang. And that's what won their organization.[5]

People who participated in the Southern labor movement were aware of the kidnappings, beatings, dynamite, riots, and massacres. They were often undereducated, profoundly poor, disconnected from one another, and legitimately afraid of people in power. Their bosses were often in cahoots with local police and political leadership. Sometimes the bosses even owned their employees' homes, schools, and the general store where they bought their groceries (and thus they owned their employees' debt). The powerlessness was real and pervasive.

In those early years, especially, the dramatics program was a powerful tool for giving workers an opportunity to state their demands out loud and hear another human being react to them.

It also gave them the skills needed to see any unfolding drama— in the workplace, in the public square, in their own home—from the outside, inside, and directorial perspectives, always with more empathy for everyone involved. These were tools for life inside and outside of work, giving people a foundation from which to be more empowered in the world and to shift the culture around them.

ZILPHIA'S EDUCATION CONTINUED in 1936 when she returned to Arkansas to take graduate classes in voice at the College of the Ozarks, moving in with a cousin and her sisters, Elsie Newell and Ermon Fay.[6] Newly committed to the labor movement, Zilphia pitched in on organizing efforts with union locals near Clarksville when she wasn't in class, leading the singing in union halls with the help of her sisters.

It was also during this brief time back in Arkansas that Zilphia began a lifelong project of song collecting. With the experience she had gained at Highlander, with the clear intention of staying there for the long term and building an effective culture program, she knew she needed to learn more about the music of the proletariat.

She wrote to scholars, songwriters, and folklorists in the region that spanned from the Ozarks to the Appalachians, seeking songs that could be sung and played with Highlander students. She sought funding too, selling her project to potential benefactors as an attempt to amplify the dignity of working people throughout the region by reintroducing them to their own culture.

Zilphia's songbook plan would get a boost in September 1938, when she and Myles drove to Birmingham, Alabama, for a convention of the International Typographical Union (ITU), a division of the somewhat newly formed Congress of Industrial Organizations (CIO).[7]

To understand what ensued, it's necessary to consider the context of the Southern industrial labor movement, such as it was, at the time.

UNTIL 1935, the American Federation of Labor (AFL) was dominant among the unions for organized craftspeople. The AFL granted its member unions a greater well of solidarity and thus bargaining power, but it was choosy about its membership, preferring to focus on highly skilled labor and thus snubbing the everyday folks who did the grunt work, exploited by greedy bosses who assumed they were too ignorant and afraid to organize.

Still, by 1935, the AFL had grown beyond any manageable size and the industrial member unions were feeling snubbed. That summer, ITU-AFL president Charles Howard joined with John L. Lewis of the Chicago-based United Mine Workers and several others to form an AFL Committee for Industrial Organizations. They thought it would be beneficial for their like-minded workers to join forces in a smaller union-of-unions, under the umbrella of the big union-of-unions, to offer their overlooked, underprivileged tradespeople greater bargaining power.

If it all seems a bit convoluted and difficult to navigate, that's because it was. The AFL embodied the comically oxymoronic "too big to fail" long before that phrase was coined.

AFL leadership was not thrilled with this Committee for Industrial Organizations and, in 1937, voted to kick out the eight member unions who had formed the committee. Those groups were undeterred, however, and spun off into their own more manageable upstart, changing their name ever-so-slightly to the Congress of Industrial Organizations (CIO).

To help the CIO find its footing, John L. Lewis had to distance himself from anti-Communist rhetoric he had spread in the

1920s because the Communist Party had been so successful with industrial workers across the country. If he wanted his union to take hold, he didn't necessarily have to join or even embrace the CPUSA, but he certainly had to look the other way—a consolation he dutifully performed, at least for a while.

Immediately, the CIO had some success with organizing industrial shops in cities like Chicago and San Francisco, but the South was a hurdle Lewis didn't know how to surmount. So around the time of the ITU convention in 1938, Myles and Zilphia began to talk with the CIO about developing a partnership.

The CIO had just announced a $2 million initiative to organize unions in Southern industrial centers, though the leadership wasn't sure exactly what it would do with the funds.[8] Regardless, this initiative seemed tailor-made for Highlander's staff, and Zilphia encouraged Myles to move forward with it.[9] Any alliance would provide Highlander with a reliable source of students and income and would offer the CIO the opportunity to populate its shops with some of the best-educated labor organizers in the South. The win-win arrangement would keep Highlander afloat during some of the harshest years of the Depression and World War II. In 1938, the relationship was new and exciting.

The Hortons returned from the Alabama ITU-CIO conference abuzz with new assignments and connections: Zilphia was commissioned by the Textile Workers Organizing Committee (TWOC) to publish an official songbook and took an assignment to continue the organizing efforts she had already begun in La-Folette, Tennessee. Myles committed to organizing some shops in North Carolina even as he recruited a few speakers for the school's winter term.

Zilphia's songbook assignment lit a new fire under her song-collecting project, which had all but fizzled at the fundraising stage. Until now, her lack of income kept that effort small and concentrated as she mimeographed song sheets for use only at Highlander and the union halls to which the staff was invited. With CIO backing, though, she could devote more time to the project, and she could claim more legitimacy behind her requests for songs.

In 1939, she created a work plan that suggests that she had been collecting songs of the Southern mountains for four years and that she intended to publish four separate volumes: one each for the Smokies, Ozarks, Cumberland region, and Southern industrial areas.

> I should go to southern industrial cities and towns which are populated by the migration of the people of the mountains above mentioned. First, I should determine how many of the folk songs found in the mountains are sung or can be recalled by the older generation who are now or have been engaged in history.
>
> From here, I should proceed to the younger generation and record the songs they are singing today. . . . The main purpose of the study, aside from the value of recording the songs, would be to attempt to show that there is a definite carry-over or influence of the old folk songs on the songs spontaneously sung by southern workers today. . . .
>
> I should not carry on the work at any university but should expect to consult recognized folk music authorities such as Annibel [*sic*] Morris Buchanan, Allen [*sic*] Lomax, and people connected with the southern folk lore society concerning the music.[10]

She closed by stating her intention to remain in the South and commit her career to folk music, which makes her mention of Annabel Morris Buchanan and Alan Lomax worth highlighting in particular.

ANNABEL BUCHANAN WAS a Texan by birth and, like Zilphia, a classical pianist.[11] She was also a composer who taught music classes in Oklahoma before marrying a Virginia lawyer and state senator named John Preston Buchanan. The couple moved to Marion, Virginia, where they raised a passel of children.

Annabel created the Virginia State Choral Festival in 1928 and later the White Top Folk Festival. She published a book, *Folk Hymns of America*, with which Zilphia would have been familiar. Annabel was also instrumental in creating the Southeastern, Kentucky, and American Folklore Societies.

Alan Lomax was a second-generation song collector who had grown up collecting songs in Texas with his father. A pioneer in the field of folklore, John Lomax was particularly interested in cowboy songs and the songs of the Black prisoners on Texas chain gangs. John took his son and daughter Bess with him on his collecting missions. On occasion, Bess would transcribe the music because her father could neither read nor write notation.[12]

One of John's greatest discoveries was Huddie Ledbetter, a sharecropper in prison on a murder charge. Ledbetter, who became friends with Zilphia, was known to audiences as Lead Belly. John Lomax had famously sponsored Lead Belly for release from prison in 1934 because of his musical talent.

In adulthood, Alan would lead the American Folk Music office at the Smithsonian Institution and become celebrated for his song collection. Alan and Bess Lomax were good friends with Lead Belly, Woody Guthrie, and Pete Seeger—all of whom Alan recorded at great length during his time at the Smithsonian.

Zilphia had probably become acquainted with the Lomaxes' work through the wider folk music community of New York, and possibly through Lee Hays, an old friend whom she had come to know well when both were attending the College of the Ozarks. Hays, perhaps best known for his work in The Weavers and for cowriting "If I Had a Hammer" with Pete Seeger, was also a student of Claude C. Williams and his philosophy club. The letters Hays and Zilphia wrote back and forth over the years reveal a kind of intimate friendship that was almost familial, with her often telling him that she hoped he was kicked back in a comfortable chair because she had a lot to report to her old friend.

Later in life, Lee wrote:

Claude and Zilphia did more to help change and shape my life than any people I can recall. I was still in Arkansas when Zilphia told me of her experiences in New York and it was through her that I learned of the New Theater League and the whole process of using art as a weapon; it was a revelation. Her concepts of what might be done with music, drama, and dance opened up windows on a whole new world. She introduced me to Claude, whose vision has remained with me ever since. I'm not talking about his politics—I'm not sure I ever understood them—but about his ability to reach for the talent in people. During my brief stay at Highlander theory was fleshed out with the couple of plays we put on and by the song or two we wrote for them. . . . I remember Zilphia poaching eggs in milk and have done the same ever since. And I shall never forget her dancing on the lawn in her billowing peasant skirt. Blouse too, of course.[13]

These memories from Lee were precious, if fleeting. He spent only a couple of months at Highlander before he moved on to Commonwealth College in Arkansas and eventually New York City, where he lived with a couple of other folkies: Fred Hellerman and Pete Seeger. Greenwich Village has always been a small town for folksingers, and the roommates were close to not only Sis Cunningham but also Bess Lomax and her boyfriend, later husband, Butch Hawes.

The least celebrated of the Lomaxes, Bess was a Bryn Mawr graduate and an equal contributor to American folk music alongside her father John and her brother Alan. She eventually created the folklore division of the National Endowment of the Humanities, helped create the National Folk Festival, and became a successful folk music educator.

In his biography of Woody Guthrie, Joe Klein called her, "without doubt, the sanest person ever associated with the group. She was a sweet, plump woman, kindly and intelligent, a solid musician with a good voice and, like her brother, a vast repertoire of songs."[14] She was also a sort of den mother to this makeshift New York folk song society, which would soon enough become known as the Almanac Singers. While the Almanac men (Seeger, Hellerman, Hays, Guthrie, and Lead Belly) all eventually achieved widespread fame, Bess Lomax Hawes and Sis Cunningham were among the most important, influential members of their circle. Bess, in fact, cowrote "M.T.A." with Jacqueline Steiner about Boston's Metropolitan Transit Authority, a song that would become a major pop hit for the Kingston Trio. Like Zilphia and so many other women in history, their stories faded into the background behind those of the men with whom they spent their time.

When I spoke with Lomax Hawes for a magazine article in August 2008, she was at the end of her life, spending most of her time in bed at home outside Portland, Oregon.[15] She recalled Seeger and Guthrie arguing at her kitchen table about whether politics and social issues had any place in folk music. Considering where these men went with their careers, this may strike some fans as an unlikely scene. But it's important to remember that the early folklorists—Lomax's father, John, and Seeger's father, Charles—believed that political and topical music were in a separate field altogether from American folk music and that never the twain should meet.

Yet, as Zilphia collected songs for her folk songbook in 1939, she tapped Guthrie for a song or two that November, and he responded quickly from where he was living on Mermaid Avenue in Brooklyn:

Dear Zilphia,

You hereby have my permission to print my song, "You Gotta Go Down," in your forthcoming songbook.

I wrote the song when I was singing over radio station KFVD in Los Angeles, and sang it over the air waves there during my thirty minute program which I had every day. I sung it around at the cotton strikes around Bakersfield on special trips that Will Greer [sic] and other actors would go up on. I've been singing it ever since at all sorts of meetings, rallies, picnics, and banquets, and folks seem to like it.

I am proud that you have picked one of my songs to print in your songbook for the National CIO.

Thank you very much,
Woody W. Guthrie[16]

The following year, Seeger and Guthrie took a lengthy road trip from New York to Texas, through the South, and stopped at Highlander to hang out with Zilphia. As they drove away, Klein pointed out, "Woody was preoccupied with the idea of writing union songs."[17]

Though Guthrie had performed for countless unions in California, his visit with Zilphia gave him a sense that union songs were more than just a genre of music that could be used to entertain a downtrodden people; he and Seeger became convinced that the form was a way that they, as musicians, could effect real change in the world.

After driving away from Highlander, the pair wound up spending the next three years dedicated almost exclusively to union songs. The Almanacs were a collective that threw its musical heft behind the burgeoning labor movement. The effort would lead directly to Pete's widely influential *People's Songs* pamphlet (a precursor to *Sing Out!* magazine), to which Zilphia would regularly contribute songs and liner notes, and the groundbreaking folk-pop sensibility of The Weavers (Seeger, Hays, Hellerman, and vocalist Ronnie Gilbert).

Thus, through the careers of its members, the Almanac Singers would become one of the least known, most consequential groups in the realm of popular music in the decades to come.

Considering the personalities of its two stalwarts, Seeger and Guthrie would have filled their canons with labor songs on their own, but it's hard to ignore the fact that, at a pivotal moment in their lives, both were enamored of Zilphia Horton and inspired by her ideas and energy. The admiration went both ways.

MODELING HER BOOK AFTER Joe Hill's *Little Red Songbook*, Zilphia was determined to present the songs without their sheet music. She believed writing out the notes on staff paper would create a barrier for the average person who didn't read music. She wanted songs that were sung to a tune people already knew, and "You Gotta Go Down," which used the tune of an old hymn, was a perfect example. Another, "Solidarity Forever" (she recorded it simply as "Solidarity"), used the tune of "John Brown's Body" or "Battle Hymn of the Republic." Zilphia also included the new lyrics, written by Don West, to "My Country 'Tis of Thee":

My country 'tis of thee
land of mass misery

of thee I sing
Land where the workers toil
and bosses reap their spoil
Where children starve and freeze
from fall to spring . . .

"Casey Jones" made the cut, too, as did "We Shall Not Be Moved." In the introduction to the latter, she wrote about the strike near Chattanooga and also included this:

> Perhaps this song, more than any other one song, has held work-
> ers together when opposition was greatest. . . . Helen Norton
> Starr says, "I heard a quartette [*sic*] of Negro singers who stood
> on the steps of a country school house while the hot summer sun
> beat down on the little group of West Virginia Mine Workers
> in 1931. The mountains looked down on the little mining valley
> and the state police watched from the road above, their pistols
> riding on their hips."[18]

Zilphia wrote notes to all the songs in the book, with a little history of the song or its writer. Sometimes she would also include a story about the circumstances under which it had been
sung, so that workers picking up the book could come to understand that they were part of a line of folks who had demonstrated
for better working conditions and more freedom.

For the song "Joe Hill," about one of her heroes, she included
this introduction:

> Joe Hill, whose songs helped organize copper miners, was
> framed on a murder charge and executed in Salt Lake City, Utah,
> 1915. Ralph Chaplin, in "Joe Hill: A Biography," [1923] says,
> "When the bullet-riddled bod of Labor's singer was placed at
> rest, the outpouring of the people was spontaneous and unprece-
> dented and the grief was truly genuine. The funeral procession it-
> self was miles in length and it took hundreds of men and women
> to carry the furled banners and the floral offerings. It seemed
> that the entire working population of Chicago had turned out for

the occasion. . . . [O]ne of Chicago's biggest newspapers asked
. . . "What kind of man is this whose death is celebrated with
songs of revolt and who has at his bier more mourners than any
prince or potentate?"[19]

Another notable inclusion came from Sis Cunningham, whose
"Mister Congressman" was included in the collection: "The song
comes from Oklahoma. I wrote it for the tenant farmers years
ago while touring the state for them. A typical verse as it was
sung then, was: 'A farmer wants to own his farm. Surely that
would do no harm. So get us land and get it fast, or in Congress
you won't last.'"[20]

Other songs came from Tom Glazer, Waldemar Hille, Carl
Sandburg, and others. These familiar names alongside the familiar melodies made people feel safe and comfortable within the
song. The labor movement may have become a singing movement,
thanks in no small part to the work of Joe Hill, Zilphia Horton,
and the Almanac Singers, but it wasn't because people then felt
any more comfortable raising their voices in song on a moment's
notice than would a group gathered for any purpose today.

Sure, people were accustomed to singing in church, but this
was different. These songs were daring and new. The context in
which they were being sung was uncomfortable and scary. Joining your peers in song on the picket line was not without risk.
As she did with her dramatics program, Zilphia wanted to eliminate anything from her efforts that could get in the way of people joining in. The more voices in the choir, the grander the song,
after all.

If people couldn't read sheet music, she wouldn't use it. If they
didn't know the melody already, she would choose another song.
If they were intimidated at the request to sing out loud, she would
pull her accordion to its length and show them how easily they
could be drowned out if they didn't sing with their full voice.
Then, as now, few people wanted the accordion to be the star of
the show.

Zilphia also placed ads in various labor papers throughout the
country and implored them to write articles about the project:

More and more, union groups are realizing the need for songs in their meetings and on picket lines to enliven them, and bring them more solidly together. We are endeavoring to meet this need by publishing a song book by and for Southern workers.

In many locals, members have written new words for familiar tunes. It is our feeling that these songs should be published in order that other locals may benefit from them.

We should like to appeal to all workers through your paper to send us at once whatever songs they have written, or know about and would like to have included in a workers' songbook.[21]

The result was that union workers and leadership nationwide sent her songs and stories to accompany them, and she answered them with letters of gratitude and greater explanation.[22] She approached this effort with the same zeal she brought into a room to lead singing, indicating she believed the work of collecting songs was just as important as the practice of singing them as a means of reconnecting Southern people with their own traditions.

Picking up old songs and traditions was worthwhile, but just as important was creating something new. Zilphia knew well that, without new material written by the people living through the present situation, these traditional folk songs would just be used as mindless entertainment. Tradition alone wasn't enough. People are sustained by clearing a way forward and then actually moving in that new direction. This was as true of the lectures Highlander provided as it was of Zilphia's efforts with arts and culture.

Many locals and labor schools had their own song pamphlets from which their constituents pulled, and they had their favorite selections. Zilphia wasn't hoping to reinvent the wheel, but simply to present a book that shared with union workers in Kentucky the songs being sung by union workers in Alabama, and so on.

Her songbook also widened people's worldview and spread solidarity beyond any single union local. When you realize that your picket line in your tiny town is asking for the same fairness and dignity as that of a shop three states away, it suddenly becomes clear that what you're doing isn't wrong. There are others like you who believe as you do, who meet each day with hope and determination, and are there with you in spirit. Your plight is their plight; you are not alone.

Besides, Zilphia wanted to honor individual contributions and make people feel empowered. For union workers who had been oppressed their whole lives, working for low wages and in poor work conditions, getting a song they made up included in a nationally distributed book could be the one vote of confidence they needed to push ahead with the cause, to hold on to hope.

In the introduction to the book, which she titled simply *Labor Songs*, she included quotations from notable members of the movement family, including John L. Lewis, who wrote, "A singing army is a winning army and a singing labor movement cannot be defeated. Songs can express sorrow as well as triumph, but the fact that a man sings, shows that his spirit is still free and searching, and such a spirit will not submit to servitude."

Zilphia's own introduction was especially concise and direct: "Most of the songs in this collection were written by people who work in the mines, mills, factories, and on the farms. It is hoped that this book will encourage workers to write and sing their own songs."[23]

Privately, though, her enthusiasm was more palpable: "I've been working like mad on the new song book—it's gonna be a hum-dinger!"[24]

CHAPTER 9

CONFLICT AND WAR

IN FALL 1940, a handsome, sturdy fellow with thick, curly dark hair, glasses, and a confident smile arrived on the plateau from Black Mountain College (BMC). Emil Willimetz had been at Highlander two years earlier for a work camp—a 1930s trend that often saw left-leaning youth spending their summers doing manual labor. Work camp attendees resided in tents on a far-flung part of the property.

During his work camp, Willimetz helped to restore and paint some of the structures on the Highlander grounds. CIO resident sessions were happening at the same time, but the work camp folks stayed out of the fray with their own activities and mealtimes.

Still, Willimetz was so enthralled with the life of the school—anyway, what he saw of it—that he wrote to Myles to beg, more or less, for entry.[1] A gifted writer, Willimetz had experience working in typesetting and print shops, though not enough to earn his union card from the AFL.

Born to Austrian immigrants in the Bronx, he grew up in New York. He was a resourceful introvert and a hard worker with an adventurous spirit and a keen eye for social issues. By the time he arrived at Black Mountain College, he had hitchhiked all over the Northeast and thought he might thumb his way around the South for a while. A brief stop at BMC led to a full scholarship there. Though he embraced his academic life, Willimetz always wanted more from his Southern adventure than Black Mountain had to offer. He found what he was looking for at Highlander Folk School.

Though he had yet to discover his affinity for a camera in 1940, Willimetz took thousands of photographs at the school over the ensuing decades, chronicling life there in a more comprehensive, personal way than any other journalist ever would. His photographs captured an intimate candor; he put his subjects at ease. Thanks to his eye, we see a studious Myles reviewing papers in his easy chair, Zilphia lovingly sitting on the chair's arm, reading over his shoulder. Her long dark hair, graying in places by then, drapes down her back in contrast to the done-up style she typically sported while out in public. We see workshops in action: a diverse circle of people feverishly discussing something at a table or lounging in a circle outside on the lawn. We also see the children of the plateau running through the grass and dirt in their overalls and bare feet, past the welcoming warmth of their tin-roofed log cabins. In contrast to the stark deprivation on display in *People of the Cumberland*, Willimetz's photography depicted a Grundy County filled with compassionate humanity and ample pockets of joy.

Luckily for those willing to dig, he also left an exhaustive memoir, *Gringo: The Making of a Rebel*, recalling his time at Black Mountain College and Highlander Folk School and his service in Europe during World War II.

By the time Willimetz arrived, Highlander was firmly established as a training school for the CIO, and its union-specific, weeks-long sessions frequently included around thirty people. There was a study term for the Southern Tenant Farmers Union (STFU), one for the Textile Workers Organizing Committee (TWOC), and another altogether for the Food and Tobacco Workers (FTA). Students from Antioch College were usually present on a work term, providing the only non-union presence. (Exceptions for someone like Willimetz were made whenever Myles felt like doing so.)

Willimetz's clear recollection in his memoir is typical of descriptions in other books and former students' memories of that era of the school, and it tells us much about how Zilphia's culture program, then in its fifth year, was woven into daily life. He describes how the dinner dishes were cleared away each night as Zilphia picked up her accordion. "She would lead us in rousing union songs," he wrote. "I don't think she brought out any new talents in me, but I bellowed out the labor songs with outstanding enthusiasm."[2]

Her dramatics program had evolved quickly after Zilphia returned from New York. By the time Willimetz arrived, it had gone from the creation of full plays with set lines, characters, and scenes to something that was fully improvisational. As Willimetz wrote:

> Since I was the only student not in a union and not on strike, the class thought it great fun to cast me as the villain—boss . . . shop foreman . . . scab. It was good typecasting, I never won an Oscar, but I got to be good at it, and I really made them work hard to get the better of me. The little dramas we put on were in no need of imaginative speculation—they came directly from the students' lives.[3]

Alongside the improv program, Zilphia continued to offer costume and set design classes as groups of students put on theater performances during the evening. Some students went back to their union local inspired by the possibilities of playwriting, while others simply saw the opportunity to provide quick trainings in nonviolent resistance that could help nervous workers surmount their fears of threats and violence.

Workshop attendees also learned how to produce and print newsletters to keep members of the union locals informed. Willimetz naturally gravitated to this part of the culture curriculum. These broadsides were an effective way both to spread the word about successful negotiations quickly and to call for a strike or a walkout to show solidarity. Occasionally, the CIO wanted to broadcast a message to its members nationwide, and these messages from the parent union were always included in local newsletters and pamphlets and also reported to Highlander's alumni and supporters in the *Highlander Fling*.

Another great use of the printing instruction was the creation of song sheets that could be passed out during meetings and pickets. Of course, the music curriculum was not only focused on song sheets and songwriting, but also on song leading, which is the most well documented of Zilphia's efforts. She prepared an instructional list:

SUGGESTIONS FOR SONG LEADERS

1. Secure an accompanist who is a leader too—one who is able to support the leader. Good sight reader and one who can play by ear.
2. Start singing with a well-known song that is generally liked. Rhythmic and one that lends itself to harmonizing if possible.
3. Anticipate and plan best physical arrangement such as seating, lights, song sheets.
4. Give directions for finding song easily.
5. Be sure the pitch is low enough at first—later it could be raised to a brighter pitch.
6. Vary choice of songs—contrast, mood, etc.
7. Indicate clearly the tempo of the song by singing a few words.
8. Give decisive movement for the beginning (attack) and the ending (release).
9. Interpret the meaning of the song in the manner of singing. Could be done[,] although not as well, by accompanist.
10. "Draw pictures in the air"—indicating pitch (high and low) and rhythm.

HOW TO PRESENT A NEW SONG

1. Tell something of the background, the purpose of the song or an interesting note about the composer.
2. Sometimes good to sing the song entirely through while the group listens.
3. If chorus or refrain is rhythmical or "catchy," leader might teach it first. It is most important that everyone participating gets some reaction to this first enjoyment.

4. Every song has a design. Made up of sentences which in turn are composed as phrases. To sing a song with feeling for these phrases and sentences will simplify the learning of it and increase musical enjoyment.

5. A rhythmic approach will teach "pulse" or "swing" better sometimes than just "beating time." Clap or tap the phrases which are not sung correctly. This will get people to relax and "feel" the rhythm.

6. Present the song with enthusiasm and feeling for its meaning. A group sings a song with the same quality as the leader gives in its original presentation.

MUSIC IS *NOT* TRIMMING!

Music can be trimming but fundamentally, music is the heart of things—of beliefs, situations, of struggle, of ideas, of life itself. Music should be used as an important part in achieving the main purpose of the program. Not tagged on at the end as an after thought.[4]

Read closely, this emphasizes Zilphia's belief that, without music (and other arts and cultural elements), a movement is devoid of heart and will be difficult for outsiders to connect with.

Again, the goal was to ignite the empathy of the bosses, to encourage them to negotiate because it was, ultimately, the right thing to do. Nothing kindles empathy quite like the arts—a fact that Willimetz emphasized in his remembrance, as had Mary Lawrence Elkus noted a few years earlier. Both recalled not being particularly drawn to singing and theater before their time at Highlander, but there was something about the way Zilphia taught these skills that made sense to people who were not so inclined.

AFTER WILLIMETZ LEFT HIGHLANDER in winter 1940, Zilphia, Myles, and a handful of staff headed to Washington, DC, for a concert to benefit the school. "The sponsors of the affair read like a Who's Who of the New Deal and organized labor," wrote Willimetz, "including Supreme Court Justice Hugo Black, cabinet members, congressmen, administrators of major federal agencies, Eleanor Roosevelt, and other prominent persons . . . [and] an audience of around 500 people."[5]

Mrs. Roosevelt had become interested in the school's activity with the CIO and had recently begun a correspondence with Myles and Jim Dombrowski. Though it's not clear exactly how this benefit came together, the First Lady certainly had a hand in gathering some of the high-profile guests. She believed so strongly in Highlander's mission that, in the years after the event, she offered a scholarship for students who could not afford the time off work to attend the school.

The *Highlander Fling* newsletter that they sent to supporters reported:

> The program for the Highlander Washington benefit on December 6th consisted of the reading of "America Was Promises" by [Librarian of Congress] Archibald McLeish; a ballad poem, "And They Lynched Him on a Tree," by Katherine Garrison Chapin, sung by the Washington Choral Society and the Howard University Glee Club; mountain and workers' ballads sung by Zilphia Horton; and Negro folk songs sung by Houdie [*sic*] Ledbetter (Leadbelly).[6]

During rehearsals and then again backstage before the show, Lead Belly and Zilphia holed up in a dressing room and swapped songs, helping each other decide which ones to deliver for their audience.

"Zilphia and Lead Belly were backstage playing, just having fun," Myles remembered. "He said he wanted to try this song out on her, that he was working on . . . but he hadn't finished it. And so she liked it so much she said, 'Go ahead and use it anyway.' She persuaded him to sing it even though he wasn't quite satisfied with it. So that was the beginning of 'Bourgeois Blues,' the first time that was ever sung."[7]

Lead Belly knew he was talented—he had a virtuosic command of a wide range of instruments, including piano, violin, and melodeon (a variant of accordion)—but he was also one of the most exploited Black performers of his generation. The Lomaxes paraded him around in prison stripes to perform his "Goodnight Irene" in front of television cameras, having him sing with the cold-eyed stare of a hardened criminal.

He was a rather large Black man with a booming voice and a commanding presence. Racist conventions of the time would have expected a Southern white woman like Zilphia to shy away from such a man, but she sat and listened intently to his music. She saw in Lead Belly much more than just the legend, the exaggerated story. She saw the man and his enormous talent, and Lead Belly was incredibly appreciative. In later interviews, he gushed about her, remembering her as "the only white woman I know who could play black music."[8]

To understand the gravity of his decision to perform this song on this particular night, in Washington, DC, for members of the government, we need only look at some of the verses of this iconic composition:

> *Home of the brave*
> *Land of the free*
> *I don't wanna be mistreated*
> *By no bourgeoisie*
> *Lord, in a bourgeois town . . .*

> *Well them white folks in Washington, they know how*
> *To call a colored man a nigger just to see him bow*
> *Lord, it's a bourgeois town . . .*

This direct confrontation of race issues in Lead Belly's song offered an artistic reflection of what was on the minds of Highlander staff and supporters around the same time. Earlier in 1940, Highlander had instituted an official non-discrimination policy, which brought them into the 1940s regularly, unceremoniously—but actively—doing the work of resisting Jim Crow laws. Meeting notes reflect this, as the school determined to broadcast the message that "unions should notify in advance all students both white and Negro that there would be no discrimination."[9]

Granted, Myles had been keen on resisting Jim Crow for decades and had been open to Black union members at resident sessions from the beginning.[10] But it became clear to him that someone had to directly address the fact that Black union members and white union members were not even allowed to share a meal, much less join forces to demand better working conditions. The separation Myles had seen as a child, which had sparked his curiosity about injustice in general, was what was keeping poor people down because it was keeping them from joining forces.

WHILE MANY NOW CONSIDER the labor and civil rights movements to have occupied separate eras in American history, the grassroots reality was that they were richly intertwined—the separation of the races even in labor unions meant that there was only so much empowerment that could happen among the working class. Thus, in so many ways, one movement led to another and both ultimately proceeded in concert.

After the Washington benefit, Highlander began holding more frequent integrated labor workshops. When, on occasion, white CIO workers were uncomfortable about this fact, Myles would matter-of-factly tell them they were welcome to stay at the hotel in town, or go home altogether, at their own expense.

In her book, *The Highlander Folk School: A History of Its Major Programs, 1932–1961*, Aimee Horton noted:

> These first integrated residence terms were not, of course, free of problems. As Zilphia Horton pointed out, "When the white students arrive, the majority of them have the usual prejudices. It is the first experience . . . for the majority of Negroes and it is likewise a difficult adjustment for them to make." Yet in spite of some tense situations, especially early in a new term, and in spite of the fact that a few whites departed abruptly when they learned that they would be eating at the same tables and sharing the same cabins with Negroes, most stayed and came, surprisingly quickly, to know and accept one another.[11]

True, by the end of the workshop—with all its integrated banquets, square dances, volleyball games, sing-alongs, and debates—those who stayed had gotten over it. It would be naïve to assume that they returned home as active desegregationists, but they did leave Highlander with the experience and knowledge that white people and Black people could live together in peace—and work together toward a common goal. They had seen it with their own eyes. They could not unknow this truth.

This deliberate desegregation practice only confused and angered folks in the community outside the school, some of whom had always been suspicious. They had never known quite what to make of the activities atop the plateau. In Monteagle and Tracy City, Highlander's neighbors started gossiping anew, awash in new conspiracy theories, creating yet another wave of animosity.

AROUND 1941, THE CRUSADERS, a fundamentalist religious group based in Tracy City, were growing increasingly nervous about what they saw as threatening: the school's practice of equality, particularly the presence of well-educated women and visitors with dark skin.[12]

Though Myles was by now no stranger to the naysayers in the community beyond Highlander, the tension brought on by the Crusaders was something altogether different. The group was determined to shut down the school as a "hotbed of Communism." They passed around propaganda claiming that "the Russian flag is saluted at the end of every class and the students sing 'Keep the Red Flag Waving.'" Further, they alleged, "The school is against the U.S. government, publicizes the poverty of Grundy County, and has a demoralizing and disintegrating effect on the county generally."[13] These false accusations would have seemed laughable if they hadn't been made in such a straight-faced manner.

The Crusaders mailed death threats to Myles, along with several threats to march on the school and blow it up. As if that didn't go far enough to make a point, the Crusaders decided to drag the First Lady of the United States into it.

In 1941, for the second year in a row, Eleanor Roosevelt offered Highlander one hundred dollars as a scholarship fund. When Highlander secretary Jim Dombrowski took the check to the bank to cash it, a bank worker made a photocopy and sent it to the Crusaders, who had it published in the local paper.

Angry, vengeful editorials followed. Letters flew back and forth between Dombrowski and Mrs. Roosevelt discussing ways to deal with the situation. In one letter, Mrs. Roosevelt wrote to Dombrowski, commiserating: "As in so many other things, people can and do use only half truths."[14]

Over the course of a few days of flurried wires, the pair debated whether either should say or do anything at all in response. Ultimately, the First Lady decided to send the following letter to Dombrowski, with express instructions for him to leak it to the local press, if he saw fit. It was written on White House stationery for additional effect.

> February 1, 1941
> My dear Mr. Dombrowski:
>
> I am sending you the same amount as I sent you last year as my contribution toward a scholarship in the Highlander Folk School.
>
> I have had the school checked by people in whom I have absolute confidence and am convinced that the newspaper attack and the groups which have been opposed to you are not opposed to you because of any communist activities, but because they are opposed to labor organization and, therefore, labor education. This seems to me a most unwise and short-sighted attitude and, therefore, I am continuing my support. I hope this spring to come down to see the school myself.
>
> Very sincerely yours,
> Eleanor Roosevelt[15]

Myles was away during this particular escalation; Zilphia was home with Dombrowski and the others. Any letters or personal ruminations she composed during this time have not been preserved, but it would have been natural for her to be reminded of the threats to her father back in Paris, remembering the men who drove slowly past her house and her tall, strong father at the window, holding his pistol, peeking through the shades in the middle of the night, and hoping nothing would come of it. She would have had a visceral reaction to these threats of violence.

"Zilphia got tired sometimes and discouraged," her sister Ermon Fay noted. "When the school was attacked, she got discouraged."[16]

She probably spent a fair amount of time in the Star Cabin working on a project, when she wasn't running offense by throwing a square dance or inviting neighbors over for a meal.

Meanwhile, Highlander records suggest that the Crusaders were working with the FBI, making the school staff aware of the Bureau's now years-long investigation. A handful of letters from the school's FBI file around this time indicate that someone in Chattanooga and another person who signed their letters simply "A Citizen" were sending local newspaper clippings directly to J. Edgar Hoover, who responded with gratitude. "Your courtesy and interest in bringing this information to my attention are indeed appreciated," he gushed.[17]

That fall, an FBI "man named Lynch" spent the duration of his investigation with "C. H. Kilby, Secretary to the vice-President of the Tennessee Consolidated Coal Company at Tracy City" and a leader of the Crusaders. Though the Monteagle Hotel, where Agent Lynch stayed, was a mere two miles from the school, the agent avoided all contact with Highlander and its staff, preferring to watch from outside.

Myles was never intimidated by the consequences of well-intentioned confrontation, so he went with Highlander librarian Leon Wilson to Lynch's hotel room and provided him with names of people who could speak to the veracity of Highlander's activities. Lynch never bothered to contact any of those people. Instead, he tried to convince a local union leader to attend the school as a mole.[18] (The FBI had considered sending a mole as early as 1936.)

Myles wrote to the FBI to complain: If they were going to investigate Highlander, he wanted to make sure they bothered to visit, interview the staff, and read the school's records. He had nothing to hide and the best way to eliminate such a threat, in his view, was to welcome the scrutiny.[19]

This effort was not in vain. In January 1942, another FBI agent arrived in town. This was "a man named Hill from the Knoxville FBI office. He said that he had come because of the School's complaint to the FBI that the last investigation was not fair."[20]

Agent Hill actually spent time at Highlander, albeit one day. But Myles and Dombrowski provided him with all the requested information, including minutes from meetings and a file of student and staff records. Hill was overwhelmed with the assistance and told Myles that, in his decades of working for the FBI, he had never been treated to such thorough records. He shared that someone—probably CH Kilby—had reported that Highlander held rifle practice during its annual alumni reunions; he also said that several FBI offices had received complaints about labor organizers returning from Highlander Folk School and bringing Communism with them.[21]

As Eleanor Roosevelt had noted, and, by now, Myles, Zilphia, and everyone else at Highlander well knew, "Communist" was a word thrown around anytime someone felt threatened by the effectiveness of a labor union or the possibility of desegregation. It carried a big trigger.

As worried as he was, Myles took it all in stride. "Treat the FBI boys nice," he told his wife, "and don't over feed them on apple sauce cake."[22]

THE WHOLE THING CREATED great stress for Zilphia, who was no doubt relieved and distracted by the occasional visitor who wasn't with the FBI. A particularly notable one arrived and spent a week over Labor Day in 1941: the photographer Edward Weston and his wife and frequent model Charis, who was also the sister of Highlander librarian Leon Wilson.

Zilphia and Charis Wilson hit it off immediately. A gifted writer and artist in her own right, Wilson reminisced about her arrival at the school in her 1998 autobiography, *Through Another Lens*. "The evening of our arrival," she wrote, "there were four tables full of people at dinner. Everyone ate fast while spontaneous-combustion coffee came around in a huge pot. When gobbling had reached the lull stage, Leon stood up, tapped a coffee mug with a fork, and introduced his sister and brother-in-law to those assembled. Zilphia then led the congregation in a spirited sing-along, after which people rushed the dishes off the table and swept the floor, converting the dining hall back into a classroom."[23]

The almost familial atmosphere and daily goings-on at Highlander made a strong impression on Wilson. This was often the case for visitors used to city life or academia or influenced by the images they were shown in movies about rural Southern living. The school and the people who ran it were starkly different from the caricatures so many people expected.

The world of Highlander had evolved into somewhat of a natural outcropping of the Hortons' balanced marriage. Many people assumed, and still assume, the demands they faced took a toll on their private life from an early date. Perhaps some of the early staff witnessed their clashing personalities on occasion and passed gossip around. Yet, their personal letters suggest otherwise. Myles and Zilphia's passion for one another poured through letter after letter during their sometimes quite long stretches apart during their two decades together. Even when letters alluded to troubles within their marriage—and there were troubles from time to time, as with any marriage—these were appended by expressions of optimism, love, and forgiveness.

To that point, Wilson recalled Myles commenting on how difficult it was for the couple to have their own private time and space—to develop lesson plans or do visioning exercises around the school's future—since the students wanted to see them present all the time in the gardens or classrooms, or, at the very least, wandering the grounds. Myles and Zilphia's omnipresence made students, who were far out of their element, feel more at ease, the way a child might be soothed merely by the presence of a parent. Though in starkly different ways, both Zilphia and Myles gave the impression that they had control of a situation. They had to fit socialization in between everything else in order to maintain this persona.

"The only chance for a visit with them was before their workday started," Wilson wrote.

Leon, Edward, and I wandered down through the grape arbor, past [the pig] Rosebud's pen, and along the path through the woods carrying a coffee pot, pail of water, pitcher of milk, eggs, and bread. We had a delicious breakfast with Myles and Zilphia under the watchful eyes of their three black cats—Zollykoffer, Pippisiwa, and mother Jezebel.

The Hortons were amazing people, friendly, down-to-earth, and relaxed despite the enormous amount of work required to keep such a complex community functioning. They were a complementary couple, ideally suited to the enterprise—Myles the impassioned philosopher and Zilphia the cultural catalyst. . . . After dinner that night, the students sang another round of labor songs. Edward and I joined in, most of the songs being familiar, although I did not know "Just like a tree that's planted by the water, we shall not be moved." We sang "Joe Hill" which they dragged out to lugubrious lengths.

Wilson was accompanying her husband on his travels for work, assisting him even as she, like Zilphia, pined for her own creative pursuits.

Weston was on a journey across America, photographing its greatest features for a special edition of Walt Whitman's *Leaves of Grass*. He took a handful of photos in and around Monteagle. Among them were several photographs of Zilphia.

For the girl who grew up flipping through her mother's fashion magazines, it must have been somewhat of a dream to be asked to pose for a professional photographer. But we can see from the photos Weston took that he recognized a quality in Zilphia that would naturally fit in the context of Whitman's signature poetry.

Of the day the photographs were taken, Wilson wrote: "Sunday brought clear, sunny, blue California weather. Down to the Hortons' cabin again, this time with the Graflex [camera] in addition to breakfast fixings, and between rounds of coffee, Edward photographed Zilphia among the leafy trees. Later, he did 8 × 10s of her against the dark-stained wallboards of the outdoor shower."

Through Weston's lens, we see a young-looking Zilphia—

she was thirty-one—hair cropped to shoulder length and slightly wavy, with sharply trimmed bangs sweeping across her brow. In one shot, she's gazing toward the treetops, perhaps watching a bird glide past. Her face embodies an image of hope and faith. In another, she's staring straight at the camera with a glance of momentary disdain. In yet another, she holds a grass leaf in her mouth and tugs on it with her hand, a flirtatious, knowing look in her eyes. This is the image that appeared in the book as its final illustration, along with the last line from this stanza in Whitman's "Poem of Remembrances for a Girl or a Boy":

> *Anticipate the best women!*
> *I say an unnumbered new race of hardy and well-*
> *defined women are to spread through all*
> *These States,*
> *I say a girl fit for These States must be free,*
> *capable, dauntless, just the same as a boy.*[24]

That Walt Whitman poem was a fitting context for the woman who was so motivated by context. It called upon the youth to awaken to the legacy they had been handed, to embrace the United States Constitution as a collection of the core principles of what it means to be American, the words "signed in black and white by the Commissioners, and read by Washington at the head of the army."[25] It was a charge to young people to recognize their own context, to be proud of what changes their generation would bring, even as they honored the past Americans who had fought, sweat, and died to lay a foundation of freedom for them.

This was, in so many ways, the work of Highlander—and the work of Zilphia Horton in particular—written as a poem, nearly a century earlier.

AS WESTON AND WILSON packed away the cameras and drove off, autumn set in. Many of the trees on the plateau shed their leaves. Only the hearty evergreens retained their broad coats of color.

Within a few months, the United States joined the war against

Germany, Italy, and Japan, and the fear of a military draft was beginning to reach the Cumberland Plateau. A few of the Highlander men signed up for the Civilian Conservation Corps to avoid the draft.[26] They were patriots all, but also averse to violence in all its forms. Emil Willimetz ruminated over this fact at great length in his memoir: World War II was a difficult time for a peace-loving pacifist to juggle his aversion to war with his aversion to human suffering. Many opted, where and when they could, to dedicate their energy to the more peaceful side of the cause.

Myles was thirty-six, still young enough to be drafted (forty-four was the cutoff). He did his best to calm Zilphia's nerves as she started to hear of friends being drafted. He assured her that he was likely to be one of the last men called in the county, if he was called at all.

In a letter while she was away, he explained that his draft classification was Class III, which meant he was considered "deferred because of dependency." It's not clear who his dependents were in 1941 as his children had yet to be born, but he noted: "Unless and until I'm reclassified it will be impossible to tell when I'll be drafted. We should, however, build up a good HFS staff so that it will be possible for me to take a defense job if advisable. Don't worry sweetheart."[27] Myles never was drafted, much to Zilphia's relief.

The five years of United States involvement in the war created a quiet time at the school, with so many of the men who had populated CIO union locals drafted, serving their country. Zilphia's youngest sister Ermon Fay shared Zilphia's musical talent and had a particular skill for cultural organizing. She had already spent a fair amount of time at Highlander and officially joined the staff around this time.

Ermon Fay would later remember that Zilphia's role during the war was to be "an ear, a mother, fun, lots of ideas, capable, a whole way of approaching things gained from a mother who had six daughters, though only four survived childhood."[28]

At Myles's memorial service in 1990, Ermon Fay spoke at greater length about this period:

I came to Highlander during the War. It was a quiet time—we were a small flock of women, including Zilphia (perhaps a harem?) and Myles. Some of these young women were Antioch students on their work term, eager to be a part of the people's movement. And Myles did what he always did—he pushed and prodded to make us analyze, formulate, and defend our opinions and decisions. After that process, Zilphia put us back together. She had an ability to make people feel special—not by flattery, but by her interest in them and her enjoyment. She made people feel that they could do something, be something.

Although it was the quiet time, we carried on with union schools and community work, and we began organizing the farmers union, and staff members were borrowed by other organizations. We prevailed.[29]

Claude C. Williams (courtesy Paris Logan County Coal Mining Memorial and Museum)

Myles Horton (courtesy HREC)

Lilian Johnson (courtesy Wisconsin Historical Society)

A workshop meets in front of the main building at the Highlander Folk School (courtesy HREC)

Zilphia leading singing during a Highlander workshop in the 1930s. From left: Waldemar Hille, Mary Lawrence Elkus, and Zilphia Horton. Frankie and Charlie Wilson are at right in front. (courtesy HREC)

Zilphia Horton handing out broadsides at the LaFolette, Tennessee, Textile Workers Local (People of the Cumberland, courtesy HREC)

Recreation at the Highlander Folk School with Zilphia on the left (courtesy HREC)

Zilphia leading singing at the Textile Workers Organizing Committee Founding Convention (courtesy HREC)

Myles and Zilphia square dancing (courtesy WHS)

Emil Willimetz (courtesy EW)

Woody Guthrie at HFS in 1939 (courtesy WHS)

Joie Willimetz in the Highlander Nursery School (courtesy HREC)

Zilphia with Thorsten, Christmas (courtesy WHS)

Zilphia leading singing during a Farmers Union session (courtesy WHS)

Zilphia singing (courtesy HREC)

Zilphia and Myles (Emil Willimetz, courtesy HREC)

Zilphia Horton portrait, 1948 (courtesy HREC)

Zilphia leading singing for workshop women, Charis Horton in center (courtesy HREC)

Staff meeting at Highlander School. From left to right: Henry Shipherd, unknown, Betty Shipherd, Zilphia Horton, Septima Clark, Myles Horton, and Julie Mabee (courtesy HREC)

Esau Jenkins and Myles Horton in conversation at Highlander (courtesy HREC)

Block print by Zilphia, #1: "Strike" (courtesy Charis Horton)

CHAPTER 10

NO MORE MOURNING

PEOPLE HAD A WAY OF COMING to Highlander and staying, as happened with Claudia Lewis, Emil Willimetz, and Ermon Fay. Charis Wilson may have also stayed if it had been an option for her, but her marriage and work called her away in late 1941.

Summer 1942 brought Aleine Austin, a young coed and talented writer from Antioch College who would become one of Zilphia's close friends.[1] Austin grew up in New York and attended a high school for girls before enrolling at Antioch. As she became more and more intrigued by labor unions, she began to wonder why nobody had yet written a digestible guide to a movement that had been so integral to America's growth over the past century and a half. She thought Myles Horton might know such a book, but he did not, so she eventually took the task upon herself, authoring *The Labor Story: A Popular History of American Labor, 1786–1949.*

Austin spent her first Antioch work term at a summer work camp in New Jersey, where she met some people who had attended residential sessions at Highlander and had come away singing. She was dazzled by her new friends' use of music, how they sang whenever they pitched in with a strike, though she didn't entirely understand how or why they were choosing the songs they sang. Nonetheless, they were emphatic enough about singing that she figured there must be a practical use for songs on picket lines.

Curious, Austin requested a work-study term at Highlander

for the summer after her junior year at Antioch. Myles liked to let the Antioch students find their own way at Highlander, and that summer she naturally fell into a writing and teaching role at the school. She was also drawn to Zilphia's cause of engaging the community around Highlander.

The Summerfield News, to which Austin contributed, was not just about Highlander, however.[2] Its purpose was to build a bridge of information between the staff at the school and the neighboring community and vice-versa. This meant that Austin had to embed herself in the community, develop relationships based on trust, and learn about the ways the school was affecting its neighbors and the impressions they had. *The Summerfield News* was a vital part of the relationship between the school and its neighbors. Zilphia was one of its most frequent contributors. She appreciated the fact that it offered her neighbors another view into the truth about what was happening at Highlander. She saw in the newspaper a potential to open minds through truthful, engaging reporting.

Myles made a lasting impression on Austin—they were close for the rest of their lives. About Zilphia, she said:

> [W]hen [Zilphia] sang, it was a deep contralto voice and the spirituals—that was, I think where her full potential came out in the spiritual songs. I mean that dug into me in a way. . . . The singing was just like it is in church—a way for people to get to their innermost feelings about what they were doing and living for. And Zilphia could communicate that just because she felt it. Nothing manipulative about it, it just came through. She made a profound emotional impact on me.

One of the songs Austin remembered learning from Zilphia that summer was "No More Mourning," which was one of the songs Zilphia held most dear. Over time, "No More Mourning" became famous as "Oh Freedom," a song recorded in the 1950s by Odetta and Harry Belafonte and sung by Joan Baez on the steps of the US Capitol on August 28, 1963, the same morning Martin Luther King Jr. gave his "I Have a Dream" speech.

Zilphia learned it from a Black sharecropper named John Handcox, "a natural song-maker [who] used songs to help organize the Southern Tenant Farmers."[3] She spent hours over the years singing through it on her own, working her full, round alto around the deep spiritual declarations of the song's lyrics—its optimism, determination, the way it colored the universal human impulse toward hope.

No more mournin'
No more mournin'
No more mournin' after while
Before I'll be a slave
I'll be buried in my grave
Take my place with those who loved and fought before.[4]

Someone gave her a home recording device and Zilphia recorded herself singing the song a number of ways—long, drawn-out notes like the bellows of a sob, sliding into some notes and pouncing on others. It's unlikely this is the only song she toyed with in this way. Zilphia was a bit of a perfectionist, and she wanted to make sure she knew what she was doing with a song—what the song said, what potential it held—before she bothered to introduce it to others.

In fact, the recordings of her rehearsing "No More Mourning" provide a stunning view into her studiousness—how dedicated she was to not only understanding what she was singing, but also to embodying it. To Zilphia, context and delivery were everything.

She might sing the song hundreds of times in her life, but for the people who were at Highlander for a few weeks, it might be the only time they ever heard it. Zilphia knew that whether the students were affected by a song would be determined by the way she sang it for them that one time. She was determined to place it in her muscle memory so that it might travel into theirs.

She also knew that the way she learned to sing as a white woman taking lessons and studying music in college was markedly different from the way Black women sang in church. She wanted to sing this song the way they did—not to appropriate their musical attack, but to honor it, so that anyone listening might know that it was more than just a song, that it had come from a culture that demanded understanding and respect. She wasn't using it for her own benefit, but rather acting as a conduit between the culture from which the song came and her audience, so that their view of the world might expand.

Zilphia knew this particular song had come from a cultural tradition that stretched into chattel slavery. The kind of terrifying circumstances to which the song referred was something that she, as a white woman, would never experience or truly understand.

And there were other tendrils of oppression that wrapped other people in lives of seemingly insurmountable servitude. The labor movement was, to her, an avenue toward empowering those people—Black and white workers alike—to refuse to be so trapped. The work she was doing was a continuation of the movement for justice and equality that had been central to America from its founding and that had taken so many turns, including revolution, slave rebellion, and labor organizing.

So rather than appropriate the culture of Black abolitionists, Zilphia wanted to join her students to their legacy, to link the plight of struggling workers to the plight of every single one of "those who loved and fought before." To extend the movement for justice to all humans, all members of the big human family.

Zilphia saw the ways these old songs provided links from the present to the past, and she viewed the plight of impoverished people as intimately linked—something that she first came to understand during the desegregated philosophy club back at Claude Williams's house in Paris.

On one recording of "No More Mourning," she closes with a dissonant conclusion on the accordion that sounds like a team of fiddlers on a funeral march.[5] The instrument's melody barely rises above the din of its drone notes. It's a tremendous moment for an accordion, as it does the sonic work of depicting the struggle a single soul faces in its attempt to win freedom from the forces of oppression. This instrumental arrangement is no accident. When Zilphia Horton picked up any musical instrument, she knew exactly what she was doing.

And once she had connected with a song like "No More Mourning," she took it with her wherever she went—whether union halls in LaFolette or Chicago or school fundraisers in New York City. The more she sang it, she knew, the more it could *do*.

DURING SPRING 1942, just before Austin arrived at Highlander, Zilphia had been back in New York. Now that she knew her way around, the city was one of her favorite places to visit. She had come to love New York with a special passion, relishing any opportunity to take in a few shows, visit the galleries, and drop in at Cafe Society, the trendy nightclub in the Village. She made the most of her limited time there and, on the way back to Monteagle, she wrote to Myles that she was starting to wonder about the way she was feeling: "Darling, I've been thinking that by the time I get to Washington, another month will have passed and if nothing has 'happened' by then, I might see a doctor recommended by Camille. Maybe I'm too impatient. What do you think? It seems that if we want any children we shouldn't wait any unnecessary time."[6]

So eager for news about the possibility that she could be pregnant, Miles closed every letter he wrote to her for the next week with the smiling nag, "Have you seen the doctor yet?"

There's reason to suspect this was not Zilphia's first pregnancy, as letters across the previous years were occasionally peppered with questions about her doctor visits. Charis Wilson remembered Zilphia being pregnant when she visited Highlander with Edward Weston in 1941.[7] Charis Horton and Zilphia's friend Anne Romasco both recalled her having terribly challenging menstrual cycles. "Like go-to-bed-with-cramps bad," Charis recalled. "And she was tough, but that's how bad they were."[8] Whether Zilphia was suffering from endometriosis, fibroids, or some other reproductive ailment, Myles frequently addressed her health and wellness in his letters.

Zilphia Horton was a tough woman with physical strength to match that of her emotional wellness, so it might almost seem as though these missives about her health were akin to the hysterical musings of "the weaker sex" in Victorian literature. But it seems clear that her health was only of real concern around reproductive issues. Myles sent her extra affection when it was time for her "monthly illness," a phrase he took to using not as innuendo, but rather to refer to how ill she actually became. It's possible that she was seeing a doctor to help regulate her cycle, but reproductive health issues ran in the family. With all this in mind, it also seems Zilphia may have experienced at least one miscarriage.

In a letter to Myles in 1936, she reported, "Perhaps I shouldn't put this in a letter but when I arose, I felt a certain tenderness about my breasts which is not common to this time of the month."[9] A pregnancy did not come to fruition at that point, but that was the first indication we have that the couple was interested in starting a family.

Clearly, something within the Hortons' relationship had shifted in their seven years of marriage. "At first," Myles wrote, "just being together and being able to work together was enough, but we soon began to think of children. I was well past 30 and Zilphia only five years younger when we realized that to do justice and to enjoy children, we shouldn't wait too long."[10]

Zilphia was thirty-two by the time she wrote that letter from Washington, DC, and Myles was thirty-seven. At that time, the median maternal age for a first birth was twenty-one.[11] By that measure, Zilphia was viewed by society as somewhat of a curiosity by the time she first carried a pregnancy to term.

The Hortons must have been trying to conceive for a while, in-between highly stressful workshops and their many weeks-long trips apart. Whether their timing was off or there was a reproductive ailment for Zilphia to overcome is hard to say. Women didn't exactly record or advertise these details in the 1940s, even women like Zilphia who thought it important to talk forthrightly with other women about birth control.

Regardless, in summer 1942, Zilphia was indeed pregnant. She bought Myles a book about parenting and repeatedly insisted he read every page. She told him she was "chompin' at the bit" and was excited with the possibility that "'it' could be twins."[12]

Myles's response was equally enthusiastic, if somewhat flustered. When he received a letter from her confirming the pregnancy, he shot back: "Darling; your letter came this morning and oh boy what news. Makes me dizzy though to think of it. But happy. There is really nothing to say is there?"[13]

With a baby due the following spring, the couple finally moved into their new home. Zilphia's nesting phase ensured the family would be well equipped with all the conveniences in their out-of-place modern abode. In a county where most people didn't even have a flushing toilet in their house, the Hortons would have a full-service kitchen and bathroom, bathtub, and washer and dryer.[14]

As the holidays passed and the winter set in, Myles and Zilphia were alone at the school with only one other staff member, Eve Milton. Milton's memory of those months shows us how quiet and still life atop the plateau was in the days before the children when no residential session was taking place:

> One cold, wintry evening at the beginning of 1943, Myles, Zilphia and I were alone in the main house. The day's chores were done. We had finished supper and had cleaned the kitchen and we now sat peacefully before the large fireplace. A soft fire warmed us and the room. John, Lilian Johnson's old rheumy collie, snoozed and wheezed at our feet. Zilphia whittled small oak birds, the beginnings of a mobile she was constructing for their eagerly awaited first child. Myles was reading to us. The three of us were all the staff there would be for several months.
>
> The war had decimated our staff, our funding sources and many of our projects. We were peaceful just the same. We had much to look forward to and laugh about.[15]

Toward the end of that season, with parenting books read and impatience dutifully surmounted, Thorsten Wayne Horton was born at the Vanderbilt Medical Center in Nashville, Tennessee, on February 22, 1943. His name derived from a common Danish surname that Myles appreciated from his travels there years ago.[16]

Myles, who was over the moon, headed back up the plateau to try to get some work done, but could hardly focus without first writing his wife, who would remain in the hospital for a few more days. His confession of fear over her well-being during the delivery—along with the fact that the Hortons drove an hour and a half to the Vanderbilt hospital for delivery despite there being a hospital in Sewanee—seems to underscore how serious her reproductive health had been to this point:

> Dear deflated sweetheart; This is my first letter to you and Thorsten Wayne so don't forget to tell him about it. Leon beat me home and told them about you and Thorsten. The staff still had a lot of questions though and were pretty excited. . . .
>
> Honey, I am rambling on because it is impossible to say what I feel. The afternoon and evening before Thorsten was born I was numb with fear that something would happen to you. The news that we had a healthy boy effected [*sic*] me much less than word that you were alright. It was only later that I could enjoy the thrilling experience of our having a child. Already though the anxious hours over you are pushed into the background by thoughts of raising a child. We are in for a lot of fun, enough I hope to repay you for all that indescribable suffering. Your courage darling was grand. I will never forget it. I didn't realize that anything could make me love you more but something did—little red faced Thorsten with his wrinkled brow. Give my regards to your intern and the nurses.[17]

Despite Myles's fears for her health, Zilphia recovered from the pregnancy, telling him within a day or two that she was ready to get back to work.

She was completely smitten with the child. She couldn't stop staring at his little body and face, smiling every time he cooed. From the beginning, Zilphia knew she was going to adore being a mother. She relished watching her son grow and develop.

Luckily, the quiet left behind on the plateau due to the war years created the perfect space for Zilphia and Myles to focus on their firstborn, and Thorsten was a much photographed, much written-about new wonder in their world. Every noise he made and step he took added to Zilphia's lust for life, and she relished orienting her son to the world around him. In photographs taken by Emil Willimetz, we see her lifting Thorsten over her head, carrying him on picnics, and holding him on her lap, making playful faces while he smiled.[18]

Though Zilphia was certainly happy to pour herself into motherhood, she was also relieved to have a visit from Emil Willimetz that September. It was a visit he remembered clearly and held dear for the rest of his life:

> In the morning, Zilphia Horton came over to fill me full of
> school gossip and buttermilk pancakes with black walnuts, sour-
> wood honey, and wild muscadine grape jelly. There were now
> 12 members of the Highlander Board, and Zilphia was rais-
> ing a goose named after each. She served me a single goose egg
> that filled the platter. This goose, she said, was Board Member
> Paul R. Christopher, my ex-boss and good friend. . . . The mem-
> ory of that breakfast stayed with me all through my Army expe-
> rience—as it does to this day!
>
> How good it was to be with friends. And Zilphia was one of
> the best. As we talked, mindless army discipline and chickenshit
> brass slid into oblivion. I told her about life in an Army camp,
> and we chuckled over the story of my friend the Tennessee hill-
> billy who was discharged from the army because he couldn't
> shoot a rifle. Owning and shooting a rifle was as common as
> chewing tobacco in the mountains. Zilphia admitted modestly
> that, personally, she wasn't such a bad shot herself.[19]

The first two years of Thorsten's life were full of outings, with parents swapping home time so that the other could get away. But even with all their duties, the couple did not wait long before trying for a second child. They got their wish on March 24, 1945, a little more than two years after Thorsten was born.

Karis Ermon Horton was named after her grandmother Ora Ermon, her aunt Ermon Fay, and Leon's sister Charis Wilson. Wilson recalled the change of spelling in her autobiography: "Zilphia . . . said if she had a girl she would call her Charis. I urged her to be more merciful and spell the name 'Karis' to spare her daughter a lifetime of mispronunciation and misspelling."[20]

Charis Horton would learn of this and insist her parents change her name to the correct spelling. Her argument was convincing enough that Zilphia had her daughter's birth certificate legally amended.

AS HER CHILDREN GREW, Zilphia settled into a life that had categorically changed. The babies were too much of a distraction for the workshop hall, so she began spending a fair amount of time away from the events of the school. Though she remained deeply entwined with the culture program, her role was irreversibly changing. As Myles wrote:

> New problems of carrying on independent professional lives naturally arose. We had our professional interests, our personal lives, and the children to work into a pattern. The basic operating principle was that we would equally share in all responsibilities when possible. The responsibilities of a mother that could only be dealt with by the mother were attempted to be balanced off by my doing as much of the housework, etc., as I could. An effort was made to share all other responsibilities equally including taking care of the children. . . . I always had the feeling that I wasn't doing my full share, and looking back, I can see how I could have done more.[21]

An effort was certainly made, but the children had no recollection of their father doing anything along the lines of washing dishes or cooking. Things in the outside world were heating up, the school was under constant threat, and Myles had, somewhat necessarily, long since become a benevolent dictator in terms of how Highlander was run. Intentions are always one thing; reality another. And it is clear from various accounts that Zilphia took over the lion's share of parenting during the early years—not that she especially minded. "They're both in wonderful form," she reported once when Myles was out of town. "Both demanding every second of mother's time and of course she loves it."[22]

Zilphia would bring the children to the workshop space in time for dinner and other people would hold them while she led the after-dinner singing. Otherwise, she was focused on making home a wonderful place and orienting Thorsten and Charis to life on the plateau. She especially enjoyed hiking with them through the woods, the way her parents had done with her.

As Thorsten kicked into toddlerhood with boyish aplomb, Charis seemed a jovial, happy knockoff of her mother. Myles and Thorsten made noises at her just to get her attention, then hid behind a door or wall in a protracted game of hide-and-seek. She would foist herself up on her elbows and look at them quizzically, then fall off her hands, laughing, and try again.

When she was at home alone with the children, Zilphia peppered her letters with choice vignettes, labeling them as "Thorstenote" and "Charisnote" and recording the children's physical and intellectual developments with the good humor of a doting mother. She was moved by Charis's cries in the middle of the night and thoroughly amused with the way Thorsten was beginning to verbalize everything.

Both she and Myles waxed poetic about how the births of their children metamorphosed their marriage in beautiful, heartwarming, exciting ways. They instantly felt more deeply connected, through the visible, physical incarnations of their partnership. They shared updates about the children at the same feverish, inspired pace of their early love letters that first winter when Zilphia was in New York and Myles was a young, heartsick beau.

The Hortons raised their children with the mindful intentions of two people determined to leave behind a world better off than they had found it. In a bit of autobiographical writing, Myles reminisced:

> Part of the reason [Thorsten and Charis] were ready for dealing with the adult world was that they had grown up in the presence of both adults and children and had never been told there were some things for children and others for adults. . . .
>
> Perhaps the main thing was that everybody could share in work and responsibilities and that you could make do with what you had in a material way and deal with circumstances as they

arose. They . . . helped us with cooking, gardening, etc. They also learned that they were not the center of our world or should be. They knew we had to work and they were beginning to learn why we felt what we do was important, that in many instances you work because you wanted to and liked to, not because you had to. That work could be done voluntarily and not because it had to be done at the behest of some force outside.[23]

As the children grew and the school shifted focus, the work kept evolving and the world kept turning. A few states away, on the east coast of South Carolina, change was brewing in the five-story warehouse at the American Tobacco Company.

CHAPTER 11

WE WILL OVERCOME

THERE WAS NO UNION at the American Tobacco Company in Charleston, South Carolina, when Lillie Mae Marsh Doster started working there in 1943.[1] The shop took a "no-strike pledge" during the war, as did most industrial workers around the country, despite the fact that its workers were unsatisfied with the conditions of their labor and pay.[2] But they were also aware that a national movement was simmering around low wages and poor working conditions—particularly at tobacco plants, where Black workers were treated like slaves by abusive, demanding white foremen.

The same year that Doster landed at American Tobacco, a young Black woman named Theodosia Gaither Simpson raised hell—and won the union—just a few hours away, at the R. J. Reynolds Tobacco Company in Winston-Salem, North Carolina.[3] One day, Simpson noticed one of her coworkers was sick and not working as fast as expected. The foreman leaned into the sick woman, letting her know that if she didn't pick up the pace, she would be fired.

Simpson decided she had had enough. She talked to a couple of women in the ladies' bathroom and together they staged a sit-in the next day. Their action inspired others to join them throughout the factory, forcing its closure, forcing the bosses to the bargaining table, and establishing Local 22 of the Food, Tobacco, Agricultural, and Allied Workers of America (FTA), a branch of the CIO.

Doster had heard about Simpson's leadership and became interested in organizing something similar where she worked, on the fifth floor at American Tobacco.

Each of the company's twenty-three hundred workers was responsible for some small part of processing tobacco into cigars, then boxing them up to be shipped. They called the fifth floor the "Box Shop." Doster's job was to "label a box, turn it over, put it in the machine, and mash a bell." She recalled: "It was three people. One would put the box on the belt, come down, and I would flip it over and put it in the machine, [which] would wrap the box and somebody else would wipe it off." All day long, every day.[4]

This was mind-numbing, demoralizing work, for ten cents an hour. Forget that the Fair Labor Standards Act of 1938 had set forty cents an hour as the bare minimum for tobacco workers. When it came to what Black women were paid, the bosses were willing to ignore the law, assuming the women would either not know better or that they would not dare defy their white male bosses.

Like Theodosia Simpson, the women of American Tobacco were tired of such fears. Knowing that many of their coworkers—the white women and at least some of the white men—were sympathetic to their cause, they thought it was high time to demand a desegregated factory floor. It was also time for more pay. Their ten-cent wage was equivalent to today's dollar-fifty; it was enough to buy bread and little else; enough to keep them alive and in poverty.

With a clear mission—a twenty-five-cent raise, six days of sick leave, "a closed [union] shop and uniform working conditions in all the company's factories"[5]—the workers of American Tobacco organized that fall as part of the FTA-CIO, as had their peers in Winston-Salem. Doster became one of the union stewards in the Box Shop. The other was Lucille Simmons, a young woman who sang in the choir at the Jerusalem Baptist Church. Like Doster, Simmons was a socially aware, well-educated Black woman at a time when there wasn't supposed to be such a thing, certainly not in a factory hall in South Carolina.

As stewards, the women were responsible for following up on grievances and collaborating with the workers and bosses to mediate solutions to any problems. There was, for example, no air conditioning in the factory, so they agitated for fans. The issues of increased pay and sick leave, however, were too big for any single mediation. So, on Monday, October 22, 1945, they walked off the job, setting into motion what was to be a strike of historic proportions.

The newspaper reported: "Most of the machines at the American Tobacco company's plant ground to a stop shortly after noon today when some 1,000 employees . . . walked out of the factory at the direction of Local 15 of the Food, Tobacco, Agricultural, and Allied Workers Union."[6]

IT WAS UNSEASONABLY WARM that October day, but as autumn 1945 unfolded, the air turned chilly and humid in Charleston, giving way to a colder, wetter winter. For the women of American Tobacco's FTA-CIO, it was not the best season for a strike, but they were willing to stand out in the cold rain in order to make a point—an indication that other, more comfortable avenues toward success had failed.

These women knew, because they had organized with the CIO, that people elsewhere were making more money for the same job. They knew that there were laws in the United States that ensured factory workers a fair wage and a safe workplace. This may have been the City of Charleston's first labor union strike, but it was by no means an early moment in the American labor movement. These workers were fighting on the tail end of the movement's heyday, long after the eight-hour workday had been won and after Roosevelt's New Deal had ensured protections for union workers, safeguarding their right to organize and bargain collectively via the 1935 Wagner Act.

They knew there was nothing to lose. They saw it in the eyes of their children, who were hungry and poor, who wanted more, and who would eventually take up the cause and face beatings and worse, surmounting fear to bring the battle for civil rights to the national stage. It would be easy, on this side of history, to imagine that these women had all that in mind, and perhaps they did. But, more immediately, they wanted good pay and respect. They struck for five months that winter.

At first, the decision to strike takes some cajoling, but once everyone's on board, there's a passion, a wave that passes over people. A sense that *we can do this, together.* These women showed up day after day, refusing to work, not taking home any pay. Doster remembers being on the picket line from six in the morning until six at night, every day, from October to March, except one: Easter Monday.

She, Simmons, and the others didn't have savings to tap. As the days dragged on into weeks and then months, the bosses refused to cave, and the rain refused to quit.

When Pete Seeger told his version of this story to Tim Robbins for Pacifica Radio in 2006, he placed them standing around a big metal drum with a fire burning in it for warmth, asking each other, *Is this strike sustainable? How do we know when we should give up?*[7]

Discouraged, broke, tired, and demoralized, some picketers started going back to work, willing to take the fifteen cents an hour the company offered them as a consolation. Other strikers felt angry and betrayed, some threatening the "scabs" with violence.

"Some of the girls didn't want to come in through the front door," Doster said, "because we were picketing. Because, I mean, they put the beating on some of those girls one day. A friend of mine was in bed for two weeks. . . . The strikers [were] going to beat the people who went back in the plant."

So, instead, the workers who decided to defy the strike and return to work would sneak in through the back door to avoid any altercations. Hundreds of others remained on the line, though, huddled in soup kitchens[8] for warmth and subsisting on spare change from fellow workers, who sent them funds via the CIO.

Simmons closed each picketing day by singing out, long and slow, low and haunting, like a meditation, an old, old hymn with new words:

> *We'll be all right*
> *We'll be all right*
> *We'll be all right someday*

Whoever was there, huddled in the cold, holding their coats together across their tired chests, joined in. Simmons insisted they couldn't leave until they sang. "Every afternoon we would fuss with Lucille," said Doster. They had been on their feet all day and rolled their eyes at her persistence. But, once she started singing, they relented and joined in. There was something about the song that just refueled them.

Down in my heart
I do believe
We'll overcome someday

"You think about that, it's almost like a prayer of relief," Doster explained. "We didn't make up the song. We just started singing it as a struggle song."[9]

"We sang 'I'll be all right . . . we will win our rights . . . we will win this fight . . . we will organize . . . we will overcome.' We sang it with a clap and a shout until sometimes the cops would quiet us down."

SIMMONS'S APPROACH TO this old melody and lyric was likely drawn from "If My Jesus Wills," a hymn written by Louise Shropshire sometime in the 1930s.[10] Shropshire, a Black woman who was born to a sharecropper family in Alabama but grew up in Cincinnati, Ohio, sang with and composed hymns for the choir at her local Baptist church.

For decades, the history of this song was traced to a white man named Charles Tindley, who published a song called "I'll Overcome Someday" in 1901. Though the spirit of Tindley's song is similar, it doesn't match "We Shall Overcome" in lyrical or melodic pattern, while Shropshire's composition is almost exactly the song that came to Zilphia Horton from the women of American Tobacco. Its melody can be traced back to a Catholic hymn from the Middle Ages, "O Sanctissima," and had likely been through a hundred lyrical incarnations before Shropshire's update.

Regardless, as those five months passed, the song became

somewhat of a theme for the strike, and while the union did not achieve all its demands from the American Tobacco Company, the workers were successful in winning a slight pay raise. They also experienced the power of singing, using parts of their culture to change the conversation, to empower themselves and each other, and to fuel their resistance day in and day out.

When the strike ended in late March 1946, Doster, Simmons, and the others returned to work, but they had changed. They had not prevailed in their demands. In fact, what amounted to a less-than-successful strike is perhaps one of the most important parts of their story. The eight-cent raise they were granted was far lower than the twenty-five cents they were demanding,[11] but the women of American Tobacco had learned a vital lesson through this momentary failure. They hungered for a better way and now knew one was possible. They knew from experience that when they organized, people in power would listen and respond. This would carry the Black population of Charleston through other labor disputes and into the thick of the civil rights era on the wings of the experience they now had with collective power.

Though history has lost track of Simmons's story, Doster became heavily involved in the civil rights movement that unfolded in the ensuing years, helping to organize Black nurses in Charleston and working with other groups to lift their voices and overcome. A couple of their coworkers from American Tobacco traveled to Monteagle to attend a workshop at Highlander that summer after the strike. Accounts about who, exactly, brought the song and how it even came up during a Highlander workshop vary.

In a pamphlet written in the 1970s about the history of what by then was the unofficial anthem of the civil rights movement, Guy and Candie Carawan shared the version of the story they had been told. Neither was present for that 1946 workshop, but it is possible that at least part of the story Guy picked up came directly from Zilphia, if not from Myles. Both Hortons were prone to exaggerate their stories in order to make a point, though, so it's hard to know what details are accurate.

Regardless, as Guy recalled:

It is one of the ironies of history that the song was brought by two white workers, who had probably not sung it themselves but had heard it sung by the black strikers. The song was drawn from them at the workshop by Zilphia. . . . Zilphia had to ask several times before the Charleston workers told about "We Will Overcome," and based on their rendition of it she had to imagine what it must have sounded like in black tradition on the picket line. . . . It had a slow, free, anthem-like feeling to it, and wherever she taught it people loved the song.[12]

The "slow, free, anthem-like feeling" is certainly an accurate description of the recordings Zilphia made with her home-recording device. But the memory that it had been brought to Highlander by white workers from American Tobacco is the point that's likely not true, as intriguing an irony as it may have been.

Other sources point to the likelihood that the Charleston FTA-CIO workers who taught the song to Zilphia were Black.[13] Some reports suggest that it was Simmons and a woman named Delphine Brown who delivered the song. Brown was also known for leading the song on the picket, though she attacked it with a more spirited tempo than that of Simmons's drawn-out dirge.

Aleine Austin, who was present on the plateau that year, told Highlander interviewer Sue Thrasher in 1982 that she also recalled that the Charleston FTA members who came to the workshop were Black.

It was a mixed group; and part of the program was just having them describe what their problems were. They had just had a strike and they were describing the conditions of the strike and then they . . . started singing some of the songs they sang on the picket line. And one of the songs was [she sings] "We shall overcome; we shall overcome." And then "The union will see us through, the union will see us through." And the final verse, "We are on to victory, we are on to victory." And Zilphia just felt the power of that song, "We shall overcome." That first verse, but the rest of it was sort of banal and you know, she got us together one night and told us how powerful she felt this song was and she played it on the piano with the chords, and . . . the whole workshop was there, and she said, "I think we could find better words for some of those middle verses." She says, "So why doesn't each person here—now that you know the melody—sit down and write what you think would be a good verse?" And so we sat there and then each of us sang our little portion. Well, there [were] marvelous lines that came out of it. I think one of them was "The truth will set us free." That was Myles. I'm not sure, but I think that was Myles.[14]

Ermon Fay, meanwhile, remembered going into the Highlander library with Zilphia and the two FTA-CIO workers and coming up with new verses, just the four of them.[15] Perhaps somewhere in the center of the Venn diagram of these memories lies the truth about how "We Will Overcome" was reborn at Highlander.

One thing all the memories have in common is that several people came together at the Highlander Folk School in spring 1946, under Zilphia's leadership and encouragement, and metamorphosed this hymn into a song that would ultimately change the world.

Zilphia knew an important song when she heard it. She adopted "We Will Overcome" as a sort of personal anthem, printing it in song sheet broadsides. From that moment on, she taught it to everyone who came through Highlander. She closed every meeting with it. She sang it as a sort of closing prayer at every event and gathering when a song seemed necessary. The song struck a perfect balance between public declaration and personal meditation. It was a reminder to all those listening of the persistence of the human spirit, just as it was a reminder to the singer that no momentary struggle could kill a person.

As long as I'm alive, the song seemed to say, *I can sing this song.*

Every word in the song was important. Every note, drawn out the way she sang them, was like a boldfaced underline.

We.

Will.

Overcome.

The song was effective because it did what it said it was going to do. For every individual singing along with the refrain, it was easy to feel that injustice both could and would be overcome.

Sing the song in a group and look around the room. Noticing other people sing the words, "we will overcome," you begin to understand, intrinsically, without epiphany, that you want to overcome. A light turns on in your soul, showing you the truth of your humanity: You are not interested in resignation. As you sing "we" with everyone else singing "we," you understand you are making a promise together, to one another, to yourselves, to anyone listening. There doesn't even need to be eye contact because you hear these voices.

Not "we *can* overcome," but "we *will*."

By the end of the song, those singing are indelibly linked. The promise has been made. The refrain cannot be unsung. There is a knowledge shared with the others who sing, and with anyone standing nearby.

Being present for "We Will Overcome" means bearing witness to the power of collective determination. Together, the song tells us, we will transform the impossible into the accomplished. Indeed, that is the story of human history—from migration around the globe to the building of civilization, the pursuit of freedom and equity, and the exploration of space.

Humans are social creatures, not just because we enjoy each other's company, but also because we cannot do much alone. We cannot survive alone, and we certainly cannot build a more just, peaceful, and equitable world alone.

The vitality of cultural organizing, the way that Zilphia developed the discipline, cut to the core of this truth about our common humanity: Organizing a successful movement is practice for the way the world will be once that movement is successful. The labor movement organized by empowering working-class people, teaching them how to be leaders, and illustrating to them the value of their knowledge and experience—things that would become necessary for them to employ when they wielded more power in the workplace.

The civil rights movement was organized by bringing Black folks together with white to strategize, to see in one another the

value of shared experience—something that would become necessary once Jim Crow laws were off the books.

Both of these movements remain ongoing, but the lessons
these organizers learned and shared at various turning points remain for us to improve upon as we continue to organize around
these goals. And where the narrative details of labor and civil
rights history are confined to books and lecture series, the songs
that came out of these movements can be recalled and employed
without anyone in the room requiring an explanation. Without
any necessary context. When we sing, we are joining our voices
not only with those in the room, but also with all those who sang
before.

As Zilphia impressed upon all the people to whom she taught
"We Will Overcome," singing it now connects us—the "we"
here—to those who sang it before, at Highlander, in Charleston,
or anywhere else. "It's a way of laughing," she told her students,
"but it's very serious, too, you see."[16]

When we sing, we join the long chain of people who saw no
other way but to come together and promise to overcome. We
are joined to their successes and thus the way forward becomes
clearer.

IN AUTUMN 1948, in New York, Zilphia taught the song to
Pete Seeger, who remembered her singing it "slower than anyone had ever heard it." It's easy to imagine the pair of them sitting together in a room, Zilphia singing it for Seeger with no accompaniment, Seeger picking up his banjo and finding a melodic
rhythm that felt like a match. It's easy to imagine that they then
sang it through together a few times and that Zilphia left him
with a list of the lyrics, maybe notated the sung melody for him.
It's possible they sang it together at a fundraising event for the
school during that same trip, since Zilphia frequently had well-
known folksingers join her for such occasions, and Seeger was always happy to pitch in.

Regardless, the Almanac Singers had long since parted ways,
after many of its men were drafted—Seeger spent much of the
war serving in the army in the Pacific. Upon his return to New

York, newly married with a young son, he began publishing the monthly pamphlet *People's Songs* and asked Zilphia to write about "We Will Overcome" for inclusion in Bulletin No. 3. That printing, in September 1948, included a brief introduction written by Zilphia: "Many a visitor to the South has never . . . forgotten hearing the rich harmonies of some little band, and the determination in these words, even though surrounded on all sides by hate, Jim Crow, and all the forces of power and money. Its strong emotional appeal and simple dignity never fails to hit people. It sort of stops them cold silent."[17]

Whether Zilphia knew she was setting the foundation for what would become one of the most consequential songs of the twentieth century is unclear. But she certainly believed it was one of the most important songs *she* had ever heard—if not the most important.

In 1947, the year before she taught the song to Seeger, she spoke to a gathering of CIO members about the importance of "We Will Overcome," telling them:

> Although you may never have expressed these big world ideas in just the way we are talking about them tonight, I think that they are perhaps the reason you put such feeling into such simple words as we sing "We Will Overcome."
>
> For I think you know that it is only when working men and women everywhere realize not only their rights but their duties as union members, as citizens of a democracy, as citizens of a free world, and work together to that end, that we will overcome.[18]

Seeger, for his part, was so stirred by the song that he added it to his own repertoire, as did folksingers Joe Glazer and Guy Carawan, who had learned it from folksinger and song collector Frank Hamilton, who had learned it from Zilphia.[19]

As stage performers, however, Seeger and Carawan knew the importance of keeping an audience's attention. They felt there needed to be a more accessible rhythm and the song had to be easier to sing, more natural, less dramatic, lest it tire or exasperate an audience. Carawan perked up the melody, adding a triplet rhythm that felt like a heart racing from the adrenaline of determination. In this 12/8 time signature, the syllables of "We Will Overcome" became like the tolling of a bell, a calling to the table. The song became a marching hymn.

Seeger liked the way a "sh" sound pulled the rhythm forward, the way the sound of the letter "a" opened up the singer's mouth.[20] He felt it created a progression of openness that matched the song's message. When you sing the words "We Shall Overcome," you can feel your mouth opening wider and wider still, with each syllable. He changed the "will" to "shall" and adopted Carawan's triplet rhythm, turning Zilphia's way of emphasizing the lyrics into something anyone could sing with as much gusto as she, and then he took the song around the world.

"WE SHALL OVERCOME" has been celebrated as the defining anthem of the civil rights movement. When Carawan introduced it to the Student Nonviolent Coordinating Committee (SNCC) in 1960, those present instinctively, unprompted, linked arms and swayed as they sang. They sang the song on picket lines and marches, in paddy wagons and jail cells, until it became synonymous with the effort to recognize the humanity of Black lives.

SNCC's commitment to Gandhism—active resistance that calls for people to practice agape love for their oppressors as equal victims of an oppressive system—made the song even more powerful. *Beat us and sic the dogs on us*, the song implicitly declared, *but we shall overcome.*

Martin Luther King Jr. heard SNCC members sing the song and found some truth in it as well. He worked it into one of his most memorable speeches:

> We shall overcome because the arc of the moral universe is long but it bends towards justice. We shall overcome because Carlisle is right: "No lie can live forever." We shall overcome because William Cullen Bryant is right: "Truth crushed to earth will rise again." We shall overcome because James Russell Lowell is right: "Truth forever on the scaffold, wrong forever on the throne." Yet

that scaffold sways the future. We shall overcome because the Bible is right: "You shall reap what you sow."[21]

So powerful and effective was the use of this little song and its prevailing, persisting refrain that it was quoted in a joint session of Congress on March 15, 1965, when President Lyndon Baines Johnson announced that he was sending the National Guard to Selma, Alabama, to accompany civil rights activists on their route to Montgomery as they made history in the effort to win voting rights for Black citizens.

"Their cause must be our cause, too," Johnson told Congress. "Because it is not just Negroes, but really it is all of us, who must overcome the crippling legacy of bigotry and injustice, and the harsh judgment of history on our acts. And we shall overcome."[22]

Johnson knew that this song came from Black churches and labor activists. Invoking their import in the halls of Congress added a certain strength to the message he was sharing. In so doing, he linked himself for all of history with Lucille Simmons, Delphine Brown, Lillie Mae Marsh Doster, Ermon Fay Duschenes, Zilphia Horton, Pete Seeger, Frank Hamilton, Guy Carawan, and Martin Luther King Jr.

CHAPTER 12

GETTING OUT OF TOWN

THE CIVIL RIGHTS MOVEMENT, which would dominate Highlander's resources for years to come, was beginning to take shape with Black and white workers organizing together in more and more shops like American Tobacco. And though this required a lot of flexibility and time for the Hortons and their staff to re-imagine Highlander's vision, Zilphia and Myles were finding it increasingly necessary to fit some leisure into their harried lives.

"Ethel Clyde . . . gave them lots and lots of money," says Charis. "She wanted to bring Myles to Mexico and Guatemala, and he said she had to bring Zilphia, which Ethel did not want to do. She was eighty or something. She just wanted to have her boy toy. [Maybe] boy toy is the wrong word—she was giving him money, he was going to accompany her around, so he made her take Zilphia."[1]

Clyde was a colorful character, and she loomed large in the memories of most people who were closely involved with Highlander. The Horton children remembered her for the gifts she sent them and the affection she harbored for their father. She was in her eighties by the time they knew her, but others at Highlander remembered her as a sixty-something woman whose husband's grandfather had founded the Clyde Steamship Lines.

Late in life, Jim Dombrowski recalled the first time she invited him to her home in Huntington, Long Island. In his biography of Dombroski, former Highlander board president Frank Adams wrote that Clyde "was among the few wealthy Americans who gave to liberal causes and was well-known to most socialists."

The wealthy widow "took sociology courses at Columbia University, mostly to satisfy an easily bored, inquisitive mind. A liveried chauffeur drove her to classes in a limousine flying the Clyde Line flag on its fender."[2]

These classes opened Clyde's eyes to the plight of the common person who was not afforded the luxury and privilege she enjoyed. She became dedicated to workers' rights, especially after visiting a West Virginia coal mine and feeling heartsick over the working conditions of the miners.

Clyde displayed the kind of garish wealth that usually turned Zilphia's stomach. But Myles's ability to straddle the fence between hillbilly radical and New York intellectual tugged hard on Clyde's heart and she became one of his most ardent supporters. She visited Highlander on occasion but was quite out of place in Monteagle. More often, she made him come to her. Thus, her Long Island estate was one of his first stops whenever he traveled to New York to raise funds for the school.

Clyde would parade Myles around various society functions, bragging both about the extraordinary effect he was having on the helpless Southerners to whom his school catered and the fact that she helped to cover his expenses. It must have been equal parts exhausting and entertaining for no-frills Myles to be party to her grandiose nature. But once he had submitted to the show and done his part, he was able to head home with a hefty check for the school.

Supporting the school wasn't enough, though. Clyde cared deeply about Myles, specifically, as an individual, and wanted to support not only his intellectual mission but also his children and his leisure time. She wanted to make sure that Myles had enough time to play and relax, away from the school with all its threats and demands.

So, in December 1947, Clyde eagerly sent Myles—and reluctantly also paid for Zilphia—to take a trip to Mexico's Yucatan Peninsula and Guatemala.

MYLES AND ZILPHIA LEFT their children with Mom and Dad Horton and boarded a train to New Orleans, where they transferred to a flight across the Gulf of Mexico for a two-and-a-half-week vacation. They spent two days near Mérida, Mexico, before traveling on to Antigua, Guatemala, where they visited Lake Amatitlán, Palin, the Agua Volcano, and the village of Santa María de Jesús. From there, they moved on to Chichicastenango and the open-air markets run by indigenous communities in Sololá and Panjachel and then to Guatemala City in time for a parade to celebrate the Day of the Virgin of Guadalupe. Their last scheduled stop was Cobán, before they flew back to New Orleans and took the train home to Monteagle, reams of textiles and other souvenirs in their additional luggage.[3]

We can imagine Zilphia at her kitchen table, looking over this itinerary before they left, delighting at the foreign words and phrases, becoming excited with all the wide-open unknown adventures that awaited her. The girl from rural Arkansas had never been on a plane before. In fact, at that point, most Americans had not flown, certainly not those who lived in small, rural areas. Zilphia did the math and figured out it would have taken them seven days to arrive in Guatemala City by train, so she was eager for the opportunity to go so far in so little time. It would be markedly different from riding the train over the Mississippi River or pulling into the Washington, DC, bus station.

She had been to Canada twice, taking the train from New York to Montreal for two summers of leading the music at Camp Laquemac, a YWCA adult camp.[4] But to this point in her life, all her travel had been to places where most people looked and behaved more or less like her: white, middle class, fluent in English. She had read a couple of books about local history. But, as with all things, Zilphia was eager to finally immerse herself.

With equal parts nostalgia and an interest in educating her otherwise isolated neighbors about foreign cultures, Zilphia upon her return wrote about their Latin American adventures for *The Summerfield News* in two installments:

How hot New Orleans was! Like a steam bath. We were glad to get out of the heat as we walked up the ramp at 9 a.m. into the big four-motored plane. . . . The plane rose higher and higher until it reached 8,000 ft. By this time we are leaving the coast and

as we looked down, the waves and white caps on the deep blue .
ocean looked very tiny. The only thing we saw besides the ocean
and white clouds in the bright sun were two freighters which left
long paths in the water behind. It took us only four hours to fly
across the Gulf. About one o'clock our ears began to pop as the
plane lowered and we crossed over the coast line into Yucatan.
We could see nothing but flat, flat country as far as the eye could
see. Most of it was covered with bushes and patches here and
there of corn and sisal which looks something like a big century
plant. (Most of our hemp and rope comes from sisal.) . . .

As we left the airport, we drove on into Merida, a city of
about 150,000. It didn't look this big however. There were no big
signs outside the stores—no neon lights. The stuccoed houses—
pink, green, yellow, and blue, came up to the edge of the narrow
sidewalks which lined the cobble stone streets. They had a law
requiring the houses to be painted once each year so the stucco
looked clean and fresh. The city seemed quiet with Indians walking leisurely along. An occasional old-fashioned buggy jogging
on the cobble stones (they were used for taxis) and very few cars.
So few, in fact, that we felt conspicuous riding in one.

Our driver never slowed down for a corner. He honked his
horn long and loud as it echoed against the solid wall of houses.
At the first intersection, I shut my eyes expecting to hear a crash
and land upon the sidewalk or something worse. But nothing
happened and I finally found out that they do have a set of traffic
signals which works very well. If you honk first, you don't have
to slow down. It's up to the other fellow to let you pass or else.

We soon passed through the city and out over the country
road toward the ruins of the ancient city, Chichen Itza, 80 miles
away. . . .

We stopped in several villages and watched the Indians
around their "cenote" or well which was their meeting place and
community center. Bright-eyed, black-haired children smiled
shyly at us as they peeped out from behind their mother's skirts
or clung to big brother's hand. There were no toe heads [sic]
there like Thorsten and other Summerfield children—no fair
skins either. They were the color of rich copper. (I had a movie

camera along and took a picture at one of these wells. If you'd like to see this and other pictures I took, let me know and we'll show them some night.)

The men, dressed in white cotton pants, had come from their corn fields, and were gathered in small groups near the well.

Women with hair in long black braids and dressed in white square-necked mother-hubbards balanced water jugs on their heads as they left the well and went toward home.

One fourteen-year-old girl was cross-stitching a beautiful rose border for the skirt of her new white dress. (They're always white.) Our guide asked her about it since we couldn't speak Mayan and she said it was her dress for "fiestas" which is their word for celebrations or parties. They put this colored cross-stitch around the square necks of the dresses too.

Their huts had palm leaf thatched roofs and the walls were made of mud or adobe, or corn stalks bound together with vines. In the country villages, a hut would usually have one dirt-floored room. This was not as crowded as it seemed for the entire family slept on hammocks which could be swung up to the ceiling out of the way during the day. Smoke curled out under the thatched roof as they cooked their tortillas over an open fire on the ground inside the hut. The few pots and pans plus the corn-grinding stone, and a brightly painted wooden box to store their clothing and few personal belongings such as ribbon for the women's hair, made up the furnishings of the household. In spite of these primitive conditions, the Indians in Yucatan are very clean with their bodies, taking a bath at least once a day.

We drove on through sisal plantations and the neat rows of cactus-like sisal made pointed shadows in the late afternoon sun. (Sisal is like hemp and they make grass rope and twine with it.)

Myles looked at the corn fields and suddenly said, "That corn is growing in nothing but a rock pile." And sure enough, we got out of the car and looked down the corn rows and the stalks were growing in lime stone rocks. Our driver told us they take sharp-pointed sticks, punch a hole in the ground, and drop about 6 grains of corn. They cut the weeds down with a big machete (a long knife) once or twice during the growing season. Corn is planted during their rainy season when it rains every afternoon about one hour. The moisture and the little soil in the rocks plus the heat make the corn grow very high.

We passed Indians coming home from the fields and they all had water-gourds slung across their shoulders. They were shaped like this and the rope was tied around the middle.

When the gourds were still green and growing they had placed a grass rope around the middle so they had grown like this. Most of the men wore hand made sandals—soles cut out of old rubber tires and laced on the foot with leather strings. I noticed a few of the men wore short knee-length skirts. When I asked the driver about this, he said they wore these in the field to save their white pants.

We reached the lodge where we were to spend the night and which was near the ruins of the city Chichen Itza, just before dark. We slept in a palm leaf thatched hut which had banana trees and lemon and orange trees just outside the window. There were long-tailed birds with bright blue feathers and the night air made the jasmine growing near the tall ferns smell a heavy sweet.

As we pulled the mosquito nets swung from a rack above, over our beds, birds made strange night calls and I could hardly sleep with all the new noises and smells. I was even more anxious to wake up to see the beautifully carved old temples which we had come so far to see.[5]

This says much about the way Zilphia soaked up culture and tradition during her travels. She points out the cleanliness of the indigenous people and the fact that the men wore skirts—both points that challenged her white American assumptions and certainly those of her readers.

People on the Cumberland Plateau were afraid of outsiders because their culture had taught them to be afraid of outsiders. But Zilphia wanted to impress upon them, through her stories, the ways in which people everywhere are essentially the same: they work hard, love their families, value things like faith and cleanliness, and make beautiful art.

Her mention of gourds, sisal, and tortilla-making is also notable. She and Myles—who especially had an affection for gourds—brought these remnants of Mayan culture home with them to Monteagle.

Zilphia asked local women in the Yucatan to teach her how to make tortillas and would regularly prepare them for her family's dinner, walking her children through the lengthy, detailed process, soaking the corn in lime water, and grinding it down into a batter. She also acquired dozens of yards of Mayan fabric, which she turned into curtains and oversized pillows for their living room. The curtains adorned the floor-to-ceiling window on the south side and the pillows doubled as sleep cushions, adding as well to their collection of floor cushions for her piano-playing afternoons.

Zilphia explored the Mayan ruins in both Mexico and Guatemala, marveling at the construction, the large stones that were hauled up and set in place one at a time, and the great height of the pyramids, which naturally draw the eye toward the heavens. Though she never ascribed to any specific religion, Zilphia had an affection for spirituality and was enamored of how these ancient people created a world that required them to bend over in reverence as they climbed the steep, wide stairs to throw their heads back and gaze upon the glory of heaven, squinting against the holy power of the sun god.

It wasn't just the spiritual architecture that she admired, however; she also developed an affinity for the area's traditional food and beverages.

"What a beautiful country," she wrote to a friend. "I think I could live there. . . . Your advice about the beer was right. We liked it so much, we forgot about water. And thanks to your advice about Tequila, we tried it 'native' style with lime and salt and drank practically nothing else besides tequila and beer."[6]

The couple made a point of venturing outside of Antigua, exploring the colorful textile markets and lush gardens of Chichicastenango and going off-schedule to take a tour provided by the United Fruit Company. The tour exposed the couple to the real work and life conditions of the Guatemalan working class. Zilphia found this very similar to the poverty she had seen among the attendees of Highlander workshops. She always had an eye for connections, and these intersections would have sparked her interest. She knew, on a gut level, how poverty affected hard-working people, whether those people were in the US South or elsewhere in the world.

Before heading home, the couple went deep-sea fishing. A photograph from the end of that trip shows Myles and Zilphia with their three guides, standing next to their catches. Myles, in baggy long pants and a button-down shirt, stands with a pleased but restrained grin on his face. Zilphia is to his right, in her bathing suit top and a shin-length skirt, hair tied up on her head, eyes squinting and with a laughingly wide gap-toothed smile. Hanging from a wood frame are three giant sailfish, and the photograph is inscribed: *245 LBS, 9 FEET LONG.*

THE OPPORTUNITY TO LEAVE the school was welcome in light of the FBI scrutiny and suspicions from the community. Toss in the round-the-clock demands of parenting small children, and the Hortons were hungry for a break. The trips that Ethel Clyde would send them on in coming years would prove a necessary distraction from what would only become an increasingly stressful life back home. Indeed, as Zilphia quite literally whittled and carved her way into the culture of the plateau, she found that leaving was one of the best ways for her to stay.

In April 1949, the couple celebrated her thirty-ninth birthday with the children at the nursery school and then Zilphia and Myles boarded a train for Montgomery, Alabama, where they met up with friends to celebrate. On their third day in Alabama, they met Clyde at the train station and she swept them away on "one of her 'surprise' trips. This seems to be one of her strong 'fortes,'" Zilphia wrote in a recollection to her parents and sisters, "taking you on a trip and not telling you what or where you are going."[7]

On the first evening, Clyde brought them to the Tuskegee Institute. Back home, Zilphia had been sitting in on discussions about desegregation and all the troubles and hurdles faced by Black Southerners, from their point of view. Now at Tuskegee, she found herself in someone else's world, the minority in their room. "I experienced an unexpected and new feeling," she wrote. "For the first time, I felt completely surrounded by Negroes and in fact we were the only white people in a little Negro city."

Notably, she doesn't say she was afraid, which suggests that on some level she was aware of her privilege—that she had a choice to be the minority in the room, unlike so many Black folks in so many other rooms across the South. Thus, the experience may have helped build the empathy that was essential to her work on civil rights.

From Tuskegee, Clyde and the Hortons traveled to Savannah, Georgia, which Zilphia adored for all its tree-lined streets and public squares: "The rows of palm trees and the old, old live oaks with moss hanging from them, completely shading the streets for miles. There was a feeling of open space and quiet that was very satisfying."

But the pinnacle of the trip was a visit the trio then made to St. Augustine, Florida. A letter to her family illustrates the kind of long, drawn-out tales Zilphia was known to tell over dinner or drinks. She veered off in various directions, but always eventually returned to her point. Her attention to detail and her pervasive sense of humor show not only what repulsed and amused her, but also the way she carried her audience with her through these rather lengthy stories.

This particular letter went on for many pages, with stops and starts as she noted that she had to take care of various tasks such as cooking meals, putting the children to bed, and sleeping through the night.

About St. Augustine, she wrote:

We saw the oldest house in America. Ponce de Leon's fountain of youth, and a most beautiful old fort. Never thought of a fort as being beautiful but the lines are magnificent. Spent the night in the Ponce de Leon Hotel which is the most amazing and schmaltzy hotel I've ever seen. With its plazas, fountains and tennis court it covered something like four blocks. It was built in 18 something or other and looks as though the owner said to himself when he built it, "I'm going to build the most expensive hotel in the world—it is to be the ultimate in hotels." Then he proceeded to cover every single square inch with gold leaf, marble, hand carved curlycues, cupid murals on the ceilings, mirrors, and chandeliers. The ball room was an art gallery—exhibiting one droopy drapy artist's work all over the walls. It was fun staying there one night but more would give me nightmares.

From there, it was on to the Alligator Farm, Marineland, and Okefenokee Swamp. In all three places, Zilphia reveled in not only the new-to-her exoticism of various animals and vegetation, but also in her budding relationship with the cameras she carried with her. Though she had taken her camera to Guatemala, it was during this trip to Florida that Zilphia first reported on her passion for filming things. She took documentary video of alligators, swamp animals, and marine life for hours at a time. The film she recorded is lost to history, but the language she used to discuss it indicates where her life may have led her, had she lived longer.

"I'd like to learn how to use the 16 mm and shoot enough footage to make a colored short," she wrote. "I may feel differently about movies when I see the results of this trip. Just now, however, I feel very invigorated. There was real excitement in working with the camera this time."

THE HORTONS MADE A POINT of traveling even without Clyde's help. Over time, they would drive away from Highlander more and more frequently, taking the children on road trips to national parks, the Outer Banks of North Carolina, and particularly memorable visits to the Grand Canyon and Yellowstone. The family went fishing on the beach near Kitty Hawk, putting out crab traps and gobbling up their spoils at the end of a long day, after Zilphia had prepared a dinner of vegetables and lemon butter for dipping their catches.

When they couldn't squeeze in a vacation, the Hortons would take their children with them to union conventions and organizing conferences. They would take turns—one attending the events while the other played tour guide. It was important to expose the children to the world beyond Highlander, lest Thorsten and Charis begin to think most children grew up in what was a rather unusual context.

Christmas always provided a welcome getaway as well. That's when the Johnson Girls would gather everyone together, with their husbands and all their children in one place for a vibrant family reunion. The women would work together in the kitchen, then sit at the table late into the night, trading stories about their childhoods and laughing through Zilphia's humorous, dramatic embellishments—a tradition that continued long after Zilphia was gone, when the stories would revolve around her memory.

CHAPTER 13

CHANGING DIRECTION

IN THE MID-1940S, with World War II ending, the Communist Party USA was seeing a surge in interest and the US government was getting nervous. In 1948, Alger Hiss, a State Department official, was accused of spying for the Soviet Union, and, the next year, the Soviets responded to America's display of atomic warfare by testing their own atomic bomb.

In the wake of all this, President Truman filed an executive order requiring that all federal employees be screened for loyalty, with disloyalty defined by any affiliation with socialist or communist organizations. Wisconsin Senator Joseph McCarthy published a list of State Department workers suspected of disloyalty. Various committees in the US Senate and House of Representatives—the House Un-American Activities Committee, McCarthy's Senate Permanent Subcommittee on Investigations, and others—began investigating individuals and groups outside the government.

During this time, in an effort to display loyalty, the CIO, under the leadership of John L. Lewis, was not only informing on its membership, but also red-baiting, which angered both Myles and Zilphia. They believed in democracy and America, but also believed that McCarthyism was going too far in a dangerous direction. They had been inclined toward breaking their tie with the CIO for a few years, and the red-baiting that began in the 1940s sealed the deal.

Zilphia's affection for labor leadership had been on the wane even before Thorsten was born. Unions were getting bigger and more corporate, and in the process were taking on many of the corrupt practices that fueled so many of the corporations against which labor stood. Zilphia sensed there had to be more to the social struggle than just what she had been doing. If labor unions didn't solve social inequity, then people concerned about freedom for all were going to have to go deeper, to the roots of injustice.

The United Nations, which had been founded in 1945, held a few workshops at Highlander. Zilphia was very interested in the work of the UN.[1] She had long been deeply moved by the connections between far-flung peoples, an interest sparked by her father's dinner table stories about members of the IWW, with their colorful personalities and thick accents.

She had witnessed the parallels between the Southern working poor and those of Guatemala on her travels, and she was beginning to wonder: If people organized across national boundaries, what might they achieve? The cause of world peace ignited Zilphia's soul. For the rest of her life, she would pepper her speeches and public appearances with talk of its possibilities. But Myles, ever the more pragmatic, wasn't so sure world peace was attainable when there were more practical, immediate concerns right there at home in the American South—a point that he was hearing mentioned by students more and more in integrated Highlander workshops.

Highlander had educated most Southern unions about labor organizing, and Myles knew the school needed to find another focus if it was going to continue operating. He was beginning to believe that Black civil rights were the next great barrier in the march toward a more peaceful and just world.

Highlander's mission has long been attributed entirely to Myles, but the Hortons were very much partners in deciding a way forward for the school. Sure, he got the final word, but it was important to him that Zilphia believe in his vision to be able to carry out her culture work with integrity. Indeed, that was the only way she could be effective. So, while Zilphia was interested in more holistic worldwide concerns, Myles made plans for Highlander's role in civil rights work with his two-eyed approach to popular education: one eye on world peace and another on upending institutional and interpersonal American racism.

Myles knew that the workplaces where Highlander and CIO organizing principles hadn't been especially effective were the ones where white workers and Black workers were at odds, ensnared in the long tentacles of systemic racism.

Zilphia and Myles understood the connection between the South's past and its present. They were aware of the work being done by the National Association for the Advancement of Colored People, as well as by Black labor activists like A. Philip Randolph of the Brotherhood of Sleeping Car Porters and Bayard Rustin, who had worked with Randolph to plan a civil rights march on Washington in 1941.[2] The Hortons were beginning to realize that their approach to education and organizing could be even more useful and effective in building a freer world if they worked together with these individuals and groups.

"We had made the decision to do something about racism," Myles wrote. "We were having workshops with black and white people to figure out some answers—but we didn't know how to tackle the problem. The Highlander staff didn't approach it theoretically or intellectually, they just decided to get the people together and trust that the solution would arise from them."[3]

Though objectives like Black civil rights and world peace were lofty goals, the Hortons both sensed that there were small steps that needed to be taken before the larger changes could occur. For starters, poor folks in and around the South needed to be better connected—an objective that was achieved in part by Southern unionization—but they also needed enough free time in their lives to be able to see other ways toward empowerment. And their children needed to be educated well enough that they would be ready to take up whatever struggle was going to be next in the American movement.

WITH HER OWN CHILDREN approaching school age, Zilphia concentrated on the education objective, a purpose that felt especially personal to her. As the 1940s wound down, she placed some renewed energy in the nursery school that Dr. Johnson had created and Claudia Lewis had helped to grow during the '30s.

In 1947, at Zilphia's request, Lewis brought a fresh group of Bank Street School for Teachers graduates into the South to tour the Tennessee Valley Authority's dams and other projects. Zilphia hoped that one of the students would be capable of and interested in picking up where Lewis had left off with the nursery school.

To help her choose, Lewis enlisted her old friend Emil Willimetz, whom she had met at Highlander, to come along on the trip as a photographer. On the trip, Willimetz was drawn to a young woman named Joanna Creighton, who went by "Joie."

Creighton had a striking, kind face framed with light brown hair and a frequent, easy smile. Confident and easy to talk to, she was the kind of person who makes both children and adults instantly feel at ease. She was also probably the only person on that bus who wasn't already sympathetic to the cause of labor unions, much less labor schools, making her stand out from the crowd in a way that must have seemed curious to Willimetz.[4]

Creighton's father was an executive at Bethlehem Steel, and he was skeptical about his daughter's decision to move to a labor school known for organizing in the South for the CIO. She had to convince him to let her take the teaching job, going to great lengths to impress upon him that she would have nothing to do with the labor movement or any other radical activities. She was only going to run a nursery school for the children of poor Southern mountaineers. Sold on her argument, Mr. Creighton reluctantly relented and wished his daughter well.

When Joie Creighton arrived for her staff position, she found the main hall dark and quiet. She wondered if anyone was even there. Knocking for the third and fourth time, she was surprised when the door opened and an arm came out of the dark to grab her inside. She was shoved under a table and asked to keep quiet and still. Nervous already about what she was getting herself into, Creighton thought this was an alarming welcome to a school she knew to be under federal scrutiny. But, as it turned out, Creighton had arrived while the staff was thick in the middle of a game of Sardines.

When the game ended and Zilphia came to walk Creighton to her room upstairs, she told the new recruit, tongue in cheek, "I have to apologize for your introduction to the school—you came at a mistimed moment." And then they shared a good laugh, knowing instantly they were going to get along.

Willimetz was working on a film in Washington, DC, at the time so he and Creighton commenced a love letter exchange that would lead to their marriage. Meanwhile, Creighton dove into her role as "director-janitor-cook-plumber of the Highlander nursery school."[5] Among her students were Thorsten and Charis Horton, a fact that endeared her even more to the family and drew her even closer to Zilphia.

Creighton began to learn that progressive organizers were not the monsters her father, nor even she at one time, believed them to be. She found herself in good company, surrounded by easy friendships and warm welcomes.[6] Labor activists, she was beginning to see, were merely people who wanted to live better lives and who saw organizing as the best, or maybe the only, way to do that.

In an article for the Wellesley alumni newsletter, she described the late 1940s and early 1950s at Highlander. Through her words, we can see how the culture in and around the school—under Zilphia's leadership—had changed since its founding in the early 1930s, and in what important ways it had stayed the same.

Besides our teaching staff, which numbered five instructors during our last resident session, we have a Film Center (my husband is the photographer), a secretary, a maintenance man and farm manager, and for three-month periods, an Antioch College student assistant.

During our summer resident sessions, which are usually interracial, the students have classes in union-building, parliamentary law, grievance procedure, political action, recreation etc. The current Farmers Union term studies FU cooperatives, insurance, and their own special problems.

. . . All of the community women spend busy summers canning. In many of the houses rows of beans, kraut, apples and berries are stored underneath the beds. Even the tiniest children have done their share of berry-picking and field work. But this adds only a little variation to the monotonous diet of biscuits and gravy. . . .

[The] extensive community program provides a library, a small newspaper, square dances, and the new nursery school . . . [whose] wide porch and big yard are a teacher's dream, providing plenty of room for the work and play of 2–5 year-olds. One of its most delightful features is a flush toilet which is ignored by most of my cherubs. . . . Running water is a constant joy to these children since most of them help haul water up "from the branch" or carry it from a neighbor's well. . . . Besides nursery planning with parents, distributing clothing and Christmas toys, visiting dentists and doctors, my job includes such miscellaneous activities as chasing fifty bats out of the school and catching a runaway horse and wagon. It even includes biological research in the breeding of hamsters or rushing expectant mothers to the hospital in the next county.[7]

In many ways, Creighton's background as a primary school educator helped her to be far more consequential within the community of Summerfield than many of the other Northern activists and intellectuals who cycled through the school in those days. The fact that Highlander ran a nursery school, alongside Zilphia's other cultural outreach efforts, helped to soften the view that many of its local detractors had developed. It also provided these parents with a little extra space for extra work and, consequently, extra pay. Highlander could be viewed as a group of crazy radicals, sure, but at least they were crazy radicals who were genuinely interested in helping their neighbors improve their lives.

Even today, with Highlander pushing up against its ninth decade, the school has neighbors in close proximity whose sociopolitical worldview is equal and opposite that of the school's staff. And yet, by being good neighbors and respecting their differences—prizing a welcoming spirit and the Golden Rule over the need to convert anyone to any specific way of thinking—the Highlander staff is able to peacefully coexist with people who adamantly disagree.[8]

Despite what their detractors would insist to the media and the FBI, Zilphia and Myles envisioned the kind of society that modeled world peace, where people could hold vastly different worldviews while, at the same time, making progress for the betterment of all humans everywhere.

HELPING TO AMPLIFY the Hortons' pluralistic worldview, and feeding it handily, was the fact that the federal government frequently sent international diplomats and other foreign government representatives to the Hortons' home.[9] These people would come to the United States to meet with the president, State Department officials, or United Nations representatives, and then ask to take a tour of the country, to experience the breadth and beauty of American culture across its many different regions. Yet, the South was not the most welcoming place for non-white visitors, even if one was wealthy, foreign, and surrounded by aides.

The government couldn't countenance sending African diplomats, for example, to the kinds of Southern hotels and boarding-houses that typically welcomed people of color in the days of Jim Crow. Since Highlander Folk School had been known to host integrated workshops for years, which were supported and funded in part by Eleanor Roosevelt, it was an easy and attractive alternative. The Hortons' neighbors were perhaps uncomfortable with the school's integration, but they were at least used to it by now. Further, the house Zilphia had designed was equipped with plenty of modern conveniences, which made the diplomats' interest in exploring the South much more comfortable than they would have experienced otherwise.

It was ironic that, in the 1940s, the US Department of State and United Nations ambassador trusted Highlander so completely while at the same time the Department of Justice was investigating it with such deep suspicion due to Truman's loyalty order. With hindsight, we can see that the 1,107 pages of Highlander's McCarthy-era FBI file ended unceremoniously with all individuals and groups being cleared of suspicion. But that great clearing would not come for another decade or more. Thus, the government's use of the Horton house as a destination for international visitors had to be at least as curious to Zilphia as it was exciting.

Zilphia never met a visitor she didn't like. These international diplomats were no exception. She seized on the opportunity to listen to them speak in their own language, picking up their slang and other choice phrases the same way she picked up musical interludes. She would ply them for bits of their native culture, learning songs and stories that she would re-purpose for her many speeches in the years to come.

She also learned quite a bit by doing. Rather than fill the diplomats' bellies with Southern cooking, for example, she would ask them what kind of food they missed from back home. She would pump them for recipes and then try her best to create those dishes for them. It helped that Zilphia had spices she had purchased in New York or that were given to her as gifts from other visitors. Certainly, no market in Monteagle sold things like Indian curry powder or harissa.

"We had people from Africa, India, China," Thorsten recalls. "I remember my mom would . . . try to cook things that they wanted to eat. I remember catching a big bass—a largemouth bass—for a guy from India who wanted this fish dish with curry. My mom [made] it. She was a really good cook." Like Grandmother Howard, Zilphia "was a person who understood how to cook without looking at a recipe. She understood the chemistry of cooking."[10]

Ask anyone who knew Zilphia to describe her and they are sure to mention three things: her remarkable musical skill, the warmth of her personality, and her talent as a cook. Over the years, Zilphia developed an affinity for cooking for large groups—international diplomats as well as students at the school.

Feeding people, Zilphia learned, is an important part of organizing any group of people to do anything. By the time the international visitors were coming to Highlander, she had come to view her role as cook in the same vein that she viewed her role as song leader. If folks were going to throw themselves into a workshop, in the middle of nowhere, many miles from anything or anyone familiar, they deserved to be taken care of so that they weren't sitting in a challenging discussion with a growling belly and a mind hankering for a home-cooked meal. Highlander was weird enough without making people wonder if they were going to have enough to eat.

Zilphia was one of many people—the students included—who contributed to cooking meals at the school, but one thing she instituted early on was a parting banquet during the last night of a residential session. Willimetz's photos show women in their Sunday best and men with their hair slicked back, bow ties handsomely taut. One shows Zilphia in a particularly fashionable taffeta dress, standing at the front of the room with her accordion strapped on, bent backward slightly at the waist, singing out in her most emphatic alto as everyone else remains seated, sans songbooks, singing and smiling along.

After clearing the tables from the feast, the staff presented awards to students who achieved brave new feats, whether they mastered *Robert's Rules of Order*, contributed a particularly catchy song, or made a memorable craft project. All contributions were celebrated—big, small, and in-between.

Further, the boundaries between Zilphia's home and the school being malleable, she frequently invited students and neighbors alike to her home for an enormous spaghetti dinner or to grill beef from one of her recently slaughtered Black Herefords on the outdoor barbecue.

She knew how to extend recipes without landing all the food in a flavorless clump. She figured out how to make yogurt from scratch, and when she went to restaurants in Nashville and Chattanooga, she always ended the night in the kitchen, asking the chef for tips. Moreover, she always shared recipes. Until Joie Willimetz died in 2017, she regularly made Zilphia's mushroom pie recipe for potlucks and always left with an empty pan.[11]

Zilphia had an eggnog recipe that called for fifty eggs. She once skinned and grilled three dozen squirrels after some friends came back from a hunt. "Tonight we're having the 'block works' for supper," she wrote to Myles in October 1946. "The treat to be a coon which they killed last week. It was beautiful—first one I ever saw up close—hate to cook it. . . . 'He' is now being parboiled after which he will be rubbed with sage, black pepper, salt, and surrounded by sweet potatoes and baked. Almost sounds good, doesn't it?"[12]

Certainly Zilphia is celebrated among those who knew her for her contributions to modern music and singing social justice movements, but it's worth noting that her predilection toward culture change was at least as deeply rooted in other areas of the arts, as well as in the very human practice of everyone sitting down at a table to enjoy a good meal.

Ermon Fay remembered, "Zilphia was a fabulous cook, but she left the kitchen in an upheaval."[13] This is not surprising, given the large meals she frequently prepared. Sometimes she would come home with everyone at the workshop; other times it was a select few who were in the thick of an important discussion, which would spill back over to the house and continue late into the night. Besides, on the plateau, where every experience was an exercise in cooperation and culture change, there were always plenty of hands to contribute to the after-dinner cleanup. This collaborative atmosphere was so omnipresent and pervasive, it was easy to just get swept up into it, to help out before you even realized you were doing the work.

Thorsten recalls another visitor, an education minister from Kenya, who pitched in with cleaning up after dinner, then begged the young Horton not to tell the story. "He was helping with the dishes," Thorsten recalls, "and he said don't tell anybody I did this. In my country, men don't do this—wash dishes. And there was somebody taking pictures and he said, 'Don't take a picture of me.' That was interesting."

The man didn't want anyone to know he was willingly pitching in on the "women's work." There was something about Zilphia that welcomed him into the task despite his lifelong prejudices. That same disarming, nonthreatening quality that made men so enamored of her, in general, made people feel comfortable enough to let down their guard. And anyway, welcoming people into tasks despite their prejudices was just what Zilphia did.

IT'S INTERESTING TO IMAGINE what these diplomatic visitors thought of Zilphia, Myles, and their little experiment on the plateau. With an eye on Zilphia's allegiance to context, it's worth stepping aside and looking at the bigger picture.

After all, it wasn't news to the outside world that the American South had a human rights problem. Black activists had been organizing for civil rights since before Reconstruction.[14] While the IWW allowed Black membership, Black labor groups over time became disenchanted with the more mainstream AFL and broke from them in the 1920s to form their own unions such as the Brotherhood of Sleeping Car Porters (BSCP) and American Negro Labor Congress (ANLC).

The latter is of note because its founder, Lovett Fort-Whiteman, formed the ANLC after returning from Russia, where he studied at the Communist University of Toilers of the East (KUTV). Indeed, many of the accusations of Communism leveled at organizations like Highlander that were working toward desegregation stemmed directly from the fact that a significant part of the American Communist movement of the 1920s and 1930s worked toward realizing Black equality. Where others saw widespread systemic oppression, the Russian propaganda machine saw an opportunity to turn a desperate people to a non-democratic way of life. This was in part thanks to the radical Black power perspective of Fort-Whiteman, who had been brought to Moscow to experience Communism firsthand and then go back and inform American Blacks about it.

Fort-Whiteman had been a Wobbly before joining the Communist Party in 1919. In 1924, the year before he launched the ANLC, he provided an educational lecture to the Fifth World Congress of the Third International, a Communist Party conference whose attendees included Joseph Stalin and Ho Chi Minh. According to Glenda Gilmore in her thorough history *Defying Dixie: The Radical Roots of Civil Rights, 1919–1950*, he addressed "the Negro question. He outlined the Great Migration of black Southerners to the North and pointed out that these new black industrial workers were difficult to organize. He advised the Party to move into the South and 'exploit' rising dissatisfaction among sharecroppers, a strategy that would pay off, since the 'negroes are destined to be the most revolutionary class in America.'" As Gilmore notes:

US citizens poured into the USSR in the late 1920s and 1930s at a rate of five thousand each year. . . . African Americans, especially, wanted to see the Soviet experiment in racial equality. NAACP founder W.E.B. DuBois wrote from Moscow in the summer of 1926, "I stand in astonishment and wonder at the revelation of Russia that has come to me." After "less than two months . . . and two thousand miles" in the country, he allowed that he might "be partially deceived and half-informed. . . . But if what I have seen with my eyes and heard with my ears in Russia is Bolshevism, I am a Bolshevik."[15]

And of course, to some extent, DuBois was played. Though, considered from another angle, it's possible to also conclude that this "playing" of Black sentiment resulted in connecting previously disconnected communities in valuable ways. It gave them the useful experience of their own empowerment, even as many came to decide that Communism wasn't the ultimate answer to surmounting their oppression.

Time would convince many that Karl Marx's ideas about socialist equality were more intriguing in theory than they were effective in practice, but at least a few prominent Black Americans were won over to the ideas of Communist Russia. It didn't hurt that the Kremlin fed and clothed them, filling their heads with ideas about Black power.

A few Black activists even remained in Russia, finding it more amenable to their worldview than life back home in Alabama or Georgia. Others, like DuBois, eventually parted ways with the CPUSA, seeing that, as BSCP founder A. Philip Randolph had declared: "We cannot temporize with the Communist menace. It's a sinister and destructive crowd."[16] Still, this period of relationship between some Black activists and Russia gave Highlander's detractors some basis for their fear of Communism spreading across the South via these desegregationists, even if that fear was extraordinarily misplaced.

IN THE 1940S, DuBois's National Association for the Advancement of Colored People came even more to the fore. Founded in

1909 as a radically integrated group of activists, the organization was hard-pressed to compete with the allure of the Communist Party on its meteoric, propaganda-fueled rise among the desperate and frustrated Southern Black communities. The NAACP was more interested in making slow, steady progress as a way of fostering change, which is often less attractive to the masses, who want and usually deserve to see immediate improvements in their lives. And while the NAACP's big-picture approach is often successful, it works best when accompanied by louder, more high-profile movements, both of the mainstream and radical variety.

As the American Communist Party became confused in its anti-fascist mission once Stalin signed a pact with Hitler in 1939, the NAACP began doing the practical work of plodding through the American courts to try to overturn unjust race laws. Nearly a half-century after the Supreme Court *Plessy v. Ferguson* decision set the stage for the "separate but equal" Jim Crow laws of the South, the NAACP was committed to proving the unconstitutionality of segregation, one court case at a time. It first focused on integrating institutions of higher education, believing that adult students could grasp such a change more readily than could elementary students. This appealed to many big picture-oriented radicals, Black and white alike—among them, Zilphia and Myles Horton—who viewed the rise of the CPUSA as short-sighted.

World War II effectively paused the NAACP's progress on educational desegregation, just as it paused the labor movement via wartime no-strike pledges. However, the organization's effort was not lost on sympathetic white leaders who could contribute to the cause of equality immediately after the war. Among them was the Hortons and Highlander's old benefactor Eleanor Roosevelt.

The United Nations, which was one of Franklin Roosevelt's last great visions, convened for the first time one week after his death in 1945. Even as Stalin sought to spread Communism across Europe, representatives from the USSR and several other countries were gathering with Eleanor Roosevelt, who chaired the committee to draft what became known as the Universal Declaration of Human Rights.[17] The final document declared that all humans are equal in the eyes of the international community, specifically listing their freedoms of religion, race, ethnicity, and general personhood.

Once it was completed and ratified by the UN, the Universal Declaration of Human Rights was held up as a goal toward which all sponsoring nations should strive to adhere, including the United States. And while this broader context has taken us momentarily away from Highlander into the wider world, we can be certain that, out in the middle of nowhere, on the Cumberland Plateau, Zilphia Horton was paying attention.

CHAPTER 14

TRAUMA

AFTER THE WAR, the school became fully staffed again, to the relief of Zilphia and Myles. Joie, who was by now a Willimetz, was running the nursery school, and her husband Emil was again running the film center. A steady flow of labor, United Nations, and civil rights meetings kept things humming.

The Hortons were entering middle age and had found their stride, both in their work and in their marriage. The vacations Ethel Clyde had been funding, and the ones they managed to take on their own, were a welcome break from Highlander. When they returned from Florida after Zilphia's birthday in spring 1949, they were feeling optimistic about the decade ahead, abuzz with new ideas and inspiration from their time away.

Yet, in the ensuing seven years, the time that would mark the end of their life together, their need for a break would become more and more frequent and pressing. For even as they boarded the train home from Florida that spring, the tumult that would rock the rest of Zilphia's life, one small event at a time, had already been set in motion.

The Hortons always met adversity with a zipped-up public face of courage and optimism. But, for years to come, it's likely that Myles and Zilphia would privately yearn, time and again, for their life before the day they returned from this trip in particular.

That day, they rolled up the plateau in the school's old, beat-up Chevy wagon. Whoever picked them up from the station no doubt got an earful about the couple's surprise adventure and the Alligator Farm. But the minute they walked through the front door, their relaxing, soul-feeding experience came to a screeching halt.

Charis, their younger child, now almost four years old, was sitting on a chair, a large telephone pressed to her small ear, listening to the party line. She had a can of grapefruit segments on her lap and was spooning them into her mouth. It was a cute and silly scene until they noticed she was having trouble swallowing. After checking her to make sure she didn't have something lodged in her throat, Zilphia realized the grapefruit wasn't the culprit; Charis's throat was simply closed.

"That's when they realized I had polio," Charis says. "And they rushed me to the hospital—the night they came back from the trip."[1]

THE VACCINE FOR POLIOMYELITIS would not be introduced until 1955. By then, however, the virus had taken root in the immune systems of children all over the United States.[2] Highly contagious and transferred through contaminated food and water, the strain of polio that infected Charis Horton primarily focused on her head, neck, shoulders, and upper respiratory system. It's likely that she picked it up from swimming in the lakes and creeks, though local lore of the time posited that the Horton children would be safe because "polio couldn't travel up a mountain."

The virus killed other children in the area, Monteagle being so isolated from the trappings of civilization. The nearest doctor was in another town, and while the nearest hospital was just ten minutes up the road in a neighboring county, most people on the plateau did not have a car.

That night, darting down the plateau in the old Chevy, Zilphia and Myles got Charis to the hospital in Sewanee, where she had a spinal tap and then was sent to Vanderbilt Hospital in Nashville. Zilphia climbed in the ambulance with her and they traveled down the long country roads toward the big city, unsure of whether Charis's life could be saved.

At Vanderbilt, Charis was diagnosed with paralytic polio, and the doctor warned Zilphia that her daughter might never fully recover. Later, Charis's parents told her they had decided that, if she was going to be paralyzed, they hoped she would die instead. But as long as there was hope, they weren't going to leave her side.

Zilphia got a room in Nashville and hunkered down for the duration, spending every day with her daughter, eschewing any duties for the school. She focused instead on protecting this little life.

Plenty of photographs feature Zilphia's big, broad smile, but it's easy to imagine her sitting quietly in the corner of her daughter's hospital room, reading or sketching in a book, staring out the window, thinking about how life remained normal on the other side of those walls, and observing the world as it went by— the world that was unaffected by the possible tragedy she and her daughter, whose life had barely begun, were facing.

Isolation was not a new experience for Zilphia, who had become accustomed to the long, quiet winters on the plateau. But as she sat in that room and watched her daughter maintain a vise grip on life, what was she thinking? Did she cry alone, quickly wiping a tear away when she saw Charis stir from a dream? What a strange, awful dream this was.

She may have thought about how her mother Ora, who lost two daughters in infancy, grieved quietly and alone, even as she pressed on with the other children and all of life's work. Watching her own child struggle to hold on to life through such a sickness would have certainly broken Zilphia's heart. But Charis simply remembers her mother being attentive, doing what must be done.

Thankfully, after a few weeks at Vanderbilt, Charis took a turn for the better. She remained in the hospital for more than a month, her little toddler body hooked up to the big iron lung, straining to remember how to breathe and generally convalescing.

When Charis was finally discharged from the hospital, Zilphia relied on a neighbor woman named Mattie to keep house and babysit while she got back to work at the school. Disabled with a clubfoot and a hunched back, Mattie would wash the clothes and dishes and clean up "sort of," but she mostly kept Charis company and helped the Hortons maintain some semblance of cleanliness and balance as they tried to transition back to normal. "I thought [Mattie] was just fabulous," Charis recalls. "But she wasn't a nanny in any sense of the word 'nanny.' She came and cleaned the house badly and did some of the laundry and was sort of there."

Though present, kind, and reliable, Mattie was incapable of helping Charis with her physical therapy exercises, so Zilphia would wake early every morning and spend more than an hour helping her daughter remember how to walk, helping her body heal, doing the exercises right alongside her. When Zilphia had to be at the school, May Justus or another neighbor would come over and exercise with Charis.

As the community pitched in, the school charged ahead. A good thing, since it was hardly a quiet time.

ONE DAY TWO YEARS LATER, six-year-old Charis donned a ruffly skirt and went outside to play. She remembers, "We had made a small fire on the lawn outside of the main building at Highlander where an evening meeting was going on. Somehow the hem of my dress caught fire and a boy who was playing with us tried to stomp out the inflamed skirt. Thorsten ran into the building ahead of me. I ran in and Myles hugged me to put out the fire." Myles's quick reaction probably saved his daughter's life. He set her in the car and drove her back to Sewanee for what would be a few more months in the hospital.

Thorsten, who was eight, was not allowed to visit his sister. "They didn't allow kids in hospitals at the time, at all," he says. "So I would sneak up the fire escape and talk to her in the window," peeking his towhead through the glass and offering her small gifts he had collected.[3] Zilphia again put aside her responsibilities around Highlander until her daughter improved.

The girl was injured with third-degree burns over much of her body, though time has dulled the scarring. It's not visible on her face or hands as she sits at my kitchen table telling me stories about what was a tumultuous, traumatic time in her childhood.

But, with the resilience she no doubt learned from her parents, Charis brushes it off. "It wasn't boring," she says—a description Zilphia often used herself whenever someone asked her what it was like to be married to Myles and to dedicate her life to the cause of Highlander.

Zilphia was becoming accustomed to the balancing act of citizenship and parenthood. She kept herself abreast of developments in the wider world and found in Charis, even as she convalesced from polio and the burns, a willing and able playmate, a young person with as much energy as she, who was always willing to assist her mother and explore her creativity. "She was always doing these projects," Charis says. "So I was her foil." For a while after her first discharge from the hospital, Charis was unable to walk. Though even as a preschooler she was already generally inclined toward projects, the temporary handicap meant that there wasn't much else to do to fill Charis's time other than to dive into the complex projects created by her mother.

"One of the reasons I was so close to her was because she wanted somebody to do projects with," says Charis. "She came back from Mexico and decided to make these hammered-cut tin candelabras. [We] soldered tin things. We made all the Christmas decorations—these Polish stars where it took a week to make each one."

Zilphia had spotted the stars during one of her trips to New York City. Thorsten, who was with her in the city, recalls, "I remember going to the United Nations with my mom and looking at the big Christmas tree," he says. "It had ornaments from all over the world."

These days, a tourist might snap a photo of such a curiosity with their iPhone, then share it on Pinterest and find their way to someone halfway across the world who could provide instructions on how to recreate the ornaments. But Zilphia had none of that. She simply drew from her childhood of making things by hand with her mother Ora and Grandmother Howard.

She "came home and we sat down and made them. We made all these ornaments that she'd looked at and she knew how to make them. These incredibly delicate and ornate things. . . . The way it was made was to take a circle of paper and make these pointy [tubes] out from the paper, maybe twenty of those, and put a string through the center and pull it tight. It turned into a star. . . . Very delicate. If you just went like that it would be gone," Thorsten explains, clapping his hands. "We spent hours. You couldn't save them unless you hung them up somewhere."

"We'd sit around with tissue paper," Charis adds, "and it took forever. Our whole Christmas tree was like that."

The energy Zilphia had previously put into projects in the Star Cabin could now thrive in her own home with her children. The whole upstairs in their house was a wide-open loft space, a sort of project zone, with Zilphia's weaving loom that always had an unfinished project on it. While Thorsten preferred to be outside exploring, shooting squirrels, and indulging in nature, Charis was happy to be her mother's playmate.

One day Charis got the idea that she might like to put on a puppet show, and Zilphia, having studied puppets with Helen Fishlander in New York, knew just what to do. She led her daughter through the construction of a puppet theater, the writing and staging of a play, rehearsals, and so forth. What could have been an afternoon indulgence turned into a weeks-long project.

"We made a puppet theater out of a refrigerator box that had velvet curtains," Charis recalls. Zilphia searched carefully for the velvet during a day trip to Chattanooga or Nashville, then sewed the curtains herself. "We made puppets and we wrote the puppet show, and then we showed Myles, who was the only audience we could find. It took us weeks to do the production. She just loved that stuff."

It must have seemed a great relief for Zilphia to be able to watch her daughter, who had so recently been struggling for her life, now thriving in a childhood surrounded by such creativity and aplomb.

BARELY A YEAR AFTER CHARIS recovered from the burns, Zilphia woke in the middle of one night to yet another traumatic event. To describe it, we have a letter she wrote to her mother and sisters.

It happened at 10:30 at night on Feb. 13 [1952]. Fortunately Myles was home. We were all in bed. The night was sultry and still—atmospheric pressure unbelievably low. When I awoke there was an eerie flood of light outside—not bolts of lightening. Almost immediately I heard a strange roar of wind and the double doors in front of Karis' bed blew open. Tremendous hail stones hit the roof like a machine gun volley. Karis screamed and while I gathered her up in my arms, Myles pushed with all his weight on the doors. At that moment the two tremendous oaks just outside came down through the roof over our heads—just two feet from Myles' head.

The thing that saved our lives was the magnificent old hand-hewn chestnut beam which runs the length of the old log house. At the same moment I felt a wrenching of the house and heard a pounding of stones in the direction of the living room. Opening the door to the living room, I saw a swirling mass of flames. The suction was so great that I slammed the door as quickly as possible in order to keep from being sucked into it. (The next day, I found that I had pushed the door completely over the sill where it jammed and the lock was hanging.) I threw something over the children and yelled to Myles that we should get out the back window before the house burned over our heads. Just as we were about to crawl out the back window, I saw through the kitchen window that the "flaming mass" (which had been the Guatemalan curtain) was swirling on the terrace. The tornado had taken it outside. At this point, Myles and I walked over the broken glass into the living room. There was a down pour of rain and when I said to Myles, "The windows are all broken out," he looked up to the sky and said, "The roof is gone." And so it was. The rain let up in about half an hour and our neighbor, Ike, came over to help us move the piano and furniture into the kitchen. In another half hour, the moon was shining brightly. I had a strange, almost detached feeling looking at the ruins, the huge oak trees over and around us in the moonlight. I really didn't care at the time—I was so thankful we were still alive.

Fortunately, nothing else was damaged as much as our house. Apparently the center of the tornado had swooped down at the down-hill side of our living room—else the rest would have been gone too. I had a line of clothes hanging on the back porch. Half were socks with no pins. Not a single sock was disturbed! Everything was hanging in place as if there had not even been a wind. The roofing was stripped off the library, nursery school and the roofing was ruined on the main building. Trees fell on the porches of three cabins. The porch of the cabin near the library was swept off and we found it deposited inside the library—it had gone through the big plate glass window.

Literally hundreds of trees were twisted down. I counted the rings on one of the big oaks in front of our house and there were almost 300. It's saddening to think a tree having been standing since before 1700 was bent over like a match stick in three or four minutes.

A big expense which I hadn't thought of, is the rewiring of the place—all the poles and wires were completely ruined.

The children have been simply wonderful—haven't complained and have remained cheerful. They probably have controlled their feelings too much. Evidence of their shock has come out in many little ways. I have had to sleep with Karis until last night and literally hold her hands while she was sleeping to keep her from "clawing" the skin off her scar tissue. She slept in peace last night and I was surprised that the itching subsided as quickly as it did. Up until last night, we were without lights and water and the house was uncomfortably cold with a partition of felt separating the kitchen from what was the living room. The first time Thorsten has said anything to indicate how he felt was last night when he said plaintively, "and to think we'll never be able to sit in that beautiful living room and look at the lake," then I told him we would rebuild it, he looked at me in wide-eyed wonder and I realized that he had accepted a future without a living room.

Before the tornado hit us, it hit a small town at the foot of the mountain, shattering a row of tenement shacks and killing four people!

I asked a contractor friend, if he thought it would have made any difference if the house had been constructed differently.

He laughed and said, "If it had been steel it would have been twisted."

Dear Ethel Clyde called before she had heard from us to see if we were in the tornado—wanted to know if we had clothes on our backs. I think she was ready to call Macy's and have an out-fitting sent down. When I assured her that none of our clothes were touched, she said she would send down a contribution of $1,000. Jim Warburg sent a wire saying the same thing. John Thompson, Dean of the Chapel at the University of Chicago, is coming in tomorrow to look at the damage so as to be able to make a first-hand report at the March 3 luncheon for Highlander in Chicago.

I made some pictures and when they are developed, will send you one.

Much, much, love—in fact, I'm glad to be able to "send love."[4]

The National Weather Service noted that the February 13, 1952, storm that eventually hit the Hortons' house began as an F4 (on a scale of F0–6), or "Devastating Tornado." F4 tornadoes can have winds as high as 260 miles per hour, and this one in partic-ular damaged more than one hundred farms and homes in Frank-lin County, Tennessee. "A church, a school, a store, and a home are destroyed at Beech Hill," read the report. As the storm tore through the area, it lost some strength but still "rip[ped] a path from Monteagle to Tracy City. The damage in Monteagle is esti-mated at $110,000, and $90,000 in Tracy City. About 150 build-ings are affected. One person is injured in each town. A total of 4 fatalities are reported in the three counties, with 46 injuries."[5]

It's a wonder that the Hortons survived at all. Charis remem-bers Zilphia seemed cool and collected through all these horri-ble days, but it's hard to believe any mother could brush off such events as over-and-done. Nonetheless, there was always another thing awaiting Zilphia's attention. It was her responsibility to make sure the children were not only safe but also well-adjusted.[6]

She had learned from her mother and grandmother that one does not wallow in times of sorrow. To whatever extent she felt this stress, outwardly, Zilphia simply carried on.

CHAPTER 15

LUNGING TOWARD CIVIL RIGHTS

BY 1949, Highlander had fully severed its ties with the CIO.[1] A few years earlier, its staff—including Zilphia, who took on a leadership role as a member of the Executive Council—had begun to fan out to organize Black and white farmers throughout the South into an integrated Southern Farmers Union.[2] Zilphia and Myles had been working with sharecroppers via the Southern Tenant Farmers Union since the early 1940s. They had come to believe that working on racial equality within this realm made the most sense, as it would allow them to build on the work they had been doing for so long with organized labor.

Even as they were convening UN meetings of Black and white activists to discuss desegregation, they saw the Southern Farmers Union as another way to connect poor whites with poor Blacks, and to do so through something as vital to the national interest as the Southern food supply. This effort, while noble, never quite developed the muscle the Hortons hoped it would.

It's important to recognize the failures. With both the strike at American Tobacco and Zilphia and Myles's attempt to organize an integrated union of farmers, the objectives were not achieved but led to transformational progress nonetheless. The former gave us "We Shall Overcome" and the latter placed Highlander staff in the position of actively engaging and organizing around desegregation, albeit through a labor union. The lessons they learned from bringing Blacks and whites together, working under their

leadership, informed the Hortons' work around desegregation going forward.

While the school had held integrated meetings ever since Zilphia's first year, the Southern Farmers Union terms were among
the first integrated residential sessions at Highlander. At these sessions, Zilphia introduced songs from farmers in faraway places
like Palestine, even as she also taught Southern farmers the folk
songs of similar communities in the western United States.[3]

Because of the depth of racial inequity in American history,
Zilphia knew she was going to have to bridge cultural chasms
to unmask the humanity of both sides before any work could be
done toward the cause of justice. Members of the mostly white
unions with whom Highlander worked in the 1930s and '40s via
their connection with the CIO had a shared cultural foundation.
Thus, in those years, Zilphia's focus was on acquainting Highlander attendees with the value of their own cultural line, even
as she tried to expand their understanding of the world around
them. She always peppered her singing sessions with popular
songs of the day to help people relax and feel comfortable with
something that felt timely and familiar. Yet, the educational feature of Highlander sing-alongs was her introduction of a song she
had plucked from the history of the people in the room.

For example, in the 1930s, if there were folks who had grown
up along the Mississippi River in Arkansas, she would lead them
in a round of "The Crawdad Song":

You get a line and I'll get a pole, honey
You get a line and I'll get a pole, babe
You get a line and I'll get a pole
We'll go fishing in a crawdad hole
Honey, baby, mine

Then she would explain how this song sounds like a fun little flirtatious ditty, but a closer listen reveals that it's actually a work
song: you take this task and I'll take another task, and then we'll
come together and get something done.

"The Crawdad Song" emerged from communities of Black and white workers alike, who were building levees in that part of the country. Once Zilphia had employed it to gain the attention of people in the room—perhaps they remembered the song from their childhood—she would tell the story of the song, probably also embellishing for effect.

In reacquainting people with their own local traditions, Zilphia was able to empower them by showing how their ancestors surmounted fear and anxiety with songs, food, dancing, and other local traditions and by coming together across their differences and working toward a common goal.

But as her interest in world peace grew, as the school broadened its scope, and as she became more worldly through her own travels and her conversations with State Department visitors, Zilphia began to see music, food, and dance as an opportunity to open people's eyes wider to the greater world beyond their own traditions. She hoped that presenting local traditions alongside those of foreigners—or their fellow Americans of a different race, region, or ethnicity—would help people to understand that *they* come from a line of valuable ideas, but so does everyone else in the world. If we can recognize the value of our own culture, she would emphasize, then we also have the capacity to see the equal value of other cultures.

Zilphia's culture program focused on broadening the worldviews of the workshop attendees—a practice that ultimately began to chip away at racist ideas, a necessity when Jim Crow whites shared dorm rooms with their darker-skinned Highlander peers. The songs they sang together helped everyone sleep better.

Outside Highlander, though, Myles was frustrated at how difficult it was to organize Southern Black folks around any cause. There were pockets of organization—Charleston was one—but when it came to educating the organizers so they might continue to effect positive changes in their community, many people outside the plateau were skeptical. They had, for so many years, been led to believe that Highlander was a toxic environment bent on spreading Communism throughout the region. Black leaders, especially those in the NAACP who were carefully trying cases to upend segregation, cautioned distance from anything related to the CPUSA. Besides, propaganda that focused on keeping people separate and in their place was remarkably effective during this time.

BOTH THE LABOR AND civil rights movements had their own distinct goals, but two objectives were remarkably similar: lifting up people who have been kept down and granting freedom to more people instead of just those in power positions.

Working people in the South were so often kept under the thumbs of their bosses by the convenience of Jim Crow. It was hard for white and Black workers to rise together if they weren't permitted to even share a table. Thus, it wasn't unusual for a white local and a Black local of the same union to be in the same shop. They would meet in the same room, Blacks on one side and whites on the other, their leaders in front of the room at adjacent tables.[4] In this way, they would technically adhere to Jim Crow laws while having the same meeting about the same issues. But separate wasn't equal, no matter to what extent the workers tried to get around it.

It's important to recognize that Zilphia and Myles Horton, who were deeply involved in both movements, never exactly put labor in a drawer to move on to civil rights, and they weren't alone in that. They broke ties with the CIO over irreconcilable differences, but they continued to organize and educate labor unions well into the 1950s. One of the last events of Zilphia's life, even as she was energized by work she was doing around Black civil rights, was a speech to a farmers union.

The tactics the Hortons and Highlander staff used during the labor movement of the 1930s and '40s—picketing, civil disobedience, the culture program—were continuously employed in the civil rights demonstrations that were to come. This was not one movement borrowing from another, but rather one line continuing, expanding its focus, calling more people to the table, making connections outside its comfort zone. In many cases, the same people with the same skills shifted their personal priorities.

On August 28, 1963, nearly a decade after Zilphia died, the

songs she brought forward were sung on the National Mall the day Martin Luther King Jr. made his "I Have a Dream" speech. The March on Washington for Jobs and Freedom, a labor and civil rights march wrapped in one, was organized by Bayard Rustin, who worked closely with A. Philip Randolph, a leader of the Brotherhood of Sleeping Car Porters. The night before King was assassinated, he spoke to a sanitation workers' gathering about the need for Black folks and white folks alike to put aside their differences and rise together. It was a labor union speech.

When white folks today talk about civil rights, we are still talking about skin color, despite the fact that King asked us to focus instead on content of character. His emphasis, especially at the end of his life, was on the way systemic racism had separated whites and Blacks for the purpose of keeping poor people down.

The United States has moved, not as the result of any of a series of separate, competing movements, but because across more than two hundred years, the nation has rolled over the old ideas that children belong in the mines, that bosses should have all the power, that Black folks should live in chains, that women should be subservient to men, that the natural world exists to be exploited, and so forth. To Myles and Zilphia, these things were all part of one long American movement, where one thing leads to another and where people learn from one another—from their own traditions as well as those they see around them—how to *move*.

So, in the thick of this transitional period, Zilphia, Myles, and the Highlander staff knew that it was not a big leap to get from one cause to another.

Myles took a second job in 1952 as the educational director for the United Packinghouse Workers of America (UPWA), which "had a high proportion of Negro members," for the purpose of making some extra money at the same time that he was becoming more deeply embedded in desegregationist circles.[5]

Myles also sent out calls beyond labor unions to groups like the Southern Regional Council (SRC). The Council succeeded the Commission on Interracial Cooperation, which, in parallel with the NAACP, had helped promote racial equality in the South since 1919. He was hoping that, by actively inviting predominantly Black organizations to Highlander, he could bring in new ideas and new minds, as well as new hands, to help point the way forward.

And while it may have looked to the outside world as though Highlander was wandering aimless, Myles saw this as a period of "getting ready," shifting priorities in the school and creating workshops that might represent "a kind of microcosm of the democratic society which the South would become."[6]

DURING SUMMER 1952, an integrated gathering of activists workshopped at Highlander about race relations, community organizing, and the peaceful uses of nuclear energy. One of the attendees was Anna D. Kelly of Charleston, South Carolina. Kelly had a large, kind face with jubilant, determined eyes and a warm smile. She was working as a youth coordinator for the Charleston YWCA and was a longtime member of the SRC.

When Kelly received an SRC newsletter that included information about the Highlander workshop, she became curious. Though most of her life had been spent in Charleston, she had lived a few years in Atlanta and had developed an interest in the way other people in other places dealt with the challenges of their lives. If the newsletter information was correct, Highlander sounded to her like a rare opportunity to get away, immerse herself in new ideas, and expand her horizons.

"I talked with the executive director [at the YWCA] and she did not exactly approve but she had no reason to disapprove," Kelly recalled. "She knew about Highlander and had been there, and some people said it was Communistic. She didn't know if I wanted to go, but if I went, I would have to put somebody in my place at the Cumming Street Branch while I was gone. Septima Clark was available."[7]

That summer, Kelly drove to Highlander, stopping in Columbia, South Carolina, to pick up another woman from the SRC who was also heading to the workshop. The two Black women rolled alone along the country roads that led to Monteagle, turning the corner toward Highlander right around dusk, the sun setting over the distant horizon in this sundown town.[8]

Decades later, Kelly remembered that they "drove in the yard and blew the horn and this woman came out who was white, with long, straggly white hair and no shoes on. And I looked at her and said 'It *is* Communistic,' and I was ready to leave." She laughed in the retelling of this story, but the laughter trailed off with the memory of discomfort.

Nonetheless, she and her new friend went inside and sat down for a meal. Zilphia welcomed them, as she had everyone, and stood up to lead the singing when dinner had wound down.

"Everything was really very warm and pleasant," Kelly says. "We sang songs and talked and enjoyed the experience. . . . But I was a little taken aback when we got there because we weren't exactly country folk and we didn't know what they were doing. . . . They sang after each meal and at night, and it was really a different experience."

This memory, while just one person's impression, makes clear to what extent Zilphia's program of group singing took some getting used to. With the hindsight of history and the wealth of documentary films that have since proliferated about the singing labor and civil rights movements, it's easy to imagine previous generations had some kind of natural comfort around using music as an avenue toward empowerment. But it was neither normal nor natural. Zilphia was acutely aware of this:

> For people who come from the hurry and anxieties of modern life, such singing is good recreation. Soothing rhythms help them to relax, and when they dance to the music of their songs, as well as sing them, they get good physical exercise too.
>
> Groups of varied cultural backgrounds can sing together and achieve a unity often not otherwise possible. The strong emotional element in music has a power to bring people together. Because people can sing what they would never speak, music will often unify groups that would be divided in discussion.[9]

Thus, people who attended Highlander came away with an understanding that music and the arts were part of their organizing toolbox, alongside, for example, how to file a grievance, how to challenge a law, how to run a meeting, and how to make a rousing speech. Through Zilphia's work—along with the vision of others who came later, like Fannie Lou Hamer and the Freedom Singers—most people now understand almost instinctively that movements sing. But for so many people who left their lives to come to this unconventional place, the invitation to sing after every meal required an adjustment. Singing for the movement was one of many new habits they would learn and develop in their holistic, immersive education on the plateau.

The enveloping culture of the school warmed Anna Kelly to the experience, as it did everyone who visited. She went back to Charleston at the end of that week, buzzing from all that she had learned and seen on the plateau.

"When [Anna] came back," Septima Clark wrote in her memoir, "she said, 'Oh that's a wonderful place. You don't even have to spend a nickel. You go up there, and they feed you, and they sleep you, and they ride you, and so everything is wonderful.'

"I decided I should go to a place like that, so the next summer I went up, and I found what she said was true. I even found that blacks and whites were sleeping in the same room—that surprised me."[10]

Clark, fifty-five at the time and a seasoned teacher, was tall and full-bodied, gray-haired, with horn-rimmed glasses and a thoughtful face. She had never imagined that there could be such a thing as this kind of natural-feeling integration, though all she wrote about her response to Highlander's approach was that it "surprised" her.

More surprising to her was the extent of prejudice she discovered when she finally moved to Highlander full time in June 1956. "At Highlander," she wrote, "I found out that black people weren't the only ones discriminated against. I found out that whites were against whites. The low-income whites were considered dirt under the feet of the wealthy whites, just like blacks were. . . . I thought that everything white was right. But I found differently. I found out that they had a lot of prejudice against each other."[11]

To some extent, Highlander's desegregation tactic—presenting integrated bunk rooms, bathrooms, and dining tables as a plain reality—was radical, and at the same time, it was willfully naive. It didn't bother Myles or Zilphia to share a room with Black folks, but the people they were welcoming to the school were coming from separate worlds, where they lived in a daily reality of visible, constant white supremacy. The white folks had to submit to coming down from their imagined pedestal while the Black folks had to trust they wouldn't be harmed in their sleep.

Imagine what it must have been like then that first night for someone like Septima Clark, who had lived more than five decades under the reality of Jim Crow and whose father Peter had been born a slave. Imagine the gulf she had to traverse in order to fall asleep that night in a room full of white folks. This is near impossible, especially for modern white folks.

Nonetheless, by the end of her first week at Highlander, Clark too saw great promise in the school's approach to desegregation and was feeling optimistic about its possibilities. This would be part of why she would later return to Highlander to stay as education director and perhaps also why she made her own choice about lodging. "When a new stone residence was constructed out back behind the main building, Myles Horton offered me that, but I wouldn't take it. Blacks had always been put out back in the woods. I wanted to be up front where I could see and be seen."[12]

Clark would eventually become rather close with Zilphia, and she would challenge Zilphia to step far outside her comfort zone in the interest of racial justice. She would create a literacy program that would earn her great respect from Martin Luther King Jr., who called Clark the "Mother of the Movement." But that was still a couple of years away. In the meantime, her life and the lives of the Hortons had to take a few twists and turns.

CHAPTER 16

CHICAGO

THE YEAR SEPTIMA CLARK first arrived on the plateau, Zilphia and Myles were in the middle of a house remodel, thanks to the tornado, and were beginning to think it was time to do something about Thorsten's troubles in school. Now old enough to be in third grade, the boy had failed first grade twice.

"We went to this little one-room school with one teacher, sort of across the yard from May Justus's house," says Charis. "When I was in first grade, I could read really well, so [the teacher] let me teach the other first graders to read. I played school at school all day; it was fabulous. But Thorsten couldn't read, and it was horrible for him. . . . He was so massively dyslexic, always struggling."[1]

"I got help," Thorsten explains. "I had help all the time, seriously. May Justus, who was this wonderful teacher . . . tutored me forever, trying to find a way to get me to do reading. I still have difficulty reading."[2]

In a family of voracious readers—Myles often read a book cover to cover before going to bed at night—Thorsten was handicapped by dyslexia, and Zilphia and Myles had to face the fact that the Summerfield school was not equipped to empower him to surmount it. For Myles and Zilphia, the realization that their son was having trouble learning to read was nearly as dire as was the fact that their daughter had been burned in the fire. Friends in Chicago suggested that the Hortons send Thorsten to the University of Chicago Laboratory School, but since Thorsten was only ten years old, it was vital that a parent go with him.

So, as summer 1953 began, Zilphia, Charis, and Thorsten piled into a train car and headed for Chicago. They moved into a basement apartment and began to explore. Chicago was a new adventure, so markedly different from life on the plateau.

To this point, the Horton children weren't sheltered, but they also were rural children who walked dusty roads to the country schoolhouse and experienced larger towns like Chattanooga and Nashville as the primary exceptions to their middle-of-nowhere existence. Their forays into these Southern metropolises, such as they were, were mostly for the purpose of visiting the dentist, getting Zilphia's hair cut, buying shoes, getting their eyes checked. Luxuries most of their neighbors couldn't afford, but practical activities nonetheless.

Now here they were, blocks away from one of the Great Lakes, with towering skyscrapers just to the north. Chicago was a city brimming with culture and Zilphia made sure she and the children explored opportunities and learned from things that would never have been an option on the plateau.

Early that summer, to indulge her creative impulses, she picked up a black Gibson acoustic guitar and began taking lessons from a man named Richard Pick, a serious but affable man with a serious, affable mustache. Born in St. Paul, Minnesota, in 1915, he had taken on the surname of his foster family, the Picks, and had developed a lifelong affinity for classical music as a singer, an instrumentalist, and a composer. He eventually found his way to the classical guitar and, in 1952, published his first instructional book, aptly titled *First Lessons for the Classical Guitar*. By the time Zilphia began taking lessons from him the following summer, he was an accomplished classical guitarist whose lessons were only available to the highest-caliber students. Zilphia took this education very seriously and practiced daily for many hours, the same way she habitually played the piano back home.

As autumn came and school began, Charis went to live in Los Angeles with Zilphia's sister, Elsie Newell. Zilphia and Thorsten settled into a new routine. "We lived in the house of some friends who were on a sabbatical or something," he recalls. "It was the first time I ever saw a television set. We just lived in their house

with all their stuff. . . . I used to spend almost every afternoon after school at the Museum of Science and Industry. I knew every
nook and cranny in that place because it was only a block and a
half from where we lived."

There, on Harper Avenue, mere blocks from the southern
shore of Lake Michigan, Zilphia got a taste of what it might be
like to live outside of the gravitational pull of Highlander. She
was not in Chicago to raise money or hobnob with a list of the
school's most wealthy donors, as was usually her quest in her
travels. Here, she was simply a resident of a big city, there for
her child. She was a single mom, in effect, writing home to her
husband, whom she missed dearly. Despite the longing and all
the ways she was fed by her work at Highlander, she was always
haunted by the lingering knowledge that there was more to life.

There were days in Chicago when anything seemed possible.
All the ambition of America's heartland was wrapped up in those
hardscrabble streets. Its high glass buildings stood in contrast to
the working-class gumption of its cocktail bars and jazz clubs, its
cobblestones, and the spinning wheels of its zooming taxicabs.
The parity of lives, all the paths one could take. The world was
full of options for someone like Zilphia Horton.

After school, Thorsten would either ride his bike to the mu-
seum or come home to Zilphia, and they would head over to the
Goldiamonds' house for some play time. Zilphia met Betty and
Israel Goldiamond when the couple spent their honeymoon at
Highlander in 1946.

When I spoke with Betty in 2012, she was eighty-nine with
a long, clear memory. "We were living in the prefabs located on
the spot where the Graduate School of Business now sits, and Zilphia was renting a basement apartment in that block of Harper
where they have all the Halloween decorations every fall," Betty
recalled.[3]

The neighborhood where the Goldiamonds lived was full of
children, so there were always plenty of playmates, including the
Goldiamonds' own children, for Thorsten. Zilphia and Betty
Goldiamond would sit on the back porch, making small talk and
watching the children.

Goldiamond recalled, "I didn't talk personal news with her myself. People didn't do that much in those days. Honest to God, we didn't. We kept our troubles to ourselves. . . . We would just talk about anything, nothing special. Probably always both of us interested in politics. Maybe she would talk to me about my work. I assume she wasn't able to do any work while she was [in Chicago]. I think they must have been very worried about the lives of their children and the risk they were taking."

These women had known each other for years at that point and likely didn't need to do any soul baring by the time Zilphia sat in Betty's backyard in Chicago. Goldiamond had witnessed life at Highlander up close and had known the Hortons during some of the school's most interesting periods to date.

"I heard about [Highlander] from the local press while I was at Vanderbilt," Goldiamond said, "because the folk school was identified somehow with the Communists who had been active in the South in the '30s. I attended some events at the Southern Conference for Human Welfare in Nashville and met Myles there."

During her year in Chicago, Zilphia also spent a good amount of time with Ralph Helstein, president of the United Packinghouse Workers Union (UPWA), and his wife Rachel. The Helsteins lived with their two daughters, Nina and Toni, in a beautiful, distinctly modern home—with curtain walls, concrete pillars and floors, casement windows—that had been one of the last single-family homes designed by Bertrand Goldberg. The girls taught Thorsten how to ride a bicycle—there was never any use for that skill on the dirt roads back home at Highlander—and Zilphia often relaxed over cocktails with the adults.

The lot of them would go out to hear concerts in the park, usually classical music or jazz. Zilphia was no fan of the commercial country music of the day, and certainly not of the budding trend of rock and roll. Even back home in Monteagle, the only time Zilphia turned on the radio was to listen to a classical concert being broadcast from hundreds of miles away.

That Christmas, Zilphia, Myles, and Thorsten reunited with Charis in Los Angeles, as the Johnson Girls rented a Rudolph Schindler house on the coast for their sizable broods to all stay together for the holidays. They remained through New Year's Eve, when Myles and Zilphia left the children at home and went out on the town with Elsie Newell and her husband Bruce Maynes.[4]

Their marriage was aging and had long since evolved past the days of gushy love letters. In many ways, Myles and Zilphia had grown in separate directions, though they continued to be committed to one another. Nonetheless, Myles would later regret having not embraced her joie de vivre more frequently as the years wore on.[5]

CHAPTER 17

CONTEMPT AND JOHNS ISLAND

ZILPHIA RETURNED FROM CHICAGO to another new threat and controversy. To borrow a phrase Myles often used, there were new flies in the ointment.

"By the spring of 1954," writes John Glen in his history of Highlander, "Mississippi Senator James O. Eastland was linking past criticism of Highlander and similar organizations in the South with fresh invective against their advocacy of racial integration. . . . Convinced that the movement to end segregation was the work of a Communist conspiracy, Eastland thought that if he could expose those who promoted racial equality as subversives he could demolish whatever influence they had in the South and block the desegregation of public schools."[1]

As chairman of the Senate Internal Security subcommittee, Eastland compelled testimony from Myles and Jim Dombrowski because of their positions on the board of the Southern Conference Educational Fund (SCEF), suspecting its collaboration with Southern Communists. Eastland's subcommittee also subpoenaed SCEF president Aubrey Williams and Virginia Durr, who had previously been a member of the Fund's board. Durr's husband Clifford was Myles's attorney for the proceedings.

In some ways, the Eastland hearing was a culmination.[2] It had been twenty-two years since Myles opened his experimental school on the Cumberland Plateau, walking into a culture of deep suspicion toward outsiders. Zilphia had worked so hard to build friendships and trust, and Myles had made an effort to accommodate the FBI investigations to prove the school had no interest in helping to overthrow the government. Nonetheless, objectively, Highlander staff was consistently turning out organizers who would work to change the social order of the South. Given all this, sooner or later, someone was bound to haul them in to testify. So, in spring 1954, Myles was called in front of a Senate subcommittee that could determine not only his future but also the future of the school.

Zilphia didn't let the children see how it affected her, though it's hard to believe anyone could watch their spouse go through such a mess without experiencing some level of fear and anxiety. By this point, her ability to handle stress had been tested through the war draft, her daughter's struggles with polio and severe burns, and all the everyday challenges of life at Highlander Folk School. Any letters or essays she composed during this time have been lost to history, perhaps destroyed by Myles years later when the school was facing closure yet again. In the face of that trial, Myles burned many things so they couldn't be taken out of context and give the wrong impression in court.

But in his writings about the Eastland hearing, he remembered this period sort of matter-of-factly. The children, he wrote, "learn[ed] that principles sometimes got you into trouble but that you had no other alternative than to follow your truth wherever it led and whatever the price. For example, we had family conferences on the position I would take at the Eastland Committee hearing."[3]

The position he took was that he had never been a member of the Communist Party. He had friends who had been. Among them was Highlander's cofounder Don West, though Myles refused to name names. Notably, Myles recalled, "The first person [Eastland] asked about was my wife. I said I speak for nobody but myself."[4]

In his written testimony, which was never entered into the record of the hearing, Myles was even more daring and explicit. Though he wasn't permitted to read the entire statement, his firmness caused quite a bit of consternation in the courtroom.[5]

Myles was brought in to testify on the third day of the hearing and was ushered into a private office to meet with Eastland away from the spectators and media. In that moment, Eastland agreed to allow Myles to read his statement in public, but once they moved into the courtroom, he cut Myles off after fewer than five minutes on the witness stand.

Had Myles been permitted to read his entire statement, it would have included the following:

> I shall not and will not engage in any discussion before this Committee with respect to my opinions on people or issues. I am here as an expert witness holding myself out as qualified to give opinion evidence. I am here under subpoena. I have expressed my opinions and beliefs openly in the past and I shall continue to express them openly. But, as an American citizen, I believe that it is my right to express or withhold my opinions as I see fit, and to pick and choose the occasions when I will express them. I do not recognize the right of any public official or government body to require me to express them under the threat of punishment for failure to do so. Another thing I will not do is this. I will not talk about other people who are not here to protect themselves.
>
> . . . I have acted upon the Christian postulation that all men are brothers and love freedom and that a democratic society is the only way of achieving freedom and brotherhood. These things I have taught, advocated and lived and will continue to teach. . . . Communism has never tempted me because I believe in democracy, a powerful concept worthy of mankind the world over. You know, if you have made any effort to find out, that I have never been a member of the Communist party.[6]

In his memoir, Myles admitted that he had invited members of the CPUSA to Highlander to offer lectures, so students could be exposed to all manner of social perspectives in order to make informed decisions about how they might change the world around them.

In the courtroom, however, he was interrupted by Eastland's attorney, who asked Myles if Dombrowski was a Communist. Myles attempted to explain his reasons for choosing not to answer the question and Eastland cut him off, seeking a simple yes or no answer.

"Why don't you listen to an American citizen talk?" Myles asked. Eastland responded, "Answer my question. Do you decline to answer the question?"[7] After a few more rounds of this exchange, Eastland ordered the police to remove Myles from the room.

"With hammerlocks," writes Adams, "two marshals took Horton outside the courtroom and threw him on the marble steps. Behind him Eastland was saying, 'We are not going to have any self-serving declarations.'"[8]

But the fact that Myles wouldn't admit any fault or name any names in front of the Eastland committee meant that he was held in contempt—a charge that could result in up to a year of jail time. The committee had until spring 1955 to either throw him in jail or not. Though they never did, the anticipation and the uncertainty were disruptive enough to his family.

After being dragged out of the hearing, Myles headed home and told Zilphia and the children about what happened. Then, he wrote, they engaged in "humorous acceptance of the fact that I was, according to all the best legal information, to spend a year in jail for contempt. Thorsten and Charis were eagerly planning things for me to do and ways to keep in touch with me, and talking about what they would do."[9]

Though Myles may have recalled his children's acceptance of his potential year in jail as somewhat humorous, Charis remembers the knot that would form in her gut whenever a car she didn't recognize turned down the dirt road for Highlander. Every time, she worried if those were the men coming to take her father away.

Zilphia waited with similar anticipation and trepidation that year. Highlander, however, would press on. There was a lot of work to do. Myles was the school's benevolent dictator, but its purpose and his pervasive vision were, intentionally, much bigger than he.

Zilphia firmly supported her husband's position and was proud of the statement he had composed for the committee. And, anyway, people in the Hortons' social circle, all over the country, were being compelled to testify in front of committees about the aims of their organizing. Zilphia's old friend Pete Seeger was pulled in front of the House Un-American Activities Committee one year later and would appear with his banjo in hand. He too was held in contempt when he asserted his right to affiliate with any political party of his choosing, courtesy of the US Constitution's first amendment. Like Myles, Seeger also never actually served a day in jail for his charge of contempt.

Myles and Zilphia had watched history unfold through the Depression, World War II, McCarthyism, and the rise of the civil rights movement—all events that inspired fear and anxiety in so many people, as well as optimism and promise. Zilphia's approach to music was meant to help people understand that progress doesn't equal loss. *We can keep the old melodies and just change a few words*, she taught folks, *and that will help us move forward*. Granted, change is scary for every living thing, but the Hortons were unwilling to waver in their convictions. Freedom and equality were far too important to both of them.

Regardless, as 1954 unfolded, Zilphia would have been relieved to be home while her husband was entangled in this bureaucratic mess. She spent most of the year on the plateau holding all of this together, though she did return to Camp Laquemac for ten days in August to lead singing, teach song leading, and produce the closing day's "Laquemac Festival."[10] That event included the singing of French-Canadian folk songs she had taught the campers throughout the week as well as a "Zulu War Dance," French Canadian folk dances, dances of South America, and musical accompaniment by a small ensemble that included Zilphia, probably on piano.

ALSO THAT YEAR, in its *Brown v. Board of Education* decision, the Supreme Court declared that segregation in schools was unconstitutional. Then in a follow-up 1955 decision, commonly called "*Brown* II," the court ordered desegregation "with all deliberate speed."[11] The ruling was a result of the NAACP's long attempt at school desegregation that began before World War II, and it was one of the greatest early triumphs of the civil rights movement. Despite what felt like a victory for desegregation, as white schools started to admit Black students, the Black students were not given any accommodations to help them fit in and succeed aside from simply allowing them to enter the building through the front door.

For lifelong educators like Septima Clark, the ruling was a double-edged sword and didn't go far enough to create the context for actual equality in education. This was one among many reasons she became more and more active with the NAACP and refused to disavow her membership even when the South Carolina state government passed a law making it illegal for any government employees to be affiliated with civil rights groups. Clark was not only fired from her teaching job, after decades of service and despite her advanced degrees, but was also barred from being hired by any other schools. As luck would have it, she became unemployed at just about the time that Highlander was looking for someone to coordinate civil rights education efforts.

Thus, when she went up the mountain for her second summer at Highlander, in 1954, Clark did not come back down. Myles hired her as education director, and she became a pivotal force in Highlander's involvement in the movement for Black civil rights.

As Clark moved into her new room and her new role, she became the entire Black population of Monteagle, Tennessee. She knew that one of her former students, Esau Jenkins, would be a vital connection for Highlander. A member of the NAACP, Jenkins had the trust of his neighbors in the relatively isolated Gullah community where he was raised, on Johns Island, outside Charleston, South Carolina. Jenkins could open the door to a population of Black folks who were keen on the cause of freedom, if the Hortons could convince him of their integrity. They did so by spending time in and around Charleston, getting to know Jenkins and letting him get to know them.

As the relationship developed, Zilphia was delegated to go to Johns Island and connect with its Gullah community in November 1954.[12]

ZILPHIA WAS FORTY-FOUR YEARS OLD, with two small children at home and a nearly twenty-year marriage. She had been present for the 1935 All-Southern Civil and Trade Union Rights Conference, Highlander's first integrated meeting. In many ways, the school's involvement with civil rights work grew in parallel to Zilphia's life at Highlander.

She and her friends and colleagues had not just been aware of race issues for decades, they had also been living them, confronting them, feeling the backlash from federal investigators and local Klansmen alike. You might say it showed in her hair. A shock of gray stretched down from her bangs to the tips now, somewhere below her shoulders when she let it hang loose.

That first integrated meeting in 1935 had landed at Highlander because the other meeting places the All-Southern Civil and Trade Union Rights Conference considered were threatened with bombings. Because of her commitment to justice and a better life for poor Southern people, Zilphia had learned to live with legitimate fear and uncertainty. She had long ago begun to face each day with the knowledge that she could be killed by dynamite in a room full of people who just wanted answers to questions, simply because she had come to lead the singing.

When she entered Esau Jenkins's home in 1954 to spend the night, Zilphia knew the weight of what she was doing. The island's Black population kept to itself. They were "deeply suspicious of outsiders, especially whites, who came to the islands. In short, conditions on Johns Island and the other Sea Islands were such that virtually any change would be dramatic."[13]

Clark, who had taught on Johns Island for a couple of years, had told Zilphia what to expect. Zilphia knew her choice to walk through that door would shove this community from isolation into becoming a force that could compel the civil rights movement forward. After all, "the mere fact that a white friend visited the Jenkins family and stayed in their home represented a glimpse into a new world."[14]

Once Zilphia had made contact, a parade of meetings, events, and trainings followed, carrying Johns Islanders ever closer to voting rights and more freedom.[15]

JENKINS'S HOUSE WAS LARGE and wood-framed, with plenty of rooms for his big family. It was situated on a part of the island where neighbors were not close by, so Jenkins could farm in between his other numerous commitments. Although his neighbors weren't near, Jenkins had close personal relationships with all of them.

Candie Carawan remembers the first time she visited his house in the early 1960s. By then, Jenkins had moved closer to the storefront where citizenship schools—classes in literacy that helped Black folks register to vote—were being held. He kept the wood house on the farm only for guests and visiting family.

The Johns Islanders' relationship with white visitors had already been established by the time the Carawans arrived. Candie's husband Guy had been carefully primed by Jenkins about how to dress and behave in social settings there. But she remembered the warmth and care Jenkins brought to introducing her around, and the way everyone she met seemed to automatically relax because he vouched for her.[16]

In 1954, though, Zilphia's decision to cross the literal and figurative threshold was informed by her studies, her experience, her trust in Esau Jenkins, and her infectiously empathic heart. She was able to surmount the suspicions of Black folks on Johns Island in part because she had the support and trust of Jenkins and in part because she lived so fully into her determination to not be one of "those" white women. She did the work of showing up, and they could see she wasn't messing around.

She knew that history had provided legitimate reason for Black folks to be suspicious of the motives of white women. She knew she was asking members of that community to put aside their experiences and trust *her*. In so many ways, theirs was the bigger, riskier gulf to cross.

That request for trust was markedly different for the Gullah people than it would have been in a city like Montgomery, Alabama, or even Nashville.

At the time of Zilphia's visit, the Gullah had lived on the border islands near Charleston along the Southern coast since their ancestors had been kidnapped and enslaved by white Europeans in the seventeenth century.[17] Though today it is a quick drive from downtown Charleston to the center of Johns Island, it was a nine-hour boat trip until the US government built a bridge leading there after World War II.[18] The Gullah speak a Creole language and retain other hints of their West African culture. They have remained remarkably isolated from the sorts of industrial and cultural evolutions that changed the lives of Black folks in other Southern cities. Southern Blacks in other areas migrated to Northern cities like Chicago and New York, while the Gullah people stayed isolated on their islands.[19]

There were discussions among Clark, the Hortons, and Jenkins about how best to proceed. Jenkins knew the power he shouldered with his neighbors. He knew he was heavily trusted on the island and that, if he told people to trust the Hortons, they would. He did not take that lightly. After all, he had been involved in Charleston's slow march toward civil rights organizing for the better part of a decade.

In fact, when Lucille Simmons, Lillie Mae Marsh Doster, Delphine Brown, and the other women of American Tobacco struck in 1945, Jenkins had been on the outskirts of that effort. Several of his neighbors were employed by that company and he was committed to driving them over the bridge to the picket each day, before dropping the children at school. On those bus rides, he would work with them on reading, but there was never a sufficient amount of time available to get them to full literacy.

When FTA-CIO reps from American Tobacco headed to Highlander the following spring, it was the first time Jenkins became privy to the fact that there were some white people in Tennessee interested in empowering Southern Black people. Years before he attended any workshop on the plateau, Jenkins met Myles on one of the latter's many trips to Charleston to try to recruit students, and they began a long correspondence.

Strong and of average height, with a full, round face and a slight mustache, Jenkins had been a student of Septima Clark before he became her peer. Even as a fourteen-year-old in her class, he had, Clark noticed, a level of authenticity that people simply trusted.

In such an isolated community, it was important for neighbors to be closely tied to one another, to choose their leaders wisely, to know that anyone in whom they placed trust would not steer them wrong. For, even as isolated as the Gullah were, they were also tightly bound to their slave ancestors whose conditions were even more remarkably brutal *because* of the islands' separation from the mainland.

Jenkins was part of a new generation of optimistic Gullah, who watched the bridge to Charleston being built while he was still young enough to walk across it. A father of seven children, he was emotionally committed to the future of his people and determined to make sure that all Gullah children had the same opportunities he prioritized for his own. He didn't shirk. He expected people to step up, and his personality was such that folks tended to rise to the occasion.

In one photograph, we see a grown man in a bow tie and fedora playing with a crowd of children, looking over his shoulder at them with such a loving expression, you can almost hear his laugh.[20] Jenkins's commitment to the children and families of Johns Island was deep and authentic—a fact that came through in all he did and was precisely why they so trusted his word.

"I decided to myself," he once wrote, "since I'm no better than anybody, I don't feel I'm any worse than anybody. I decided to do anything I can to help people in order to help myself. . . . And I tell you one thing: every progress that I have made in life, it came to me while I was doing some good for someone."[21]

Jenkins could see that these people from Tennessee also meant to do good, and they had the connections and experience to back it up.

He brought Zilphia into his home on purpose, and she came with her songs and her instruments to lay a foundation for what, she had a strong inkling, would be a long and productive relationship between the coastal island and the inland plateau.

She also brought her camera. Indeed, lore about a documentary film that Zilphia was shooting in order to tell the story about the Gullah people—one rumor holds that D. A. Pennebaker used some of her footage—has been passed down through the generations of Highlander leadership, though nobody is sure if it's true or where the film could be located.[22] Meeting notes in the Highlander library indicate some portion of it was shown to a group while Eleanor Roosevelt was visiting the school around 1957, and the former first lady felt the film had "great promise." But nobody still living has any idea if the movie was ever finished or preserved.

Nonetheless, we could see from Zilphia's earlier letters that she was intrigued by the way photography and movies could endear people to a subject when they couldn't be present to experience it for themselves. A half-century before digital storytelling would become standard practice among movement organizers, Zilphia recognized that it might be a powerful tool for amplifying empathy in social movements.

Her work on Johns Island would eventually be taken over by Guy and Candie Carawan. Zilphia had met Guy for the first time when he was on a road trip with fellow folksingers Frank Hamilton and Ramblin' Jack Elliott in 1953, the year before she first visited Johns Island. The trio of traveling men sat in Zilphia's living room while she recorded them casually swapping songs, and then she shared with them some of the songs she had collected. She made such an impression on Carawan that, in 1959, after she died, he offered to fill her role at Highlander.

The Carawans would eventually soak up far more of the rich Southern music when they moved to Johns Island for a few years to collect songs. These songs would eventually play an important role in freedom movements and influence popular folk music during the 1960s and beyond. Thus, the last great interest of Zilphia's life was left in rather capable hands.

But those images and moving pictures that encapsulated her early impressions of the long-isolated community on Johns Island, and the way it received her impeccable gifts, are lost to time.

OVER THE YEARS, Jenkins and his neighbors kept a correspondence with the Hortons and Clark. There were so many changes Jenkins wanted to see for his neighbors that it was hard to know where to even start. But through many conversations and letters, and during a UN meeting on desegregation that Jenkins attended, it started to become clear that the most productive change he could facilitate for the Gullah people would be to empower them to choose their own representatives to the state and federal government. They needed to be able to register to vote, and in order to do so, they were going to have to pass a literacy test.

Though children from the island had been commuting into the city for school, many of the Johns Island adults were illiterate, so Clark and Jenkins began to plan a program to teach them how to read. Clark knew that their program wasn't going to get anywhere if they brought in a professional schoolteacher because it would embarrass the adults to learn from someone who taught children. Previous efforts to teach literacy on the island saw adults sitting in children's desks, and the children would make fun of them, calling them "daddy long legs."[23]

Clark and Myles agreed that the most effective educator would be a peer who could learn how to teach even as the students would be learning how to read. Clark called upon her cousin, Bernice Robinson, who had lived for a while in New York, running her own beauty salon. Now back in South Carolina, Robinson was hesitant to take on the task but determined to try.

Jenkins purchased a building on the island and opened a small grocery in its storefront. Robinson taught the classes in a room behind the grocery. The first literacy class on Johns Island, which came to be called Citizenship School, convened in 1957, the year after Zilphia died.

Clark, who worked closely with Zilphia in those early days and welcomed her into her home in Charleston on several occasions, would manage that program for years, eventually weaving it into the fabric of the Southern Christian Leadership Conference and effectively helping hundreds of thousands of Southern Black people to register and vote.

Materials evolved over the years, with teachers using local voting laws to teach people to read. But, in those first sessions, Robinson opted for another document: The Universal Declaration of Human Rights.

CHAPTER 18

SUSTAINABILITY

ZILPHIA'S INVOLVEMENT in organizing on Johns Island shows how deeply rooted her understanding of culture was by this point and in what ways she wielded it to surmount prejudice and tension. Had she lived longer, she would have been able to bring this skill further into the causes that ignited her soul: the civil rights and environmental movements.

In her view, the arts—particularly music—did not exist in a vacuum. They were an accessible, universal pathway for people of different cultures and beliefs to come to understand and truly *see* one another. The things Zilphia learned about Jenkins and his neighbors by listening to their "shouting" style of music, for example, informed how she described that community, and her reports were taken into consideration in future organizing efforts. No doubt, the Gullah people's understanding of what kind of relationship they could expect from Highlander was augmented by the songs Zilphia chose to sing for them and the feeling with which she performed them. Always emotional and maternal, her musical performances exuded understanding and vision.

The relationship individuals have to their culture is deeply intertwined with how they see themselves and how they relate to the world around them. If someone's point of view didn't make sense to Zilphia, she would consider the culture from which they came, explore the songs and stories and food they loved, and that would help her better understand how they may have formed that opinion.

We see this in her letters and writings about her trips abroad, how she came to love foreign concepts and landscapes, how she came to love people whose language she didn't speak: by looking closely at their textiles, by listening closely to their music, by having enough of a sense of adventure to dine and drink as they do. Sure, she had a certain lust for life that so many of us find elusive, but this was fed by her determination to truly discover people who were different from her through their traditional arts and culture.

During the two or three seasons she spent outside Montreal, working as the music director at Camp Laquemac, Zilphia fed this part of her imagination in ways that were inaccessible back home on the plateau, where looming forces sought to shut down the school, where such serious discussions and decisions as those around Johns Island were always swirling, where two small children were always in need of her attention.

She was invigorated by the intellectual challenge of the movement, but as an artist, she also sought spiritual refuge—not only in her explorations of other people's culture, but also in the natural landscape. Zilphia had a deep spiritual connection to nature. She respected the natural world, and she wanted to leave a smaller footprint. She frequently sought out nature to help her rebalance herself under the weight of everything that created stress at Highlander, as it had a way of clarifying her thoughts. She jumped at any opportunity to spend the rare moment alone in the woods, on a beach, or atop a mountain taking in the world and making sense of it—or trying.

In a letter from Camp Laquemac, she wrote:

The lake is miles in length, the water is a blackish blue because of its depth, and high mountains slope off to more gentle hills along the water's edge.

I arose quite early one morning before daybreak and left the camp asleep—climbed Owl's Head, the highest mountain nearby and watched the sunrise.

As I lay on the edge of the cliff and watched shadows in the deep valleys disappear and the lake reflect the early morning light, the only sound was from a tiny bird chattering away at me from the top of a wind-blown hemlock. Later I heard a distant bell tolling for early mass. I felt completely suspended. And the thoughts and feelings I've had in the last year and a half were focused much more sharply. The thing that stood out most was the importance of maintaining a balance between one's inner self and the world about him. The delicate thread which separates—and sometimes doesn't separate—sanity from insanity, of maintaining a home with all responsibilities involved and still remaining not only an individual but a more creative individual, of being able to distinguish between one's own individual freedom in relation to the whole as against individual freedom which might become destructive, of the difficulty of living in a world where scientific knowledge is so far in advance of our social patterns of behavior that we may destroy ourselves.

Refusing to shut my eyes to the delusion, the problem is whether or not, or how best, one can fit into the present world in order to move in a positive and constructive way rather than a destructive one. Being aware of such and maintaining one's sanity is no little problem in itself.[1]

Though she uses universal pronouns ("one" instead of "I") here, this is the most intensely personal view we have of Zilphia, struggling to strike a balance between self and commitments by casting herself as one person trying to navigate a confusing world. It was a revelatory moment in her life, and it begs the question of what Zilphia might have done with these revelations, if she had had more time to act upon them.

There have been women throughout history who have struggled with the question of whether it's even worth it to break the habits of tradition—which call upon us to put self aside in service to the family and home—in order to realize one's own individual potential. Maybe Zilphia did not ponder that specific question, but she wondered if she was in the best place and context for self-actualization—a lifelong quest that began the moment she first took a train away from Paris, Arkansas, to the moment of her very last breath.

She was on a long, mindful search for her true self. In her final two years, Zilphia wrestled anew with this desire to obtain a balance between what was expected of her on the plateau and what she wanted and needed. It was a riddle that, like most women and mothers—indeed, most people—she would never solve: How can I be the best person I can be to serve my family? My community? My country? My self?

She knew that, if she was struggling with these questions, there must be others struggling with something similar, though she knew most other people weren't privileged with the choices she had available to her. Nonetheless, wasn't "you are not alone" the message she had communicated to every group of struggling workers and activists she had encountered for the past twenty years? Maybe she could use her struggle with these ideas to better help others who were struggling.

Zilphia's private writings attest to the fact that she believed the most pressing thing facing working people was not the denial of their political rights or even the racial tensions that could no longer be ignored in the South, but the fiction that they should be separate from one another. This was the big-picture issue from which she could not wrest her attention.

She believed that music, painting, theater, food, and the other expressions of art and culture had a potential, if wielded with intention, to cut through all the things that purport to separate us and to coalesce individuals around the cause of world peace.

As unattainable as something like "world peace" may have seemed to most Americans during the Depression, the war, and the period after it, Zilphia found hope and some indication of a way forward when she paid close attention to details: the tiny bird chattering, the wind-blown hemlock. As she watched people interact and considered the broader context of the times, she knew that focusing on the little things would help inform her on how to move culture through the arts.

She began to compose essays and short stories that indicated this. There aren't many of these writings, and none of them were ever published. Her poetry, while earnest, was especially unremarkable. She certainly didn't consider herself a writer. But

Myles nudged her along on her writing, and she admitted eventually that she enjoyed doing it, not because she had authorial ambitions but because she had an interest in what could be learned about humanity from studying the perspective of a single person from a background different from her own. This is evident, for example, in her writing about indigenous people in Mexico or the woman she sat next to on the train, years ago, on her way home from Montreal.

Her new pursuits of photography and organizing her thoughts into a story felt, at least for a short time, as though they were pathways toward a better understanding of—and maybe even eventually an opportunity to change—the world.

There on the mountain outside Montreal she pondered how a person might "move in a positive and constructive way." How could a middle-aged white woman change the world, she wondered, if she didn't begin with herself?

CHAPTER 19

ROSA PARKS AND THE END OF THE LINE

IN LATE SUMMER 1955, Septima Clark coordinated with the United Nations Commission on Human Rights—the body that had earlier created the Universal Declaration of Human Rights—to convene another UN workshop at Highlander, this time to address the issue of school desegregation.

Since the *Brown v. Board of Education* decision a year earlier, the somewhat fractured civil rights movement was charging ahead in various directions. A component that would later form into the Black Panthers believed in the value of militant resistance. Some among that group believed that Black Americans should secede and form their own nation in the American South. Other groups preferred to travel abroad and become expatriates in places like Paris and Rome. Others still, such as the NAACP, were committed to fighting within the context of the American legal system to have old laws thrown out or reinterpreted, even as they sought new legislation that would tighten voting rights at the federal level. These groups were committed to full desegregation and envisioned a future when Black people could rise to leadership levels in the fields of science, mathematics, and even the presidency.

As Myles had long since discovered—and as ANLC founder Lovett Fort-Whiteman knew—the problem with the cause of desegregation was that the Southern Black communities, especially, were incredibly fractured along these lines. Many in those communities had grandparents who still remembered slavery, and these families were slow to embrace the notion of equality alongside whites. If it was going to lead the way on desegregation, the NAACP was going to have an uphill battle.

Meanwhile, in cities like Birmingham, Selma, and Montgomery, Alabama; Jackson, Mississippi; Atlanta, Georgia; and Little Rock, Arkansas, Black activists were beginning to push back against Jim Crow laws with a renewed vengeance, seeing an opening in federal law in the wake of the *Brown* decision that could be pried open further.

In Montgomery in particular, a middle-aged woman named Rosa Parks, the wife of Raymond Parks, one of Alabama's most radical Black men, was the secretary for the local branch of the NAACP.[1] She worked as a seamstress for a local department store and also sewed for Highlander board member and Eastland committee target Virginia Durr, who lived in Montgomery with her husband, Clifford.

After years of working on civil rights with Montgomery's NAACP, Parks was feeling demoralized and beat down. Jeanne Theoharis, in her 2013 study of Parks's life, *The Rebellious Life of Mrs. Rosa Parks*, notes that "to be an activist for racial justice in the 1940s," such as Parks had been, "meant working without any indication that your efforts would be realized in your lifetime."[2]

Parks rode the same bus every day to work at the Montgomery Fair department store and expected that, when the bus would fill up, the driver would bark at her and others to move to the back. By law, Black riders had to stand while the seats were filled with white passengers. On occasion, Parks resisted moving, and the driver became frustrated enough by her insubordination that he would threaten to put her off the bus. Parks would cause just enough of a scene to make sure the folks in the back knew she was pushing, and then she would move.[3]

It was one of many small acts she practiced in her quiet resistance against the racist culture of the South. Her cohorts at the NAACP were aware of her commitment to the cause of desegregation because she had been one of the local branch's most active members, focused on investigating sexual assault as well as being a leader in the organization's Youth Council. Indeed, by 1955, it was the latter that had most of her focus as she was interested in what she and the Youth Council could do in Montgomery to honor the *Brown* decision.

Local NAACP president E. D. Nixon and Parks's employer Virginia Durr believed that Parks could benefit from what she might learn and experience at Highlander. So, in late July 1955, Parks boarded the back of a Greyhound bus and traveled up to the plateau. To head off any trouble she might experience along the way, Durr rode part of the way with her.

The workshop for which Parks received a scholarship lasted two weeks. She participated in discussions about the conflicting views that were gaining ground among the fractured factions of the national Black community: How to organize? How to surmount the division? How to educate and agitate? Could Black folks across the South come together around any common cause? What might that be?

Every day, Parks rose in her integrated dorm room and dressed, chatted with the white women, ate breakfast across the table from the white men. She wasn't expected to avert her eyes; she was encouraged by the culture of the school and by Zilphia's culture program to pitch in and push back.

"For Parks and others," writes Theoharis, "the naturalness of Highlander's integration—evident but not belabored—was key. Parks had participated in integrated groups and meetings, in particular, Montgomery's integrated Council of Human Relations. But she had disliked those meetings, telling Virginia Durr, 'Every time I went to one of those meetings, I came away blacker than I was before, because everything was discussed in terms of race.'" At Highlander, however, Parks noted, "I found for the first time in my adult life that this could be a unified society, that there was such a thing as people of all races and backgrounds meeting and having workshops and living together in peace and harmony."[4]

Though Theoharis doesn't dig into the culture program at Highlander in specific, the relaxed atmosphere, the natural feeling of the school's approach to desegregation, can be attributed to what Zilphia had created. In Parks's own memoir, she recalled "the smell of bacon frying and coffee brewing and know[ing] that white folks were doing the preparation instead of me."[5] If it wasn't Zilphia frying the bacon and brewing the coffee those mornings in late 1955, it was certainly someone she had roped into the task.

Parks carried as much affection for Clark as she did for Myles. But she left Highlander with the sense that a peaceful world was possible precisely because Zilphia had created a culture program that perfectly melded with the intellectual program her husband, and now Clark, ran. It was the ease of desegregation outside the classrooms, in Zilphia's domain, that internalized what Parks called "peace and harmony."

In the evening, after dinner, Parks would have joined in with everyone else, singing out loud as Zilphia took to the accordion or piano with a selection of her favorite songs: "No More Mourning," "This Little Light of Mine," "We Will Overcome." Like so many students of Highlander who had come before her, Parks experienced how it felt to lift her voice alongside her neighbors. She heard the voices of white men and women, determined to join their voices with hers as they sang, "We will organize, we will overcome someday."

At the end of the two weeks, when the workshop was winding down, staff and students sat in the circle of rocking chairs and, as Highlander students continue to do now, they went around, one at a time, sharing what it was they learned and what they intended to take back into their communities.

When the sharing got to Parks, she took a deep breath and spoke in her quiet, calm voice, saying that "she didn't know what she could do 'in the cradle of the Confederacy,'" but that she knew she must do something.[6]

Septima Clark remembered, "Rosa answered . . . that nothing would happen [in Montgomery] because blacks wouldn't stick together. But she promised to work with those kids, and to tell them that they had the right to belong to the NAACP."[7]

BACK IN MONTGOMERY, Parks told her husband Raymond about the workshop. Myles Horton, she would remember for the rest of her life, was the first white man she ever trusted.

Raymond, who wasn't thrilled that she went to Highlander in the first place, was amazed that his wife had spent two weeks sleeping in the same room as white women, eating with white men, dancing and singing and playing games and sports with white folks, sharing a bathroom with white people—all activities that could get her beaten up back home, or worse.[8]

Earlier that year, in March, a fifteen-year-old girl named Claudette Colvin, whom Parks knew through the Youth Council, had refused to give up her seat on a bus.[9] Colvin had been arrested and Parks felt she wanted to join the cause. After all, it was in the interest of empowering the youth that she had attended Highlander in the first place. Moreover, her outrage over the recent murder of Emmett Till made Parks feel like something must be done, that the adults must stand up for the sake of the children.

So, on the afternoon of December 1, 1955, on the way home from work, Parks, as she had done a few times before, refused to yield her seat on the bus to a white man.

The difference this time, however, was that Parks knew there was a wide network of people across the South who would support her if she was arrested and forcibly removed from the bus. She knew she could appeal the case against her and challenge the law that segregated buses. She knew there had been a successful bus boycott in Baton Rouge, knew of the court cases pending around bus desegregation. She knew, because she had been to Highlander, that there were white people who would come to her aid, and that someone had to refuse to move or else the deficit of justice would prevail.

There was nothing inherently different about this request this time. But like the song that Zilphia Horton had led back there on the plateau—*Just like a tree that's planted by the water, we shall not be moved*—Rosa Parks would not be moved. "It was not at all pre-arranged," she told an advisory and executive meeting at Highlander a few months later. "It happened that the driver made his demand and it also happened that I didn't feel like obeying his demand." The driver told her if she didn't move, he would call the police. She told him, "You may do that."[10]

In that moment, Rosa Parks went from a seamstress in a department store and the secretary of the local NAACP to a national figure who ignited a firestorm. The other people on the bus, who stood and sat and watched her resist, saw a woman, a nonthreatening human who just wanted to sit. They saw her demonized and threatened and arrested and dragged away. It was a sight they could not un-see, and her humanity and her quiet persistence were things they could not un-know. Whatever they thought of that moment, they saw and experienced what Myles Horton had always talked about: You cannot change anyone's mind by arguing. You must put people in a situation that requires them to act on their beliefs and then they have to reckon with how to proceed. That is how minds—and lives and worlds—change.

For all those other people on that crowded bus in Montgomery that December evening, how did it feel to see Rosa Parks resist? Did they have her back? Did they sit idly by? Did they not want to get involved? When they went home that night, told their family about their day, did they regret their inaction? Did they commit to changing their minds? Did they commit to joining the movement?

Two days before Christmas 1955, in a letter to Anne Lockwood, an Antioch student who had come to Highlander on a work term and stayed, Parks wrote:

Dear Anne:

Thanks for the kind letter from you about the news of my arrest of Dec. 1 in a city bus incident. I am sorry to have been this long answering. I do appreciate so much your concern of me at this time, for friends are needed now more than ever.

The colored people here are still not riding the buses. Private car pools and taxi cabs are co-operating to help under very trying conditions. The police are arresting drivers on the least provocation, in some cases for nothing. We have mass meetings twice each week to raise funds to use for gasoline and other expenses. It is costing more than $350.00 daily to help people go to and from their jobs.

My best regards to Myles, Zilphia and other Highlander

friends. I meant to write them and send a contribution to the school. We have not made progress on school desegregation. Perhaps this crisis will pave the way for some action later on.[11]

At the time, the NAACP had been looking for an unimpeachable figure to catapult Montgomery into a bus boycott. Parks was the perfect catalyst. Her decision to refuse to yield her seat on the bus would lead to the rise of twenty-six-year-old Martin Luther King Jr. When he spoke in the wake of Parks's civil disobedience, Rev. King linked Claudette Colvin and Rosa Parks, calling for a complete boycott of the city's public bus system.

They knew it wouldn't be a short effort: the boycott lasted 385 days.

Though Rev. King and Myles would come to argue about details and tactics in the years to come, King knew that boycotters could raise money through labor unions, churches, and other avenues in order to pay for gas and car repairs for the people who were willing to drive their neighbors to work.

With the example of Rosa Parks and the boycott in Montgomery making its way to the evening news, Black folks who had spent time at Highlander, who had been stirred by the work of Zilphia and Myles Horton and their network of staff and organizers, came calling for advice and assistance as they built their own organizations and their own branches of this blown-wide-open cultural and political moment.

It was a moment that changed everything for the Hortons, in many more ways than one.

CHAPTER 20

A SUDDEN, SHOCKING ACCIDENT

WHEN PARKS'S LETTER to Lockwood arrived at the school, the Hortons were in California, spending Christmas with the Johnson Girls. After the holidays, they headed back to the plateau, ready to welcome spring.

In February 1956, Zilphia picked daffodils and planted an early garden. She traveled west to speak to a Montana Farmers' Union gathering. She was moving on from the narrow cause of labor with great intention, and in her speech she explained why:

> Somebody said to me the other day, "How about going and singing for a particular group?" And it was a union group, too. I said, "I don't care anything about it anymore." And they said, "Why!?" And I said, "Because they have become so reactionary and they are so complacent and they have lost their ideals and I don't care anything about singing for people like that." And that's true. That's the way I feel. There aren't a great many unions like that but this happened that this one was like that. When they go through the routine, they go through the formality, but if there isn't something there that they believe in, as far as I'm concerned there's not anything worth singing about either.

Later in the same speech, she underscored the connection between arts and culture and effective organizing for social justice:

> I think this thing is so important of culture, as related to what people believe. I tried to think of something to use as an illustra-

tion and when I tell you the only thing I could come up with you may think I'm trying to be poetic. I really am not.

Singing, poetry, literature—all these things that we think make life richer, are like the water lilies. Do you have water lilies up here on your ponds and lakes? You know how they grow, don't you? The flower blossoms on top of the water, but underneath that water lily is a long root that goes down to the bottom of the pond; and what determines how beautiful that water lily is and how strong it is, is what's at the bottom of that pond in that mud and how rich it is. To me, the morality, what people stand for represents the roots in the mud at the bottom of the lake. The water lily on top, which may not seem connected at all to a lot of people, is really dependent on what goes on underneath. And that's the way I think about songs that we sing. If we sing with a group of people and they lose their purpose and they lose their belief and ideals, then the water lily is cut loose and it floats and it soon withers away.[1]

Zilphia had finally landed on the perfect image for the ideas she had always had about what music and the arts could do in the world, how we can honor and perpetuate tradition even as we create progress and blossom anew. All the thinking and working and trying had landed her finally in a place where her core beliefs were articulable, just as the world was needing her perspective more than ever.

WHEN PEOPLE WHO KNEW HER talk about the last couple of years of Zilphia's life, there is always a bittersweetness to their tales. No doubt their stories are colored by the sudden and tragic loss of this woman who was so widely adored and admired. But also in there are stories of the existential threats to the school and friction within her marriage to Myles.

Though their letters continued to contain loving pronouncements, it was almost as though the Hortons were hoping to form a protective bubble with these words. What read as passionate urgency two decades earlier now read as simply urgent.

Zilphia was wrestling with the path she had chosen. Given her life story and her love affair with New York and Chicago, it's easy to wonder whether she occasionally thought about taking the kids and moving to such a city, leaving Myles back in Tennessee with his school. She loved her husband and her work, but artists thrive in community with other artists, and there were so many months of isolated quiet on the plateau.

For all that her peers and students remember Highlander as an embodiment of Zilphia as a person, at age forty-five, she was beginning to confront the questions of midlife: Am I where I belong? Am I doing what I belong doing, and with whom?

Like so many people of so many generations who have sought external relief in times of internal strife, Zilphia appreciated the momentary comfort of a glass of moonshine—never in excess, but certainly on occasion.

THOUGH THE STATE OF TENNESSEE has boasted productive wineries and a fair number of beer breweries since its founding, it was whiskey that came to define the state's alcoholic palate. It's believed that Tennessee's first distillery opened as early as 1771. By the turn of the nineteenth century, distilleries could be found in all the cities and many of the towns. Yet, after more than a century of whiskey production, the state passed a ban on distilleries in 1909 and maintained a vice grip on legal alcohol until 1937.

Even when Tennessee lifted the all-out ban, Grundy County persisted, which put a wrinkle in the drinking habits of a certain progressive community in Monteagle.

"We were in a dry county," Thorsten explains. "It wasn't legal to buy any kind of hard liquor in Grundy County." And then, to illustrate the backbone of that particular law, he adds with a grin:

> You could drive up to the Shell station and ask for a pint of gin and they'd bring it out in a brown bag. But it was a dry county.
>
> I remember this—this happened twice: The sheriff coming to our house with a quart of moonshine in a Mason jar and giving it to my dad. He was running for office. He'd say, "Oh I raided the still and now I have to give the stuff away." My dad would be

angry and never drink the stuff because it was made by using the radiator to distill it.

That's how almost all the moonshine was made. You'd use a car radiator, which means you had lead. . . . But the good stuff—you couldn't buy it in the open market. You had to have it manufactured.[2]

Manufacturing moonshine became a staple of Tennessee's black market economy, particularly during the decade of Prohibition. Bootleggers were omnipresent in the area. In fact, one of the most famous, Al Capone, built a mansion near Dr. Johnson's property in 1929. An expensive restaurant operated out of the mansion.[3] The High Point was run, it's rumored, by Capone's mistress. Secret tunnels accessed by escape hatches in the building were used into the early 1930s for moving illegal hooch.

Charis is certain Myles and Zilphia never encountered Capone because her father would have never missed the opportunity to tell such a story. But Capone's occasional rumored visits overlapped with Highlander's existence by at least a few years and the Hortons occasionally dined at the High Point, whose chef was known to turn out exquisite cuisine in a county where almost nobody could afford to consume it.[4]

At any rate, by the time Zilphia arrived at Highlander, Tennessee's bootlegging industry had deep roots and families who had been in the industry for generations. Thus, the way the illegal hooch was manufactured was almost as protected an industry as banking or any other corporate interest. It's no surprise that Myles Horton got involved in organizing for a better way.

As Thorsten describes it:

I don't know the details of this, but I do know that this happened: Enough local people who didn't want to get killed arranged to have a fairly substantial amount of moonshine made the right way. Myles was one of those people, so we had a ten-gallon oak keg in the basement, which had been burned inside so it aged the [lining]. My dad called it Jack Daniels Storage. He'd say, "Let's get some Jack Daniels."

He loved his moonshine. It was like 140 proof. He didn't drink it all the time. He drank gin most of the time. He liked gin. . . . But [Zilphia] would drink moonshine. . . . She'd be sitting around working and having some fruit juice in a glass, and put some moonshine in it. Have a little sip.

As it would turn out, a little sip would be her undoing.

AS WINTER 1956 turned to spring, Thorsten was living with Myles's sister Elsie Pearl in Murfreesboro, where he was attending public school for sixth grade. Charis was busy with her life at the Monteagle school.

To celebrate Charis's birthday in March, Zilphia took her and their friend, Anne Lockwood, to Nashville's Ryman Auditorium to see the Grand Ole Opry.[5] Zilphia was not a fan either of the show or of its highly commercialized music. Granted, she had come to appreciate the way Hank Williams toyed with folk melodies and ideas to turn them into mainstream music; she liked to tell a tale of questionable validity about how Charis turned her on to Williams's ability to bring folk music into the modern era. But Williams, who had missed appearances due to his heavy drinking, had been fired from the Opry two years earlier and was not part of the show that night.

Charis got a new pair of shoes for the occasion. Zilphia braided her daughter's hair and the three headed for Nashville on their own, staying overnight with friends Zilphia had made through the unions and with whom she had lived during the long months of Charis's convalescing from polio a few years earlier.

That trip to the Opry is Charis's last notable memory of her mother and Lockwood's last notable memory of the woman who had become her best friend.

LOCKWOOD HAD COME to Highlander a few years earlier as an Antioch student and stayed on as a member of the staff.[6] She was twenty-three years younger than Zilphia and twelve years older than Charis, but she had an instant soul connection with both mother and daughter that made the three feel like family.

The daughter of American missionaries, Lockwood had grown up in China and her first language was Cantonese. To evade the threat of war, her parents moved Lockwood and her sister to a town in the Himalayan Mountains, north of Delhi, in the 1940s. Lockwood, her sister, and her mother eventually left Calcutta on a military ship that was selling tickets to civilian passengers. They landed in California, where Lockwood went to school. When the war ended, they returned to China, and she finished high school there.

Later, back in the United States, Lockwood enrolled at Antioch College. During her first work term there, she worked for Myles's friend Saul Alinsky, and she spent the second one in her senior year at Highlander.

Zilphia was fascinated by her young friend's time abroad. She and Lockwood spent a lot of time together in that last year, just talking about life.

The month between their trip to the Opry and the onset of April passed as months tended to pass on the plateau: breakfasts and lunches, late nights in the living room singing and laughing with friends, sunsets over the lake, calls to Thorsten, letters to organizers and leaders across the South, large meals when Zilphia left the kitchen a total mess and everyone pitched in to clean up.

With a break between workshops, Myles headed out on the road to raise funds and drum up support for the movement. Zilphia and Lockwood were the only adults at the school that week, having a bit of a girls' week, mimeographing broadsides and gossiping about men.

At eight o'clock on the morning of Sunday, April 1, Zilphia was working in the office. As Lockwood recalled, Zilphia was swirling with emotions, energized by the progress happening around civil rights, missing her husband and son, and struggling with her own internal growth.[7] She grabbed a Mason jar and took a swig of moonshine. In the split second it took for the liquid to slip past her tongue and down her throat, Zilphia knew something was terribly wrong. She set down the glass and smelled its contents. It was not moonshine, but carbon tetrachloride.

It was habit for Zilphia to pour a small amount of the toxic liquid into a Mason jar, then dip an old toothbrush in, and use that to clean the gunk that mimeographing left on typewriter keys.

Such a small mistake, to have grabbed the wrong jar.

She ran to the bathroom and stuck her fingers down her own throat, vomiting out the contents of her stomach. Lockwood heard her and came to ask what was wrong. Zilphia told her friend what had happened, her silly split-second mistake.[8]

It wasn't a big sip, but it was enough. She was hopeful that making herself throw up would solve the problem. But as the morning wore on, Zilphia looked worse and worse, and she couldn't stop throwing up. After a few hours, Lockwood called Dr. Kirby Smith, the country doctor who lived two towns away in Sewanee, and told him to come immediately.

IN 2012, I VISITED Anne Lockwood Romasco's Brooklyn brownstone in the middle of a city block, near the campus of the Pratt Institute. The living room was dark and homey, full of books and more books, art on the walls, and mementos of her many decades of radical work.

After her years of interning at Highlander, after Zilphia's death, Lockwood Romasco became a teacher there, running a summer camp for high schoolers who were preparing to enter integrated schools for the first time in the fall. Harry Belafonte had bankrolled that program and asked for Lockwood Romasco, by name, to run it.

But here on the back porch, overlooking her tiny backyard, on a humid day in early July, she was an old woman, small and self-contained with the rectangular body of a gymnast and a small set of wire-rimmed glasses atop her nose. When she talked, it was with a certain quiet strength and authority that hinted at the extraordinary actions and activism of her youth.

When I steered the conversation toward the death of her best friend, Lockwood Romasco's hands were visibly trembling. She didn't want to talk about it. She had promised Myles she wouldn't tell this story to anyone, but she also realized that Myles had been dead for more than twenty years and that the reason they had agreed not to tell the story had become irrelevant decades ago.

On this day, out of habit, she was pushing back: she didn't see why it mattered. "Zilphia's life was so much more important and interesting than her death," she told me.

"I can't very well tell the story of Zilphia's life without also including the story of her death," I said. "Some people think it was suicide. The story that's out there is that she accidentally mistook a glass of carbon tetrachloride for a glass of water. I don't believe she was suicidal, but I also don't believe she was dumb enough to get a glass of a highly toxic substance to her face and into her mouth without realizing it wasn't water."

Her hands were shaking as her eyes shifted. "It wasn't a glass of water," she said, cutting off my train of thought. "It was moonshine." She went on to say that the reason they didn't tell anybody that was because, after the Eastland committee hearing, Myles knew if word got out that anyone on the plateau in the dry county of Grundy was drinking illegal alcohol, the school would be shut down.

"We were afraid people would make up stories," Lockwood Romasco explained. "But, of course, then they just made up stories anyway."

With an exhalation, she settled back into her body, thinking of how her silence inadvertently led to the rumors of suicide and other awful theories.

LOCKWOOD ROMASCO REGRETTED for the rest of her life not calling Dr. Smith sooner. She wondered if that could have saved Zilphia's life, but the medical reality was such that once the poison entered her body, there was nothing Zilphia could do to reverse its effects.

She contacted Myles, and he came home as soon as he could. Dr. Smith treated Zilphia at home for two or three days before transferring her to the hospital in Sewanee, where she had so recently sat with Charis for all that time. Zilphia was treated in Sewanee for three more days before being transferred to Nashville and the Vanderbilt Medical Center.

As hope began to wane in those final days, Myles picked up Charis from home, then went to collect Thorsten from Elsie

Pearl's house in Murfreesboro and brought them to Nashville together to visit their mother one more time. Thorsten insisted on stopping at the hospital gift shop first. He bought her a bottle of Chanel No. 5, which was her favorite perfume. He thought perhaps its sweet scent could put her at ease as her body fought against its own kidneys.

Transplant and dialysis—two advancements that could have saved Zilphia's life—were still in the experimental stages in 1956 when she lay dying of kidney failure in a Nashville hospital.[9]

Myles recalled:

> A specialist at the Vanderbilt hospital where she had been taken said that she couldn't live, and the last few days we spent together we both knew those few days were all we would have together. She calmly expressed her regrets that she would not get to see the children grow up and we could not do the many things with them we had planned. We talked about the good times we had had and the problems and fun we had had together. She felt that she had lived a useful life and hoped she had left behind some things that would continue to be useful, but most of all, she talked about the children's future and how she would like to see them develop as creative, happy people, living for something that is worthwhile and enjoying life as we had done. Her calmness held me together when the doctor said she was dead.[10]

Zilphia Horton's life had been full of energy, passion, and music. She had sung with such ease and fervor that she inspired some of the most celebrated folksingers of the twentieth century. Uninterested in the easy, well-paved path of being the boss's eldest daughter, Zilphia instead found her voice and put it to use for the betterment of the world.

She taught thousands of people across the South how to use their voices, to join their voices together. Her own voice had been one of her best attributes—its deep, rich alto and its musical rundown-the-scale, giggling laugh. Emil Willimetz remembered her laugh as "a wholehearted crescendo of musical notes—she would throw back her head and let it out."[11] All powered by the breath in her lungs and the will in her chest, both of which gave out at some point in the middle of the day on April 11, 1956, just three days before her forty-sixth birthday.

In that moment, after expressing gratitude for her experiences, love for her husband, and hope for her children, Zilphia Horton exhaled for the last time.

Myles simply sat and sobbed. The man who had built a movement with his boundless energy and ideas could suddenly neither move nor speak. His wife had let go, but he could not bear to release her. As he recalled: "Two hours later, the doctor gently told me I had cried enough and my sister had been waiting for me for a long time. He gave me some sedatives and I went home with Elsie Pearl."[12]

On the day her mother died, Charis was released from school in Monteagle and got home to find Anne Lockwood waiting for her. Myles collected Thorsten from Murfreesboro again, and braced himself to tell his children the news.

> I took Thorsten and Charis down by the side of the lake and told them Zilphia had died. After a few sobs they wanted to know what she had said about them. She had sent a specific message. I said, "Zilphia told me that she wanted 'Charis to be Charis, Thorsten to be Thorsten.'" . . .
>
> Thanks to my sister and her family and to Zilphia's sisters, Mom Horton and Gram Johnson, life in the Horton family moved on despite the fact that I went into a tailspin for a week or so and was unable to pull myself together. This was done for me by Saul Alinsky who had lost his wife by drowning a year or two before. Saul insisted that I come to Chicago and live with him under the guise of my having to get an application to the Schwardhaupt Foundation within a week. He worked with me night and day forcing me to concentrate on getting out a report and making an application to such an extent that I had little or no time for remorse.[13]

With the loss fresh in his mind, Thorsten set off with his friend Doc Paine into the woods to find the rare blooms of the mountain laurel Zilphia loved so much. They gathered all manner of spring flowers, including rhododendron from her own bushes—the ones

Myles had found in the woods and transplanted to the top of the hill, back when he and his young bride were only dreaming about building a house, back when she was in New York, that first winter of their marriage.

The boy, at thirteen, was tall and awkward. His hair was still blond but starting to darken. His voice cracked sometimes as he stood at the door of his own adolescence. He was Zilphia's firstborn, with whom she had spent so many quiet mornings alone in the early days of his infancy, just back from the hospital. So many evenings alone in the sublet house in Chicago. They had a relationship nobody else witnessed. He had seen her thriving away from the plateau; he had seen the way the Windy City brought out a twinkle in her eye.

Her young son, for whom she had made birthday cakes topped with wires and antennae to honor his fascination with electronics, picked up his camera that day, the one Emil Willimetz had given him, and photographed his mother's funeral. He captured the strings of flowers he and Paine had laid across the top of her piano. Then he quietly approached her open casket and photographed her face one last time. Her expressive face with its broad smiles, bright eyes, and dark eyebrows was now still, expressionless, alien.

Following the funeral, he and his cousin, Butch Grant, put together a special flier reporting on the service. Carrying the torch of his matriarchal line, Thorsten dealt with his grief by getting busy.

> Her funeral was held at four o'clock PM. . . . No one was to
> bring flowers but they all did. Everyone in the room saw her and
> cried. We all went to the graveyard and saw her put in her grave.
> The preacher gave a wonderful sermon for her. . . . The funeral
> was at the Highlander Folk School where the walls were covered
> with wildflowers. The Horton family walked to their house from
> the graveyard and had supper.[14]

Charis could not bring herself to attend the funeral. Just eleven years old, she was restless, gutted, heartbroken. She wanted to cry, but tears wouldn't come. Her grandmother Ora took her absence of tears as a personal slight. To mitigate the situation, Elsie Newell, with whom Charis had lived during that year in California, left her own sister's funeral and took the young girl for a walk in the woods that had been Zilphia's sanctuary so often during her life. Zilphia had once written to Myles that she had found some personal empowerment walking home through those woods by herself after dark. "I did something I've never done before," she wrote back then. "Made myself walk home alone. It sounds foolish to you perhaps but I am frightened at the panic created by aloneness in the forest in complete darkness. And to walk home calmly outwardly, if not inwardly was a small victory and one which I must cultivate."[15]

Now her sister and daughter stepped in many of the same places where Zilphia had conquered one of her fears so long ago, seeking the ability to be calm outwardly, if not inwardly. Zilphia's footfalls from back then had long since become covered over by seasons and years.

"When she died," Aleine Austin would later recall, "it was like the impossible; like the earth—she was an earth mother and how does an earth mother die, you know?"[16] Few people could make it to Monteagle on such short notice, so the funeral was attended mostly by family, a couple of friends like Austin who could make it, and locals from the community.

Over the ensuing days and weeks, Myles became a walking vessel of emotion. He remembered it as a week; others remembered his mourning going on quite a bit longer. He would be walking in the woods, working in the garden, going through his mail, and the sobbing would just come. Austin would be impressed by how thoroughly he embraced his grief. The man who was known for his ability to step back and look at any situation with cold, emotionless detachment, to find the way forward through any storm, was, in this moment, lost in a storm of his own.

BEFORE THEY GOT TO WORK that week, activists and former Highlander students paused, as the news reached them, and sent letters of mourning and support to Myles and the Highlander staff. Hundreds of them poured in, from Pete Seeger and Rosa Parks, Eleanor Roosevelt and Lee Hays, and the hundreds of people who had come to Highlander for labor union, United Nations, or civil rights workshops. All those people whose eyes had been opened wider, whose hearts had swelled with new love and hope because of something Zilphia said to them or did for them and because of the way she welcomed them to the table, fed them, taught them to sing.

The mourning was profound and palpable, and Myles leaned into it, leafing through the hundreds of expressions of solidarity in his mourning.

> Your infinite grief is shared by all of us whose lives have been en-enriched by Zilphia through acquaintance with her, be it long or short. Hers is the most beautiful and meaningful immortality I can conceive of. With the beauty and truthfulness of her life, with her warmth and great gifts, she has left an unforgettably enriching experience with all who walked with her—and there must be thousands! . . . When I think of you, I see you both as we said goodbye to you very early one morning last summer. To-gether in the early morning light you were hoeing and weeding your garden. In the years to come even though you are deprived of her physical presence, Zilphia will go on weeding and planting with you. [Lena Kaplan]

> You have sustained a very great loss, not only personally, but she was your comrade in all your work, such a mate! I just can-not visualize her without her vibrant efficient personality. [Lilian Johnson]

> Her spirit and love for the common peoples shall live on in the hearts of all of us who knew her and loved her. [Bill Marlowe]

> If it's any consolation, and of course it's not much, there is what anyone who knew her knows, that she was thoroughly alive. [Robert M. Grant]

I think of Zilphia—so alive and full of energy. I am sure all the little angels are singing and square dancing and organizing today. [Alice Mitchell]

The music that your music made for me
Was like a singing bird's:
How can I make a song for you
With only words [May Justus][17]

In Chicago, a group chaired by Studs Terkel gathered for a singing memorial, "Songs for Zilphia," where a local folksinger led the congregants in an evening of songs from Zilphia's 1939 songbook.[18]

Myles and Zilphia's close friend, the University of Chicago professor and dean of the chapel, John Thompson, was a speaker, and he had written to Myles with some of the most moving commentary about Zilphia's and his impact:

One of the things that held me here Friday was a huge meeting we had in the Chapel Friday night with the Rev. Martin Luther King of Montgomery as speaker. The university administration was much disturbed that I allowed such a meeting; but at least 1700 people came to it and King did a good job. As I tried to listen to him, I found that most of the time I was in Monteagle, but this did not disconnect; for I thought with gratitude of the strange web of influence, how Mrs. Rosa Parks had got something at Highlander and then had sparked the boycott and even at such a dark time as this, the tide rolls on and will not be stopped. This is typical of the life that you and Zilphia built there; it reaches out throughout the South and on into the wider world and no one will ever see the whole chain of influence, and no one cares so long as the awakening comes.[19]

Zilphia's legacy charged ahead through the people whose names would never be known, whose stories would never be told, but whose hearts were all the way in on a movement with which they became acquainted thanks to Myles and Zilphia Horton's partnership.

But it was Zilphia's own words in the program for the Chicago event that perhaps best encapsulated her life and work and best spoke on her behalf. She had spoken these words at nearly every gathering of singers, and they captured the spirit of her work, the intention she brought to Highlander, the inclusivity that was in everything she did, from her arrival at the school until her comment, just before she died, that she hoped her work could continue to be of use:

> I don't care if people do have one nationality, if they have one racial group, if they have one religion. There is something else that is essential before they can sing together, and that is that they believe in something.[20]

EPILOGUE

AFTER ZILPHIA DIED, there was nobody to fill her role. Myles, in his utter grief, continued to lead and showed up where he was called, but the work of empathy and connection, outreach, maintaining and evolving the culture of the school had no individual focused on it for a few years.

As Ermon Fay explained: "Myles provoked people and got them thinking. And Zilphia welcomed people. You have to have both things. You need someone to form an atmosphere and take an interest in the individual. Zilphia had a lot of energy and she was lively and curious and people reacted to her as a genuine person. . . . She encouraged any and everybody to do something creative."[1]

In an effort to stay connected with the people of Johns Island, Myles asked Zilphia's niece, Shelby Flint, if she might be willing to go there and sing with them. Shelby was at the beginning of her music career and agreed to give it a shot.[2]

Standing before a church altar, she lit into some of the songs she remembered Zilphia singing and brought new songs of her own. It wasn't a comfortable experience for her; it was not an easy audience. Shelby ultimately decided that kind of work wasn't right for her.

Other people pitched in here and there.

For the school's twentieth-fifth anniversary in 1957, the year after Zilphia's death, Pete Seeger was called upon to lead the music. As a eulogy, he noted, "Zilphia had a beautiful alto voice, an unpretentious rare voice, but not the show-off kind. She sang [folk songs] the way a mother would sing to her child. She brought out the talents of her audience and their enthusiastic participation."[3]

Newly blacklisted after being held in contempt by the House Un-American Activities Committee, Seeger hadn't been allowed to perform in concert, on the radio, or on television in two years. He had returned from an ethnographic exploration of Africa's music traditions and was beginning to tour elementary schools, singing with children in what would be one of the most fruitful folk music efforts of the second half of the twentieth century: Some of the children who sang with Seeger at school went on to be leaders of the popular folk music boom that came a decade later.

Seeger was indelibly influenced by Zilphia's work, ideas, and friendship, and he did his best to deliver music at the twenty-fifth anniversary celebration in the same spirit that Zilphia would have done it. Indeed, many of the people with whom I spoke agreed that Seeger's ability to get people to sing with him was the closest approximation of Zilphia's gift that remained after she died.

Eventually, Guy Carawan wrote to Myles that it seemed that, following Zilphia's death, a gaping hole had opened in Highlander's mission and ability to offer holistic education, a hole that had yet to be filled. Carawan offered to take on the role, and Myles accepted.

Though Carawan was a stage performer who brought with him a different set of skills from those of Zilphia, his approach to culture leadership was hugely effective and became an integral part of the civil rights movement. Zilphia had been leading labor union groups and others in "We Will Overcome" for a decade before her death, but it was Carawan who turned the song into the anthem of the civil rights movement, introducing it to the SNCC gathering in 1960. But even as those like Carawan and Seeger continued to ripple her influence out over the music world, the situation back home on the plateau started to fall apart.

During the twenty-fifth anniversary celebration, the governor of Georgia sent moles to take photographs of the festivities that could be used against the school. One photograph of Seeger's performance showed Martin Luther King Jr. seated in the audience. This photo was used on a billboard and in an advertising campaign that sought to undermine the growing appeal of the leader. In the picture, an arrow points to King under the message "Martin Luther King at Communist Training School."

A powerful propaganda campaign was then unleashed. The school's tax-exempt status was revoked. The long-held suspicions of folks in Tracy City precipitated a court case against the school. The bulk of Highlander's FBI file was focused on this period.

One evening after a long day of workshopping around desegregation, someone offered to drive over to neighboring Franklin County for a beer run. They returned with a case of beer and everyone who wanted a bottle contributed some cash to reimburse the person who did the run. A mole for the state of Tennessee happened to be present and reported that the school was effectively selling alcohol to minors.

Despite the fact that Myles and Anne Lockwood had determined to keep mum about the moonshine that killed Zilphia, it was ultimately an alcohol violation—selling beer without a license—that brought the school into court. The dramatic case featured racist, anti-union ultra-conservatism. Some of Highlander's neighbors, notably May Justus, testified on the school's behalf. Others were more easily flipped by the prosecutors' case. The Hortons' neighbor Mattie, who had been employed by Zilphia for so long, who had helped her in the days after Charis's bout with polio, and who had such a deep loyalty to the family, watched as her own husband testified against the school. He wasn't the only one.

Many to this day wonder if so many neighbors would have testified against Highlander if Zilphia had been alive at the time. Her program and practice of outreach was so genuine and effective, and when she died, there was no individual focused on picking it up with the same amount of dedication and heart. Candie Carawan would eventually step into that role but had not yet arrived. Thus, long-held relationships lapsed, trust eroded.

Without the daily interactions—Zilphia inviting people over for dinner or to dance or sing on a moment's notice—the neighbors became more detached from the school. They had more time to sit around and worry, to draw their own conclusions, to wonder if the loss of that wonderful woman had somehow meant the school was losing its way.

"She was there for the community—for people in trouble," Zilphia's friend and former Highlander staff member Lanie Melamud later told Candie Carawan. "She would drive people to hospitals. She had one of the few cars. She knew everything about everybody in the community. . . . It seemed like the school was a living embodiment of what she believed."[4]

AS THE CASE CLOSED, the State of Tennessee revoked Highlander's charter in 1961. When the Tennessee Highway Patrol came to shut the place down, they informed Myles that he and his family and the staff would need to vacate the property. And then they padlocked the meeting hall and the library.

Standing on the steps of the library as his life's work was locked away from him, Myles was defiant. "When they first came, they padlocked the building," he told Bill Moyers in 1981. "Some of the reporters said, 'Why are you laughing?' I was standing outside laughing. I said, 'My friend here, he thinks he's padlocking Highlander. But . . . Highlander's an idea. You can't padlock an idea.'"[5]

Highlander staff had already applied for a new charter under the name "Highlander Research and Education Center" (HREC) and were able to continue operations under that charter the very next day. Hearing rumors that local Klansmen planned to destroy the property in a fit of angry retribution, a group of Highlander students emptied the library of everything they could carry. While Thorsten was attending graduate school at the University of Wisconsin at Madison, Highlander staff sent the papers to the Wisconsin Historical Society at UWM, and many of the Highlander files remain there.

What papers and records didn't land in Madison were brought to a home Highlander had purchased in Knoxville, where Myles and the staff lived and functioned as HREC for a decade, doing vital organizing and strategic work that carried the civil rights movement forward in widely effective ways.

Myles continued as the director of the school until 1969, when he "retired," ceding the position to Frank Adams, who wrote an informative history of the school, *Unearthing Seeds of Fire: The Idea of Highlander.*

In 1972, Highlander acquired a sweeping piece of land in the hills outside Knoxville, near the incorporated town of New Market. Charis, Thorsten, and others worked together to build a house at the top of the hill on the property, where Myles lived for the rest of his life, a couple of boxes of Zilphia's piano books tucked away in a closet.

In 1962, Myles married Aimee Isgrig Horton, a woman he met when she came to Highlander as a student. Aimee's dissertation about Highlander for the University of Chicago has proved to be the most factual and comprehensive account of the school's programs in the early years, and she wrote fondly, if not in tremendous detail, about the woman who preceded her.

Myles developed a brain tumor in the late 1980s and died January 19, 1990. Highlander staff and others who had been touched by Myles's work through the years put up a circus tent on the property in New Market and threw a roaring party. Friends from all over the world gathered there on the hill to celebrate and honor his memory through stories and songs.

After the funeral, they planted some of his ashes, along with a tree, just over yonder from the workshop space in New Market. Thorsten and Charis filled one of the gourds he had collected on his many travels with the rest of his ashes and buried the gourd, along with his slippers and pipe and various other of his favorite objects, next to Zilphia's remains in the Monteagle graveyard.

NOW IT'S SUMMER on the hill in New Market. The air is hot and heavy. Everything is in bloom. The trees that know to go dormant for a time have unfurled their flowers and spread their leaves. Their green shines back at the sun, which in turn pushes its bright fingers against their veins—the great powerful light taking the pulse of the world.

Nature always finds balance.

The songs have been coming around again. At the doors of

immigration detention centers, they have sung "We Shall Not Be Moved."

In the streets where hundreds of thousands have marched for peace and justice, they have sung "This Little Light of Mine."

On high school campuses, they've sung "Enough is enough / we shall overcome someday," changing the song the way they know to do because they have heard it changed by previous generations in videos they can find on YouTube.

In airports in 2017, crowds gathered in protest of an executive order barring travel from a handful of predominantly Muslim countries, and the people sang Zilphia's songs.

In the statehouse in Madison, Wisconsin, a union member showed up at noon every day for many years to sing "We Shall Overcome" with anyone choosing to join him in protest against an anti-union state legislature.

Whether or not any of these people have known that a woman named Zilphia once stood in a room and impressed upon those present the value of singing these songs is irrelevant. The songs are there. People sing because they need the songs right now. They've learned to sing them because they saw and heard other people do it before. It doesn't matter where these songs came from, only that they, like these trees, were standing in wait, ready to bloom when the season came around again.

It's been more than sixty years since Zilphia's death, and walking into the Highlander meeting hall, one can still feel her presence. She never set foot on the property where Highlander sits today, but the spirit she brought to the school, the puzzle pieces she added, which became synonymous with its function, remain: Beautiful abundant flower gardens, sweeping mountain views, delicious food, and lively parties. You sing to begin a workshop and you sing to go to lunch and you sing to close the day.

Late at night, during the Zilphia Horton Cultural Organizing Institute in 2012, we cranked up the music and line danced to hip-hop songs, played Spades, and talked about our lives. We sat by the bonfire and made s'mores. Someone noodled on a mandolin, someone else on a guitar. We took to the singing pavilion—built so the voices raised there might echo back, encouraging everyone to raise their voice higher—architecture doing what Zilphia once did with an accordion. There, exercising her legacy, we turned popular activist chants into songs.

The culture of the movement prevails. So much so that my generation—part-X and part-Millennial—now takes for granted that music and the arts are an automatic part of any social movement. We have learned because it was handed down to us that if there is to be lasting change, it will come through organizing, voting, demonstrating, resisting—and singing.

ACKNOWLEDGMENTS

I must begin by acknowledging the folks who collected parts of Zilphia's story long before I arrived. This would certainly have been a much more challenging project without the notes and ruminations of Aimee and Myles Horton, Aleine Austin, Guy and Candie Carawan, Ermon Fay Johnson Duchesnes, Sue Thrasher, Frank Adams, John Glen, and Emil Willimetz. Gratitude especially to Candie, who was the first person from the inside who encouraged me to chase this story, framing it as an important contribution.

Endless gratitude to Thorsten and Charis Horton, Shelby Flint, Bonnie Guy Johnson Flint, and Rolf Duschesnes, who generously gave freely of their time, family archive, and personal memories. Charis, especially, fielded impromptu text messages and phone calls containing questions that must have seemed out of left field and always did so with kindness and intellectual curiosity.

Thanks to Anne Lockwood Romasco, Joie Willimetz, Betty Goldiamond, Les Orear, and others from Highlander's old days, all of whom are no longer with us but who patiently offered not only context but also necessary perspective.

Thanks to Susan Williams for having so many answers and knowing where to look for the ones she did not have. Thanks to Pam McMichaels, Tufara Waller-Muhammad, Marquez Rhyne, Ebony Noelle Golden, Elandria Williams, Jardana Peacock, and the wider family at the Zilphia Horton Cultural Organizing Institute.

Thanks to the folks at the Tennessee State Library and Archive, the University of Wisconsin Archive, and the University of North Carolina at Chapel Hill Wilson Library. Thanks also to Laurence Connelley and Joyce Friddle from the Paris Logan County Coal Mining Memorial and Museum for their generosity with their time and their insights.

Thanks to Adele and Eugene Jaroszlaw for fielding my questions about New York in the 1930s. Thanks to Ani DiFranco, whose music introduced me—and much of my generation—to the radical and vibrant potential of folk music, and who unwittingly pointed me in the direction of this story during a 2006 interview.

Thank you to my generous and trusting cadre of Kickstarter supporters who threw me their cash before I had any idea what I was getting myself into. Their faith in me and this project sustained me through many authorial and existential crises.

Thank you to my writers' group—Lauren Harr, Neela McDade, Clara Boza, and Glenn Court—and other early readers: Katelyn Reilly, Stacy Chandler, Mark Baumgarten, Carolyn Wallace, and Kristin Neumeyer. Thanks to Gold Leaf Literary for helping me navigate the unknown.

Abundant thanks to my editor, Casey Kittrell, for his sustained interest in this project, and for his careful, insightful edits. Thanks to the University of Texas Press for trusting an unknown author who had an untold story to tell about someone who was unknown to so many.

Thanks to my friends and colleagues at *No Depression, FreshGrass*, and *Folk Alley*, for being wonderful people—all in the business for the right reasons. Thanks, love, and indebtedness to my mother and siblings, my friends, and my cohousing neighbors, for always asking how the book was coming. And finally, to Mercedes, Quinn, and Sage, who have provided no shortage of encouragement, support, family hugs, and happy distractions when I have needed them the most: thank you doesn't cut it, but it's the best I can do with words.

NOTES

INTRODUCTION

1. Zilphia Horton, speech recorded at Montana Farmers' Union School, February 16, 1956, Zilphia Horton Folk Music Collection, 1935–1956, Box 6, Tape 7, Tennessee State Library and Archives, Nashville.

CHAPTER ONE: A LONG LINE OF STRONG WOMEN

1. Zilphia Horton, speech recorded at Montana Farmers' Union School, February 16, 1956, Zilphia Horton Folk Music Collection, 1935–1956, Box 6, Tape 7, Tennessee State Library and Archives, Nashville. Unless otherwise noted, Zilphia Horton quotations in this chapter are from this recording.

2. Zilphia's sister Ermon Fay Johnson Duschenes wished to correct a Canadian Broadcasting Corporation (CBC) radio segment about the history of "We Shall Overcome." She collected her memories in a few pages of notes before composing a letter to CBC editor Karen Levine, dated March 27, 2005. Ermon Fay's husband Rolf shared with me an envelope full of notes and drafts, as well as the final letter to the CBC. These were compiled for a segment the CBC aired to correct the record on the history of the civil rights song. Unless otherwise noted in this chapter, quotations and recollections from Ermon Fay are from these records.

3. Bonnie Guy Johnson Flint, in-person interview with author, September 2012. Unless otherwise noted in this chapter, quotations and recollections from Bonnie are from this interview.

4. United States Census Bureau, 1900.

5. Shelby Flint, phone interview with author, October 2011. Shelby, Bonnie's daughter, referenced the story that was passed down in the family.

6. No record exists of the names of the two who died in infancy. Bonnie didn't know them, and census records only name the four who survived. This indicates that the others were either never named or died before their names were recorded.

7. US Census Bureau, 1910. Taken two days after Zilphia's birth, the 1910 census listed her name as "Ida" and shows Guy and Ora Johnson living in Prairie Township, Guy working as fireman for a coal mine. The 1920 census lists him living in Spadra/Clarksville, working as a miner. It wasn't until the 1930 census that he's listed as a mine operator.

8. Zilphia Horton, personal notes, Zilphia Horton Papers, Myles Horton Papers, 1851–1990, Mss. 831, Tape 1271A, Division of Library, Archives, and Museum Collections, Wisconsin Historical Society, Madison.

9. According to historians Joyce Friddle and Lawrence Connelley, in-person interview with the author, January 2018, Paris-Logan County Coal Miners Memorial and Museum, and a photograph of the United Mine Workers's local membership that hangs on the museum wall. The UMW organized a union local in Logan County in 1899.

10. Zilphia Horton, undated personal essay, Zilphia Horton Papers, Myles Horton Papers, 1851–1990, Box 15, Division of Library, Archives, and Museum Collections, Wisconsin Historical Society, Madison.

11. Charis Horton, communications with author, 2017–2018.

12. IWW information in this section is extrapolated from stories by Utah Phillips. Also that appear in Franklin Rosemont, *Joe Hill: The IWW & the Making of a Revolutionary Workingclass Counterculture* (Chicago: Charles H. Kerr Co., 2003).

13. Full lyrics printed in *The Little Red Songbook* (Oakland, CA: PM Press, 2014). *The Big Red Songbook* (Oakland, CA: PM Press, 2016) was released as a supplement, including 250 songs, commentaries, and artwork by IWW artists.

14. Letter from Zilphia to the secretary-tresurer of the IWW (according to iww.org/headquarters/oldgst, this was Walter H. Westman), July 28, 1946. She wrote, "Gentlemen: Could you give me information as to where I could get information about the life of Joe Hill? We have been singing his songs since the school began 13 years ago and although I know what he did . . . I would like to know more details about his life." Letter from Zilphia to unknown recipient, March 12, 1946. She wrote, "It never occurred to me that there had not been more written material and I certainly think it is a great loss. It makes me wish very much that I had the time and money to really search out the remaining recorded fragments of his life and do a biography." Zilphia Horton Folk Music Collection, 1935–1956, Folder 5, Tennessee State Library and Archives, Nashville.

15. Zilphia Horton, undated personal essay, Zilphia Horton Papers, Myles Horton Papers, 1851–1990, Box 15, Division of Library, Archives, and Museum Collections, Wisconsin Historical Society, Madison.

16. According to the 1930 census, the Johnson home was worth five thousand dollars, whereas a miner who lived around the corner owned a home worth twelve dollars (United States Census Bureau, 1930).

17. *Paris Express* archive, various issues, 1928, 1929.

18. Paving Jubilee program, June 25–June 30, 1928, provided by Joyce Friddle, Paris-Logan County Coal Miners Memorial and Museum.

19. Charis Horton, in-person interview with author, September 2017. Zilphia passed the ring down to her daughter, and it was stolen from Charis's apartment when she was living in New York.

20. In an October 2016 Facebook chat with the author, Shelby Flint recalled seeing Klan robes in her grandmother's closet in Paris. Charis Horton, during a phone conversation with the author in 2018, said that this was

entirely possible because Ora was "a major racist" and a master seamstress. She agreed, however, with a statement Bonnie Guy made during an in-person interview with the author in June 2012 that it was hard to imagine that Guy Johnson ever participated in the Klan.

21. Historians Joyce Friddle and Lawrence Connelley, in-person interview with the author, January 2018, Paris-Logan County Coal Miners Memorial and Museum.

22. Zilphia Horton, undated personal essay, Zilphia Horton Papers, Myles Horton Papers, 1851–1990, Box 15, Division of Library, Archives, and Museum Collections, Wisconsin Historical Society, Madison.

23. Zilphia's children and her sister all told me that she tended to embellish her stories for dramatic effect to make a point. Thorsten Horton, in-person interview with the author, June 2013; Charis Horton, communications with author, 2017–2018; and Bonnie Guy Johnson Flint, in-person interview with author, September 2012. In her undated remembrances, collected to correct a Canadian Broadcasting Corporation segment on the history of "We Shall Overcome," Ermon Fay Johnson Duschenes also noted, "Zilphia and Dad told the most exaggerated [stories]; Bonnie Guy and mother hewed to the truth."

24. Zilphia Horton, undated personal essay, Zilphia Horton Papers, Myles Horton Papers, 1851–1990, Box 15, Division of Library, Archives, and Museum Collections, Wisconsin Historical Society, Madison.

CHAPTER TWO: GROWTH AND EXPLORATION

1. Notes, undated, collected in preparation for a letter from Ermon Fay Johnson Duschenes to Karen Levin, Canadian Broadcasting Corporation, March 27, 2005. Unless otherwise noted, all Ermon Fay quotations and recollections in this chapter are from these materials.

2. *Highlander Folk School Review*, Winter Term, 1938, 23, Zilphia Horton Files, Highlander Research and Education Center Library and Archive, New Market, Tennessee.

3. Alan Walker, *Franz Liszt: The Virtuoso Years 1811–1847*, vol. 1 (Ithaca, NY: Cornell University Press, 1988). Franz Liszt achieved celebrity status in Europe and donated much of his money to services for the poor. He penned numerous essays about an artist's responsibility to society and was emphatic about the importance of lifting up those who cannot lift themselves. Zilphia would emulate his example as her career advanced.

4. Charis Horton, communications with author, 2017–2018.

5. Shelby Flint, phone interview with author, October 2011.

6. Shelby Flint, in-person interview with author, September 2012.

7. Bonnie Guy Johnson Flint, in-person interview with author, September 2012. Unless otherwise noted in this chapter, quotations and recollections from Bonnie are from this interview.

8. As her sister Bonnie noted: "I always felt like I was in her shadow, but I think everybody in the family felt that way too. . . . She was just talented, and she was probably lucky enough to know it." Bonnie Guy Johnson Flint, phone interview with author, October 2011.

9. Claude Williams interview with Sue Thrasher, April 22, 1974, Southern Oral History Program Collection #4007, file R-0584, Southern Historical Collection, Wilson Library, University of North Carolina at Chapel Hill. Unless otherwise noted, all Claude Williams quotations in this chapter are from this interview.

10. Carrie Ann Welsh, "When We Sing Together: Zilphia Horton and the 'Folk Approach' of Highlander Folk School, 1935–1956" (master's thesis, March 2016, University of Wisconsin-Madison), references Myles Horton Papers, Division of Library, Archives, and Museum Collections, Wisconsin Historical Society, Madison.

11. Claude C. Williams biographical information was extrapolated from his obituary in the *New York Times* and the abstract included with his file at the Southern Historical Collection, Wilson Library, University of North Carolina at Chapel Hill.

12. Myles, Jim, and Claude corresponded about the possibility of labor churches—something Myles's mentor Reinhold Niebuhr had established years earlier in Illinois—throughout 1934. The discussion seemed to come to a head in an August 7, 1934, letter from Claude to Myles: "Is the Religion of Jesus truly revolutionary? If so, how can the revolutionary program of Jesus become effective in the life of the world? By working in the existing denominations? How? By a complete break with the Church? Shall we establish independent labor churches?" Highlander Research and Education Center Records, 1917–2005, Box 29, Folder 31, Division of Library, Archives, and Museum Collections, Wisconsin Historical Society, Madison.

13. Lawrence Connelley, in-person interview with the author, January 2018, Paris-Logan County Coal Miners Memorial and Museum. Connelley's father attended philosophy club with Zilphia in 1933 and '34, and he echoed Bonnie's recollection of this rumor.

14. Joyce Friddle, in-person interview with the author, January 2018, Paris-Logan County Coal Miners Memorial and Museum.

15. "Claude was trying to organize the workers in Guy Johnson's mine for the Progressive Miners' Union. They had a contract with the United Mine Workers, but it was one of those sweetheart contracts, like a lot of the contracts at the time. That's when John L. Lewis was really a dictator." Myles Horton, *The Long Haul: An Autobiography* (New York: Columbia University Press, 1990), 76.

16. Joyce Friddle, in-person interview with author, January 2018, Paris-Logan County Coal Miners Memorial and Museum.

17. Letters from Claude Williams to Myles Horton and H. L. Walpole, August 1934, Highlander Research and Education Center Records, 1917–

2005, Box 29, Folder 31, Division of Library, Archives, and Museum Collections, Wisconsin Historical Society, Madison.

18. No member of Zilphia's family with whom I spoke believed that she would have led any organizing effort before meeting Myles. Though all mentioned that Claude's organizing effort angered Guy, they all also stated Zilphia wasn't involved in it. The distinct impression was that Guy was upset that Zilphia wasn't more upset about the organizing attempt, not that she actually helped with it.

CHAPTER THREE: A RIFT

1. Bonnie Guy Johnson Flint, in-person interview with author, September 2012. Unless otherwise noted in this chapter, quotations and recollections from Bonnie are from this interview.

2. Bonnie noted that some East Coast universities had a deal with Yellowstone to send students for the seasonal work, but she believed Zilphia learned about it in a magazine.

3. Notes, undated, collected in preparation for a letter from Ermon Fay Johnson Duschenes to Karen Levin, Canadian Broadcasting Corporation, March 27, 2005. Unless otherwise noted, all Ermon Fay quotations and recollections in this chapter are from these materials.

4. This is Bonnie's suggestion. She recalled riding golf carts around the park with Elsie Newell when she got a job there in the summer of 1935. Bonnie remembered exploring the park when they weren't working and noted that Zilphia had done the same.

5. Letter from Zilphia to Myles, July 23, (the year is illegible). Zilphia Horton Papers, Myles Horton Papers 1851–1990, Division of Library, Archives, and Museum Collections, Wisconsin Historical Society, Madison. The letter is from Highlander Folk School, "Saturday Morning: Mein Gott—it's hotter than the proverbial gats [sic] of Hades and we're all sweating cobblestones. . . ." She closes by saying, "Oh yes, John, Hoyle, and I are going squirrel hunting Monday morning—I shot a cigarette in the center the other day, sort of restored my self-respect." Charis and Thorsten both insisted that if their mother shot a cigarette, it would have had to be on the ground, as Zilphia would never have shot at anyone holding anything.

6. "Claude C. Williams Organized Blacks: Presbyterian Minister, 84, Worker for Unity of Races, Had Been Expelled from Churches," *New York Times*, July 7, 1979.

7. Letter from R. B. Tefferteller to Zilphia Johnson, January 23, 1935, Zilphia Horton Papers, Myles Horton Papers, 1851–1990, Box 15, Folder 13, Division of Library, Archives, and Museum Collections, Wisconsin Historical Society, Madison.

8. Letter from Howard "Buck" Kester to Zilphia Johnson, January 24, 1935, Zilphia Horton Papers, Box 15 Folder 13, Myles Horton Papers, 1851–

1990, Division of Library, Archives, and Museum Collections, Wisconsin Historical Society, Madison.

9. Timothy Egan, *The Worst Hard Time: The Untold Story of Those Who Survived the Great American Dust Bowl* (New York: Mariner Books, 2006); William G. Roy, *Reds, Whites, and Blues: Social Movements, Folk Music, and Race in the United States* (Princeton, NJ: Princeton University Press, 2110); and Glenda Gilmore, *Defying Dixie: The Radical Roots of Civil Rights 1919–1950* (New York: W. W. Norton, 2009).

10. Letter from Zilphia to Myles, undated 1935, Zilphia Horton Papers, Myles Horton Papers, 1851–1990, Box 15, Division of Library, Archives, and Museum Collections, Wisconsin Historical Society, Madison.

CHAPTER FOUR: EVERYTHING NEW

1. Emil Willimetz, *Gringo: The Making of a Rebel* (Portsmouth, NH: Peter E. Randall Publisher, 2003).

2. Highlander librarian Susan Williams, conversation with the author, September 2018.

3. Aimee Isgrig Horton, *The Highlander Folk School: A History of Its Major Programs, 1932–1961* (Philadelphia: Carlson Publishing, 1989).

4. Rosa Parks, quoted in her interview with Cynthia Stokes Brown, *Southern Exposure* (Spring 1981), 7.

5. Myles Horton and Paolo Freire, *We Make the Road by Walking: Conversations on Education and Social Change*, ed. Brenda Bell, John Gaventa, and John Peters (Philadelphia: Temple University Press, 1990), 12. Charis Horton has since tracked Paulk's Mill down, along with her friend and former Highlander board member, Sue Thrasher, and confirms it's somewhat near Savannah, Tennessee.

6. Horton, *The Long Haul*, 1.

7. Myles Horton, undated personal essay, Myles Horton Papers, 1851–1990, Box 4 Folder 3, Division of Library, Archives, and Museum Collections, Wisconsin Historical Society, Madison.

8. Horton, *The Long Haul*, 17.

9. Ibid., 1–2.

10. Ibid., 7.

11. Myles Horton, undated personal essay, Myles Horton Papers, Division of Library, Archives, and Museum Collections, Wisconsin Historical Society, Madison. It is not clear whether this quote was from notes for *The Long Haul* or his own private ruminations.

12. Horton, *The Long Haul*, 7–8.

13. Reinhold Niebuhr, *The Irony of American History* (Chicago: University of Chicago Press, 2008), 63.

14. Horton, *The Long Haul*, 35.

15. Ibid.

16. Ibid.

17. Horton, *The Highlander Folk School*, 23–25.

18. Horton, *The Long Haul*, 55.

19. Letter from Reinhold Niebuhr to potential donors, May 1932, Myles Horton Papers, Box 15, Folder 13, Division of Library, Archives, and Museum Collections, Wisconsin Historical Society, Madison.

20. Horton, *The Long Haul*, 63.

21. Thorsten Horton, in-person interview with author, 2013.

22. Horton, *The Highlander Folk School*, 35–40.

23. Ibid., 38.

24. Horton, *The Highlander Folk School*, 33.

25. "Educational Theory: Mutual Education," Highlander Research and Education Center Records, Box 1, Division of Library, Archives, and Museum Collections, Wisconsin Historical Society, Madison, referring to the first term of the Highlander Folk School, which began November 1, 1932. This is a more reliable account than another story Myles recorded about their first student in his more autobiographical writings, where he recalled it was a woman who paid for the workshop with a cart full of vegetables she had canned herself.

26. Undated student account of her experience there, Zilphia Horton Files, Highlander Research and Education Center Library and Archive, New Market, Tennessee.

27. "An Interview with Myles Horton: Radical Hillbilly—A Wisdom Teacher for Activism and Civic Engagement," June 5 and June 11, 1981, *Bill Moyers' Journal*, PBS, youtube.com/watch?v=qSwWozc-QBQ.

28. Horton, *The Highlander Folk School*, 52–53.

29. Ibid., 53. In a letter to FERA administrator Harry C. Hopkins, TVA official Harvey P. Vaughn wrote that the grant for the Cumberland Cooperative could "make fifty families, most of them now on relief, entirely self-sustaining."

CHAPTER FIVE: NEW IN TOWN

1. Itemized list of the attendees at Zilphia's workshop from Horton, *The Highlander Folk School*, 66.

2. Horton, *The Long Haul*, 76.

3. Notes, undated, collected in preparation for a letter from Ermon Fay Johnson Duschenes to Karen Levin, Canadian Broadcasting Corporation, March 27, 2005. Unless otherwise noted, all Ermon Fay quotations and recollections in this chapter are from these materials.

4. Letter from Zilphia to Myles, "Thursday eve," likely from autumn 1935, Zilphia Horton Papers, Myles Horton Papers, 1851–1990, Box 15, Division of Library, Archives, and Museum Collections, Wisconsin Historical

Society, Madison. Note that many of the Hortons' personal letters do not indicate a year.

5. Myles Horton, "Family," undated essay, Myles Horton Papers, 1851–1990, Box 1, Division of Library, Archives, and Museum Collections, Wisconsin Historical Society, Madison.

6. Letter from Zilphia to Myles, "Monday eve," 1935, Zilphia Horton Papers, Myles Horton Papers, 1851–1990, Box 15, Division of Library, Archives, and Museum Collections, Wisconsin Historical Society, Madison.

7. Letter from Myles to Zilphia, January 16, 1936, Myles Horton Papers, 1851–1990, Box 3 Folder 8, Division of Library, Archives, and Museum Collections, Wisconsin Historical Society, Madison.

8. Letter from Zilphia to Myles, undated, Zilphia Horton Papers, Myles. Horton Papers, 1851–1990, Box 15, Division of Library, Archives, and Museum Collections, Wisconsin Historical Society, Madison. "This way" refers to the fact that she had been writing him daily and had not yet received a response.

9. Ibid.

10. Willimetz, *Gringo*, 423. Reverend DeJarnette also officiated Willimetz's wedding to Joanna Creighton.

11. Highlander librarian Susan Williams guesses "Hilda" was Hilda Hubert, then the librarian of Highlander, who was shot during the Soddy-Daisy strike and would have been recovering from her injuries at the time. "Dorothy" was possibly Dorothy Thompson, who had come to the school as a student and stayed on as staff in 1933 before returning to New York.

12. Several copies of this letter, cut off at the bottom before the writer's signature, exist in different archive locations. But one copy, found in the Zilphia Horton Papers within the Myles Horton Papers, 1851–1990, in the Wisconsin Historical Society, Madison, has the signature "Hilda" written in pencil at the bottom. It is unclear if this was written in later by someone on the HFS staff or by a researcher. Regardless, the letter is headed "Highlander Folk School, Monteagle, Tennessee, March 7, 1935." [Note: all ellipses in this letter are original to the letter-writer, not added by this author.]

13. Zilphia Horton Papers, Myles Horton Papers, 1851–1990, Box 15, Folder 12, Division of Library, Archives, and Museum Collections, Wisconsin Historical Society, Madison.

14. Horton, *The Long Haul*, 76.

15. Bonnie Guy Johnson Flint, in-person interview with the author, September 2012.

16. Letter from Rupert Hampton to Jim Dombrowski, April 2, 1935, Highlander Research and Education Center Records, 1917–2005, Box 10, Folder 25, Division of Library, Archives, and Museum Collections, Wisconsin Historical Society, Madison.

17. Letter from redacted author to J. Edgar Hoover, April 25, 1936, FBI

File, Highlander Folk School File, Section 1 of 11 Sections, 61–7511. Obtained through the Freedom of Information Act, vault.fbi.gov.

18. Letter from Rupert Hampton to Jim Dombrowski, April 2, 1935. Highlander Research and Education Center Records, 1917–2005, Box 10, Folder 25, Division of Library, Archives, and Museum Collections, Wisconsin Historical Society, Madison.

19. From undated notes in Zilphia Horton Files, Highlander Research and Education Center Library and Archive, New Market, Tennessee.

20. Myles Horton, "An Experiment," undated essay, Myles Horton Papers, 1851–1990, Box 1, Folder 4, Division of Library, Archives, and Museum Collections, Wisconsin Historical Society, Madison.

21. They each wrote fondly about the walk from their cabin to the workshop center. Letters collected in the Zilphia Horton Papers, Myles Horton Papers, 1851–1990, Division of Library, Archives, and Museum Collections, Wisconsin Historical Society, Madison.

22. Zilphia Horton Files, Highlander Research and Education Center Library and Archive, New Market, Tennessee.

23. Joie Willimetz, phone interview with author, October 2011.

24. Charis Wilson and Wendy Madar, *Through Another Lens: My Years with Edward Weston* (New York: North Point Press, 1998), 264.

25. Collected at Highlander Research and Education Center Library and Archive in file boxes labeled "Monteagle," referring to the life of the school from 1932–1959.

26. Aleine Austin interview with Sue Thrasher, August 19, 1982, 50th Anniversary Files, Highlander Research and Education Center Library and Archive, New Market, Tennessee.

27. Lyrics transcribed from Almanac Singers, *Talking Union and Other Union Songs* (Folkway Records, 1941).

28. Ralph Tefferteller, June 1979, SF audio cassette 10854, Guy and Candie Carawan Collection #200008, Southern Folklore Collection, Wilson Library, University of North Carolina at Chapel Hill. Francis James Child collected around three hundred English and Scottish ballads, which are frequently referenced as a foundation of modern English, Scottish, and American folk music.

29. Horton, *The Highlander Folk School*, 196–197.

30. Wilbur Cross, then a professor at the University of the South in nearby Sewanee, Tennessee, as quoted in John Glen, *Highlander: No Ordinary School, 1932–1962* (Lexington: University Press of Kentucky, 1988), 198.

CHAPTER SIX: CLASS AND PRIVILEGE

1. In the late 1950s and 1960s, Highlander's work in the civil rights movement would draw more and more college students and organizers with advanced degrees to its workshops.

2. Letter from redacted author to J. Edgar Hoover, April 25, 1936, FBI file, Highlander Folk School File, Section 1 of 11 sections, 1. Obtained through the Freedom of Information Act, vault.fbi.gov.

3. Zilphia Horton, undated personal essay, Zilphia Horton Papers, Myles Horton Papers, 1851–1990, Box 15 Folder 22, Division of Library, Archives, and Museum Collections, Wisconsin Historical Society, Madison.

4. Charis Horton, communications with author, 2017–2018.

5. Zilphia Horton, personal essay, Zilphia Horton Papers, Myles Horton Papers, 1851–1990, Box 16 Folder 3, Division of Library, Archives, and Museum Collections, Wisconsin Historical Society, Madison. The essay, titled "Montreal to New York," is undated, though she mentions that her son Thorsten was about eighteen months old at the time, which would place this essay in late summer 1944.

6. Willimetz, *Gringo*, 418.

7. Letter from Myles to Zilphia, Myles Horton Papers, 1851–1990, Box 3, Folder 8, Division of Library, Archives, and Museum Collections, Wisconsin Historical Society, Madison. The letter is dated "Sunday Jan 16" and though no year is attached, it is likely from 1936 while Zilphia was still in New York. Their letters during that period frequently reflected on how they might navigate their new roles as husband and wife as well as how Zilphia might adapt to her new life at Highlander.

8. Letter from Zilphia to Myles, dated "Wednesday Morning," Zilphia Horton Papers, Myles Horton Papers, 1851–1990, Box 15, Division of Library, Archives, and Museum Collections, Wisconsin Historical Society, Madison. According to Charis Horton, Dillard was a staff member at the time, though his last name is unknown. The Stars were neighbors of Highlander.

9. Letter from Zilphia to Myles, undated, Zilphia Horton Papers, Myles Horton Papers, 1851–1990, Box 15, Division of Library, Archives, and Museum Collections, Wisconsin Historical Society, Madison.

10. Charis Horton, in-person interview with author, September 2017.

11. Letter from Zilphia to Myles, dated "Wednesday night just before going to bed," Zilphia Horton Papers, Myles Horton Papers, 1851–1990, Box 15, Division of Library, Archives, and Museum Collections, Wisconsin Historical Society, Madison.

12. Charis Horton, communications with author, 2017–2018.

13. Charis Horton, in-person interview with the author, September 2017.

14. Letter from Zilphia to Myles, dated "Monday evening" likely sometime in mid-1936 after she returned from New York, Zilphia Horton Papers, Myles Horton Papers, 1851–1990, Box 15, Division of Library, Archives, and Museum Collections, Wisconsin Historical Society, Madison. According to Charis Horton, communication with author, February 2020, Dillard was a staff member and Juny Marlowe was a neighbor of the school. Neither Charis nor Highlander archivist Susan Williams was able to find Dillard's last name.

CHAPTER SEVEN: NEW YORK CITY

1. Letter from Zilphia to Myles, November 3, 1935, Zilphia Horton Folk Music Collection, 1935–1956, Box 1, Folder 16, Tennessee State Library and Archive, Nashville.

2. Letter from Zilphia to Myles, undated, Zilphia Horton Papers, Myles Horton Papers, 1851–1990, Box 15, Division of Library, Archives, and Museum Collections, Wisconsin Historical Society, Madison.

3. Glen, *Highlander*, 29.

4. Letter from Zilphia to Myles, November 4, 1935, Zilphia Horton Papers, Division of Library, Archives, and Museum Collections, Wisconsin Historical Society, Madison. Written from Sis Cunningham and Dorothy (possibly Thompson)'s apartment, #46B, 3120 Broadway, New York, NY. Zilphia here is referring to Bell Holloway's "attitude" of economic supremacy.

5. Ibid. During a phone conversation in 2017, I asked Charis if there was a chance Zilphia was woefully unhappy at the Service League, and she doubted it. Zilphia was always over the moon for anything having to do with New York, and Charis believed these remarks were in line with her mother's particular brand of sarcasm.

6. Letter from Zilphia to Myles, undated, Zilphia Horton Papers, Myles Horton Papers, 1851–1990, Box 15, Division of Library, Archives, and Museum Collections, Wisconsin Historical Society, Madison. Though this letter was undated, it matches up with a response from Myles dated January 21, presumably 1936 while Zilphia was still living in New York.

7. Letter from Zilphia to Myles, dated "Sunday evening," Zilphia Horton Papers, Myles Horton Papers, 1851–1990, Box 15, Division of Library, Archives, and Museum Collections, Wisconsin Historical Society Archives, Madison.

8. This was confirmed by both of her children, who also frequently benefited from the benevolence Zilphia's presence brought out in people. She taught her children to smile and express gratitude, so as not to make people feel embarrassed for being willing to give something of value away. She knew being on the receiving end was a privilege in itself.

9. Letter from Myles to Zilphia, dated "Saturday," Myles Horton Papers, 1851–1990, Box 3 Folder 8, Division of Library, Archives, and Museum Collections, Wisconsin Historical Society, Madison.

10. Class listing enclosed with a letter from Zilphia to Myles, November 6, 1935, Zilphia Horton Papers, Myles Horton Papers, 1851–1990, Box 15, Division of Library, Archives, and Museum Collections, Wisconsin Historical Society, Madison.

11. Possibly painter Morris Moi Solotaroff, who designed many sets in the radical Yiddish theater world of New York in the 1930s.

12. Letter from Zilphia to Myles, November 11, 1935, Zilphia Horton

Papers, Myles Horton Papers, 1851–1990, Box 15, Division of Library, Archives, and Museum Collections, Wisconsin Historical Society, Madison.

13. Letter from Zilphia to Myles, dated "Wednesday nite," Zilphia Horton Papers, Myles Horton Papers, 1851–1990, Box 15, Division of Library, Archives, and Museum Collections, Wisconsin Historical Society, Madison.

14. Letter from Zilphia to Myles, dated "Tuesday," Zilphia Horton Papers, Myles Horton Papers, 1851–1990, Box 15, Division of Library, Archives, and Museum Collections, Wisconsin Historical Society, Madison.

15. Letter from Zilphia to Myles, dated "Sunday eve," Zilphia Horton Papers, Myles Horton Papers, 1851–1990, Box 15, Division of Library, Archives, and Museum Collections, Wisconsin Historical Society, Madison.

16. Letter from Zilphia to Myles, dated "Saturday eve," Zilphia Horton Papers, Myles Horton Papers, 1851–1990, Box 15, Division of Library, Archives, and Museum Collections, Wisconsin Historical Society, Madison.

17. Ibid.

18. Shelby Flint, communications with author, 2011–2012.

19. Highlander Folk School newsletter, June 10, 1936, Zilphia Horton, Folk Music Collection, 1935–1956, Tennessee State Library and Archives, Nashville. The newsletter also notes that the Highlander Players, directed by Zilphia Horton, were enthusiastically received by audiences in Knoxville, Norris, and Atlanta.

20. Ralph Tefferteller, interview with Candie Carawan, June 1979, Guy and Candie Carawan Collection #20008, Southern Folklife Collection, Wilson Library, University of North Carolina at Chapel Hill.

21. Charis Horton, communications with author, 2017–2018. She noted that she learned of Myles and Zilla's relationship around the time of Myles's funeral and was surprised to hear it had occurred so early in Myles and Zilphia's marriage. This speaks to the openness of the marriage, especially while Myles or Zilphia were away from home.

22. Letter from Myles to Zilphia, January 19 (presumably 1936 while Zilphia was still in New York). Zilphia Horton Papers, Myles Horton Papers, 1851–1990, Box 15, Division of Library, Archives, and Museum Collections, Wisconsin Historical Society, Madison.

23. Letters from Zilphia to Myles, dated "Saturday morning," undated, "Thursday eve," respectively, during Zilphia's time in New York, 1935–1936, Zilphia Horton Papers, Myles Horton Papers, 1851–1990, Box 15, Division of Library, Archives, and Museum Collections, Wisconsin Historical Society, Madison.

24. Lanie Melamud, interview with Sue Thrasher, March 6, 1981, Lanie Melamud file, 50th Anniversary Files, Highlander Research and Education Center Library and Archives, New Market, Tennessee. Lanie said something to this effect, suggesting Zilphia wasn't entirely satisfied in her marriage.

25. Letter from Myles to Zilphia, dated "Monday morning," Myles Hor-

ton Papers, 1851–1990, Box 3, Division of Library, Archives, and Museum Collections, Wisconsin Historical Society, Madison.

26. Letter from Zilphia to Myles, undated, Zilphia Horton Papers, Myles Horton Papers, 1851–1990, Box 15, Division of Library, Archives, and Museum Collections, Wisconsin Historical Society, Madison.

27. Charis Horton, in-person interview with the author, September 2017.

28. Ralph Tefferteller, quoted in Candie Carawan, "Zilphia Horton: A Profile," Guy and Candie Carawan Collection #20008, Southern Folklife Collection, Wilson Library, University of North Carolina at Chapel Hill.

29. Letter from Lois Timmins to Guy and Candie Carawan, Guy and Candie Carawan Collection #20008, Southern Folklife Collection, Wilson Library, University of North Carolina at Chapel Hill.

30. Letter from Zilphia to Myles, undated, presumably from the end of 1935. Zilphia Horton Papers, Myles Horton Papers, 1851–1990, Box 15, Division of Library, Archives, and Museum Collections, Wisconsin Historical Society, Madison.

31. Letter from Zilphia to Myles, undated, Zilphia Horton Papers, Myles Horton Papers, 1851–1990, Division of Library, Archives, and Museum Collections, Wisconsin Historical Society, Madison.

CHAPTER EIGHT: DIGGING ROOTS

1. Ralph Tefferteller interview with Candie Carawan, June 1979, Guy and Candie Carawan Collection #20008, Southern Folklife Collection, Wilson Library, University of North Carolina at Chapel Hill.

2. Glen, *Highlander*, 36.

3. Zilphia Horton, notes, undated, Zilphia Horton Folk Music Collection, 1935–1956, Box 5, Tennessee State Library and Archives, Nashville.

4. Mary Lawrence Elkus, quoted in Candie Carawan, "Zilphia Horton: A Profile," Guy and Candie Carawan Collection #20008, Southern Folklife Collection, Wilson Library, University of North Carolina at Chapel Hill. Mary Lawrence Elkus was on the Highlander staff along with her husband Bill in the 1930s.

5. Zilphia Horton, speech recorded at Montana Farmers' Union School, recorded February 16, 1956, Zilphia Horton Folk Music Collection, 1935–1956, Tennessee State Library and Archives, Nashville.

6. Notes, undated, collected in preparation for a letter from Ermon Fay Johnson Duschenes to Karen Levin, Canadian Broadcasting Corporation, March 27, 2005.

7. Letter from Myles to Jim Dombroski, September 20, 1938, Myles Horton Papers, 1851–1990, Box 6, Division of Library, Archives, and Museum Collections, Wisconsin Historical Society, Madison. Myles wrote: "Zilphia and I spent two or three days with Roy and Neva Lawrence during the

ITU convention. Zilphia was commissioned to put out a song book for the TWOC and I lined up a number of good speakers for winter term."

8. Frank T. Adams, *James A. Dombrowski: An American Heretic, 1897–1983* (Knoxville: University of Tennessee Press, 1992), 117.

9. In letters, she prodded him to accept the partnership. In one undated letter, she backed up her encouragement with some from a mutual friend: "Charlie suggests just the thing that we were discussing . . . [that] you should offer in definite words, the HFS as CIO headquarters." Zilphia Horton Papers, Myles Horton Papers, 1851–1990, Box 15, Division of Library, Archives, and Museum Collections, Wisconsin Historical Society Archives, Madison.

10. Zilphia Horton, songbook work plan, undated, Zilphia Horton Papers, Myles Horton Papers, 1851–1990, Boxes 16 and 18, Wisconsin Historical Society, Madison. Though her work plan is not dated, it seems to have been attached to a letter she wrote to sociologist and civil rights activist Dr. Arthur Raper, Secretary for the Commission on Interracial Cooperation, Atlanta, GA, on October 4, 1939. She asked for his opinion about her plan: "Having never made a study of any kind, my mind is a-whirl as to how the course of study and work should be made out. I should appreciate it very much if you could give me some advice."

11. Annabel Morris Buchanan Papers, Southern Historical Collection, #04020, Louis Round Wilson Special Collections Library, University of North Carolina at Chapel Hill.

12. Bess Lomax Hawes, *Sing It Pretty: A Memoir* (Urbana: University of Illinois Press, 2008), 17.

13. Letter from Lee Hays to Myles Horton, 1981, Zilphia Horton Folk Music Collection, 1935–1956, Box 1, Tennessee State Library and Archive, Nashville. Hays wrote from Croton on Hudson, NY, with memories to share for the HFS fiftieth anniversary.

14. Joe Klein, *Woody Guthrie: A Life* (New York: Delta Books, 1999), 200.

15. Kim Ruehl, "The Melody Lingers," *Sound* (October 2008).

16. Letter from Woody to Zilphia, November 1939, Zilphia Horton Papers, Myles Horton Papers, 1851–1990, Box 15, Division of Library, Archives, and Museum Collections, Wisconsin Historical Society, Madison.

17. Klein, *Woody Guthrie*, 167.

18. Zilphia Horton, "Song Notes," Zilphia Horton Folk Music Collection 1935–1956, IV-D-5, Box 5.3, Tennessee State Library and Archives, Nashville, TN.

19. Ibid.

20. Ibid.

21. *Labor Advocate*, Nashville TN, October 20, 1938, Zilphia Horton Folk Music Collection, 1935–1956, Box 1, Tennessee State Library and Archives, Nashville, TN.

22. Letters to and from songwriters around the country are housed in the Zilphia Horton Folk Music Collection, 1935–1956, Box 1, Tennessee State Library and Archive, Nashville, TN.

23. Zilphia Horton, ed., *Labor Songs*, Zilphia Horton Folk Music Collection 1935–1956, Box 3, Tennessee State Library and Archive, Nashville.

24. Letter from Zilphia to Myles, undated, Zilphia Horton Papers, Myles Horton Papers, 1851–1990, Box 15, Division of Library, Archives, and Museum Collections, Wisconsin Historical Society, Madison.

CHAPTER NINE: CONFLICT AND WAR

1. Willimetz, *Gringo*, 227.

2. Willimetz, *Gringo*, 228.

3. Ibid.

4. Zilphia Horton, song-leading instructions, Zilphia Horton Folk Music Collection, 1935–1956, IV-D-2, Box 5.4, Tennessee State Library and Archives, Nashville. Another guide, found in Box 5, Folder 4, notes that song leaders must have "A selfless interest in the music" and "Should look the entire audience in the eye, if this is not done, some will feel ignored."

5. Willimetz, *Gringo*, 432.

6. *Highlander Fling*, 1941, Zilphia Horton Files, Highlander Research and Education Center Library and Archives, New Market, Tennessee.

7. "An Interview with Myles Horton: Radical Hillbilly—A Wisdom Teacher for Activism and Civic Engagement," June 5 and June 11, 1981, *Bill Moyers' Journal*, PBS, youtube.com/watch?v=qSwWozc-QBQ. Myles recalled the debut of "Bourgeois Blues" as being during a fundraiser in New York City, but other sources—including an article in *New Horizons in Adult Education*—have pegged this episode to the DC benefit. Vicki K. Carter, "The Singing Heart of Highlander School," *New Horizons in Adult Education* 8, no. 2 (Spring 1994): 4–24.

8. Huddie Ledbetter, quoted by Myles Horton, "An Interview with Myles Horton: Radical Hillbilly—A Wisdom Teacher for Activism and Civic Engagement," June 5 and June 11, 1981, *Bill Moyers' Journal*, PBS, youtube.com/watch?v=qSwWozc-QBQ.

9. Horton, *The Highlander Folk School*, 197.

10. Horton, *The Long Haul*, 17.

11. Horton, *The Highlander Folk School*, 197.

12. *Highlander Fling*, 1941, Zilphia Horton Papers, Highlander Research and Education Center, New Market, Tennessee.

13. Letter from Sawyer Mason to Eleanor Roosevelt, January 13, 1942, Highlander Research and Education Center Records, 1917–2005, Box 24, Division of Library, Archives, and Museum Collections, Wisconsin Historical Society, Madison. In the letter, Mason laid out the history of the Crusaders' propaganda campaign against Highlander.

14. Letter from Eleanor Roosevelt to Jim Dombroski, February 17, 1941, Highlander Research and Education Center Records, 1917–2005, Box 10, Division of Library, Archives, and Museum Collections, Wisconsin Historical Society, Madison.

15. Letter from Eleanor Roosevelt to Jim Dombrowski, February 1, 1941, Highlander Research and Education Center Records, 1917–2005, Box 10, Division of Library, Archives, and Museum Collections, Wisconsin Historical Society, Madison.

16. Ermon Fay Johnson Duschenes, quoted in Candie Carawan, "Zilphia Horton: A Profile," Guy and Candie Carawan Collection #20008, Southern Folklife Collection, Wilson Library, University of North Carolina at Chapel Hill.

17. Letter from J. Edgar Hoover to redacted recipient, July 8, 1940, FBI file, Highlander Folk School, Section 1, 17. Obtained through the Freedom of Information Act.

18. Letter from Sawyer Mason to Eleanor Roosevelt, January 13, 1942, Highlander Research and Education Center Records, 1917–2005, Box 24, Division of Library, Archives, and Museum Collections, Wisconsin Historical Society, Madison. In the letter, Mason noted, "Lynch offered the president of a union local in the county to pay his expenses and additional money if he would attend the school as a student and make reports to the F.B.I."

19. Letter from Myles Horton to Zilphia Horton, February 1942, Myles Horton Papers, 1851–1990, Box 3, Folder 8, Division of Library, Archives, and Museum Collections, Wisconsin Historical Society, Madison. Here, Myles explains to Zilphia that he's followed the advice of a friend to let the process play out. "He said the process should be hurried by our offering to make all information available."

20. Letter from Sawyer Mason to Eleanor Roosevelt, January 13, 1942, Highlander Research and Education Center Records, 1917–2005, Box 24 Division of Library, Archives, and Museum Collections, Wisconsin Historical Society, Madison.

21. Ibid.

22. Letter from Myles to Zilphia, February 1942, Zilphia Horton Papers, Myles Horton Papers, 1851–1990, Box 15, Division of Library, Archives, and Museum Collections, Wisconsin Historical Society, Madison.

23. Wilson and Madar, *Through Another Lens*, 264. Unless otherwise noted, all Charis Wilson quotations are from this source.

24. Walt Whitman and Edward Weston, *Edward Weston: Leaves of Grass* (London: Paddington Press, 1941, reissued 1976).

25. Ibid.

26. Charis Horton, communications with the author, 2017–2018.

27. Letter from Myles to Zilphia, March 1943, Myles Horton Papers, 1851–1990, Box 3, Division of Library, Archives, and Museum Collections, Wisconsin Historical Society, Madison.

272 NOTES TO PAGES 133–140

28. Ermon Fay Johnson Duschenes, interview with Candie Carawan, Guy and Candie Carawan Collection #20008, Southern Folklife Collection, Wilson Library, University of North Carolina at Chapel Hill.

29. Ermon Fay Johnson Duschenes, remarks from Myles Horton memorial at Highlander Research and Education Center, May 6, 1990, Guy and Candie Carawan Collection #20008, University of North Carolina at Chapel Hill.

CHAPTER TEN: NO MORE MOURNING

1. Aleine Austin interview with Sue Thrasher, August 19, 1982, 50th Anniversary Files, Highlander Research and Education Center Library and Archive, New Market, Tennessee. Unless otherwise noted in this chapter, quotations from and biographical information about Austin are from this interview.

2. Ibid. Austin said, "There wasn't a real program for us, and Myles in his usual way, you know, left it up to people to find, ask their questions and then follow it. So that's what I did. I did the newspaper." In "Fifty Years with Highlander," *Southern Changes: The Journal of the Southern Regional Council*, 4, no. 6 (1982): 4–9, Sue Thrasher notes that the paper was started by another Antioch student, Elaine Van Brink.

3. Zilphia Horton, "Song Notes," Zilphia Horton Folk Music Collection, 1935–1956, Box 5, Tennessee State Library and Archives, Nashville.

4. "No More Mourning After While" lyrics by John Handcox. Zilphia Horton and Bill Lane, recorded at the Highlander Folk School, Highlander Research and Education Center Audiovisual Materials, 1937–2008, disc 19 of 23, Southern Folklife Collection, Wilson Library, University of North Carolina, Chapel Hill. youtube.com/watch?v=TcUxPooNdmU.

5. Ibid.

6. Letter from Zilphia to Myles, dated "Saturday morning," 1942, Zilphia Horton Papers, Division of Library, Archives, and Museum Collections, Wisconsin Historical Society, Madison.

7. Wilson and Madar, *Through Another Lens*, 266.

8. Charis Horton, communications with author, 2017–2018. Charis recalled hearing about her mother visiting the doctor frequently and her father checking on Zilphia's health. She wasn't sure if her mother had real health problems, if it was just a period where she was seeking a doctor's advice about her unusually painful/heavy periods, or whether there were fertility issues. She felt it was plausibly a combination of some of the above. Anne Romasco also volunteered about Zilphia's painful periods.

9. Letter from Zilphia to Myles, December 15, 1936, Zilphia Horton Papers, Myles Horton Papers, 1851–1990, Box 15, Division of Library, Archives, and Museum Collections, Wisconsin Historical Society, Madison.

10. Myles Horton, "Family," undated essay, Myles Horton Papers, 1851–

1990, Box 1, Division of Library, Archives, and Museum Collections, Wisconsin Historical Society, Madison.

11. Sharon E. Kirmeyer, PhD and Brady Hamilton, PhD, Data Brief No. 68, Centers for Disease Control and Prevention, National Center for Health Statistics, August 2011.

12. Letters from Zilphia to Myles, undated, Zilphia Horton Papers, Myles Horton Papers, 1851–1990, Box 15, Division of Library, Archives, and Museum Collections, Wisconsin Historical Society, Madison.

13. Letter from Myles to Zilphia, undated, Myles Horton Papers 1851–1990, Box 3, Division of Library, Archives, and Museum Collections, Wisconsin Historical Society, Madison.

14. Letter from Zilphia to Myles, undated, Zilphia Horton Papers, Myles Horton Papers, 1851–1990, Box 15, Division of Library, Archives, and Museum Collections, Wisconsin Historical Society, Madison. Zilphia told Myles that his "very pregnant wife" was going out to shop for a washer/dryer, and the baby would have to at least wait until that was installed. She probably drove herself to Chattanooga for the shopping spree.

15. Letter from Eve Z. Milton to John M. Glen, June 24, 1987, in which Milton rebutted Glen's portrayal of Zilphia in an early manuscript of his book, *Highlander: No Ordinary School, 1932–1962*. In closing, Milton writes, "[Zilphia] was very beautiful. I will never stop missing her." Considering Glen's portrayal of Zilphia in the final book, he seems to have taken Milton's letter to heart. This letter was copied to Ermon Fay, Myles Horton, Thorsten Horton, Charis Horton, Aleine Austin, C. W. Male, and May Justus. It was sent to me along with a packet of Ermon Fay's other materials after her death, courtesy of her husband, Rolf Duschenes.

16. Some sources claim he was named for the economist Thorstein Veblen, but Thorsten reports that his father always told him he had heard the surname in Denmark and had saved it for his own child.

17. Letter from Myles to Zilphia, undated, Myles Horton Papers, 1851–1990, Box 3, Division of Library, Archives, and Museum Collections, Wisconsin Historical Society, Madison.

18. Emil Willimetz, Images 56252 and 56311, Zilphia Horton Papers, Myles Horton Papers 1851–1990, Division of Library, Archives, and Museum Collections, Wisconsin Historical Society, Madison.

19. Willimetz, *Gringo*, 429–430.

20. Wilson and Madar, *Through Another Lens*, 266.

21. Myles Horton, "Family," undated essay, Myles Horton Papers, 1851–1990, Box 1, Division of Library, Archives, and Museum Collections, Wisconsin Historical Society, Madison.

22. Letter from Zilphia to Myles, undated, Zilphia Horton Papers, Myles Horton Papers, 1851–1990, Box 15, Division of Library, Archives, and Museum Collections, Wisconsin Historical Society, Madison.

23. Myles Horton, undated essay (possibly unpublished), Myles Horton

Papers, 1851–1990, Box 1, Division of Library, Archives, and Museum Collections, Wisconsin Historical Society, Madison.

CHAPTER ELEVEN: WE WILL OVERCOME

1. Lillie Marsh Doster interview with Otha Jennifer Dixon, June 25, 2008, U-0386, Southern Oral History Program Interview Database, Center for the Study of the American South, University of North Carolina-Chapel Hill. Unless otherwise noted, Lillie Marsh Doster quotes in this chapter are from this interview.

2. "Charleston's Cigar Factory Strike 1945–1946," Lowcountry Digital History Initiative (LDHI) Library, College of Charleston, ldhi.library.cofc .edu/exhibits/show/cigar_factory/world_war_11_and_labor_activis.

3. "Black Women Raise Their Voices in the Tobacco Industry," *The American Postal Worker*, February 28, 2014, apwu.org/news/black-women -raise-their-voices-tobacco-industry.

4. "'We Shall Overcome' Civil Rights Anthem Rose to Prominence in Charleston Strike," *Charleston Post and Courier*, September 21, 2003.

5. "Tobacco Workers Local to Seek Wage Increase," *News and Courier*, Charleston, South Carolina, October 21, 1945. "Uniform working conditions" referred to the fact that Southern workers for American Tobacco, especially black women, were not treated the same as workers doing the same job in the company's Northern factories. It was a thinly veiled reference to the goal of a desegregated factory floor.

6. "1,000 Tobacco Plant Workers on Strike: Union Says Refusal to Negotiate Is Reason; Walkouts Reported in Two Other Cities," *Charleston Evening Post*, October 22, 1945. Per this article, walkouts also occurred at the American Tobacco factories in Trenton, New Jersey, and Philadelphia, Pennsylvania.

7. Pete Seeger interview with Tim Robbins, Pacifica Radio Archives # PZ0673.403, part 1, July 2006, youtube.com/watch?v=N-FmQEFFFko.

8. *Charleston Evening Post*, October 22, 1945.

9. "'We Shall Overcome' Civil Rights Anthem Rose to Prominence in Charleston Strike," *Charleston Post and Courier*, September 21, 2003.

10. Mark Curnutte, "Songwriter Finally Gets Her Due for Penning 'We Shall Overcome,'" *USA Today*, February 5, 2018.

11. "Tobacco Union and Company Come to Terms: Cigar Plant Workers Accept Increase of 8 Cents an Hour," *Charleston Post and Courier*, March 31, 1946.

12. "We Shall Overcome," undated pamphlet, Highlander Research and Education Center Library and Archive, New Market, Tennessee.

13. "'We Shall Overcome': Civil Rights Anthem Rose to Prominence in Charleston Strike," *Charleston Post and Courier*, September 21, 2003; Aleine Austin interview with Sue Thrasher, Aleine Austin Folder, 50th An-

niversary Files, Highlander Research and Education Center Library and Archive, New Market, Tennessee; Stuart Stotts, *We Shall Overcome: A Song That Changed the World* (New York: Clarion Books/Houghton Mifflin Harcourt, 2010).

14. Aleine Austin interview with Sue Thrasher, August 19, 1982, 50th Anniversary Files, Highlander Research and Education Center Library and Archive, New Market, Tennessee.

15. Notes, undated, collected in preparation for a letter from Ermon Fay Johnson Duschenes to Karen Levin, Canadian Broadcasting Corporation, March 27, 2005.

16. Zilphia Horton, speech recorded at Montana Farmers' Union School, February 16, 1956, Zilphia Horton Folk Music Collection, 1935–1956, Box 6, Tape 7, Tennessee State Library and Archives, Nashville.

17. *People's Songs*, Bulletin No. 3, September 1948, Zilphia Horton Folk Music Collection, Box 5, Tennessee State Library and Archives, Nashville.

18. Notes, undated, collected in preparation for a letter from Ermon Fay Johnson Duschenes to Karen Levin, Canadian Broadcasting Corporation, March 27, 2005.

19. Candie Carawan in-person conversation with author, May 2012.

20. Pete Seeger interview with Tim Robbins, Pacifica Radio Archives # PZ0673.403, part 1, July 2006, youtube.com/watch?v=N-FmQEFFFko.

21. Martin Luther King Jr., "The Other America" speech, March 14, 1968, Grosse Pointe South High School, Grosse Pointe, MI.

22. Lyndon Baines Johnson, speech, March 15, 1965, joint session of Congress, Washington, DC.

CHAPTER TWELVE: GETTING OUT OF TOWN

1. Charis Horton, communications with author, 2017–2018.

2. Adams, *James A. Dombrowski*, 60.

3. Itinerary, Zilphia Horton Papers, Myles Horton Papers, 1851–1990, Box 15, Division of Library, Archives, and Museum Collections, Wisconsin Historical Society, Madison.

4. She had become a member of the YWCA National Sub-Committee on Music in 1940. Carter, "The Singing Heart of Highlander School," 7.

5. Zilphia Horton, "Let's Fly Across to Yucatan" and "The Indians in Yucatan," *Summerfield News*, spring 1948, Zilphia Horton Papers, Myles Horton Papers, 1851–1990, Box 15, Division of Library, Archives, and Museum Collections, Wisconsin Historical Society, Madison.

6. Letter from Zilphia to ML (probably Mary Lawrence Elkus), August 2, 1948, Zilphia Horton Papers, Myles Horton Papers 1851–1990, Box 15, Division of Library, Archives, and Museum Collections, Wisconsin Historical Society, Madison.

7. Letter from Zilphia to her sisters and parents, April 28, 1949, Zilphia

Horton Papers, Myles Horton Papers, 1851–1990, Box 15, Division of Library, Archives, and Museum Collections, Wisconsin Historical Society, Madison. Unless otherwise noted in this chapter, quotations from Zilphia about this trip are taken from this letter.

CHAPTER THIRTEEN: CHANGING DIRECTION

1. Charis Horton, communications with author, 2017–2018.
2. The 1941 march, demanding the desegregation of the armed forces and increased labor opportunities for Black folks, was called off after Roosevelt issued an executive order that prohibited discrimination on the basis of race within the defense industry.
3. Horton, *The Long Haul*, 97–98.
4. Willimetz, *Gringo*, 391–410.
5. Joie Creighton, Wellesley alumni newsletter, undated, Guy and Candie Carawan Collection #20008, Southern Folklife Collection, Wilson Library, University of North Carolina-Chapel Hill. Creighton had graduated from Wellesley in 1947.
6. Letters from Joie Creighton Willimetz to family members, quoted selectively in Willimetz, *Gringo*.
7. Joie Creighton, Wellesley alumni newsletter, undated, Guy and Candie Carawan Collection #20008, Southern Folklife Collection, Wilson Library, University of North Carolina-Chapel Hill. The term "from the branch" probably refers to a branch of Dry Creek, which flows just to the north and west of the old Highlander property in Monteagle. A short walk past the end of what is now Marlowe Lane would lead to a branch off the creek, which itself branches off the Tennessee River.
8. Peacefully coexist, for the most part. In summer 2019, someone set Highlander's office building on fire and painted a symbol on the ground of its parking lot that has been traced to white supremacist organizations.
9. Charis, Thorsten, and others at Highlander remembered these visitors as being sent from the State Department. The only print mention of international visitors that I could find is in Horton, *The Long Haul*, 98–99. Myles attributed the diplomats' visits to the United Nations. Both sources seem plausible, considering the Hortons' relationship with the Roosevelts. It's possible some visitors were sent from the State Department and others from the United Nations.
10. Thorsten Horton, in-person interview with author, June 2013. Unless otherwise noted, Thorsten Horton quotations in this chapter are from this interview.
11. Joie Willimetz, phone interview with author, October 2011. According to Joie, the recipe is: "Roll out a dish crust and shell. Saute two pounds of sliced onions plus ½ pound of chopped bacon. Four ounces of butter is in

the recipe except I always use less. . . . Then you cool that mix and beat in four egg whites. Beat the egg whites and fold it in plus four ounces of cream. Sprinkle cumin in the mix and whole cumin on top. Cook 425 degrees for 15 minutes and then 375 degrees for 35 minutes."

12. Letter from Zilphia to Myles, October 21, 1946, Zilphia Horton Papers, Myles Horton Papers, 1851–1990, Box 15, Division of Library, Archives, and Museum Collections, Wisconsin Historical Society, Madison.

13. Notes, undated, collected in preparation for a letter from Ermon Fay Johnson Duschenes to Karen Levin, Canadian Broadcasting Corporation, March 27, 2005.

14. Glenda Gilmore, *Defying Dixie: The Radical Roots of Civil Rights, 1919–1950* (New York: W. W. Norton & Company, 2008), 1–9.

15. Ibid., 48–49.

16. A. Philip Randolph quoted in ibid., 52.

17. Mary Ann Glendon, *A World Made New: Eleanor Roosevelt and the Universal Declaration of Human Rights* (New York: Random House, 2001).

CHAPTER FOURTEEN: TRAUMA

1. Charis Horton, communications with author, 2017–2018. She isn't entirely certain which trip her parents were returning from when they discovered she had polio, but she is certain she was four. Her age and the dates of the Florida trip are the most likely correlation for this part of the timeline. Unless otherwise noted in this chapter, quotations and recollections from Charis are from these communications.

2. Centers for Disease Control and Prevention, "Global Health: What Is Polio?" September 19, 2012, cdc.gov/polio/about/.

3. Thorsten Horton, in-person interview with author, 2013. Unless otherwise noted in this chapter, quotations and recollections from Thorsten are from this interview.

4. Letter from Zilphia to Ora Johnson, Bonnie Guy, Elsie Newell, and Ermon Fay, undated, Zilphia Horton Papers, Myles Horton Papers 1851–1990, Box 15, Division of Library, Archives, and Museum Collections, Wisconsin Historical Society, Madison.

5. National Weather Service/NOAA/Calendar of Significant Weather Events in Middle Tennessee, weather.gov/ohx/calendar.

6. Letter from Zilphia to Myles, February 29, 1952, Zilphia Horton Papers, Myles Horton Papers, 1851–1990, Box 15, Division of Library, Archives, and Museum Collections, Wisconsin Historical Society, Madison. Zilphia continued to be concerned about the children a few weeks after the storm. She told Myles, "In general, the children have been fine. . . . Karis is still frightened at night. Last night she came into my bed saying, 'I'm afraid a tornado is coming and can't sleep.' The diesel was making a roaring noise."

CHAPTER FIFTEEN: LUNGING TOWARD CIVIL RIGHTS

1. Horton, *The Long Haul*, 96. Though the school continued to work with local unions and participate with labor organizing well into the 1950s, "Highlander had to break with the CIO in 1949. We had been their official education center for the South at the time they decided to kick out all the so-called left-wing unions in the late 1940s and early 1950s. Highlander was opposed to this attempt to prohibit Communists from holding union office."

2. Horton, *The Highlander Folk School*, 79.

3. In a recording of a February 16, 1956, speech Zilphia gave to farmers, she teaches them a Palestinian farming song as a method of understanding that the concerns of farmers are the same all over the world. Zilphia Horton Folk Music Collection, 1935–1956, Box 6, Tape 7, Tennessee State Library and Archives, Nashville.

4. Pete Seeger interview with Tim Robbins, Pacifica Radio Archives # PZ0673.403, part 1, July 2006, youtube.com/watch?v=N-FmQEFFFko.

5. Horton, *The Highlander Folk School*, 198.

6. Ibid.

7. Anna D. Kelly interview with Edmond L. Drago, August 20, 1984, Lowcountry Digital Library, AMN 500.001.014, Avery Normal Institute Oral History Project, Avery Research Center at the College of Charleston, lcdl.library.cofc.edu/lcdl/catalog/lcdl:23394. Unless otherwise noted, Anna D. Kelly quotations and recollections in this chapter are from this interview.

8. "Sundown town" refers to the convention in the South, especially during Jim Crow years, when it was illegal or unconventional for Black folks to be in the town after sundown. Sometimes this was enforced by police, sometimes by Klansmen, sometimes simply by the creation of oppressive fear. Highlander resisted it openly, despite the fact that the entirety of Grundy County was populated exclusively by white people.

9. From her personal, undated notes about leading singing at Camp Laquemac in Montreal, Zilphia Horton Papers, Division of Library, Archives, and Museum Collections, Wisconsin Historical Society, Madison.

10. Septima Clark, *Ready from Within: A First Person Narrative* (Lawrenceville, NJ: Africa World Press, 1990), 30.

11. Ibid., 42.

12. Ibid., 41.

CHAPTER SIXTEEN: CHICAGO

1. Charis Horton, communications with the author, 2017–2018. Unless otherwise noted in this chapter, quotations and recollections from Charis are from these communications.

2. Thorsten Horton in-person interview with author, June 2013. Unless

otherwise noted in this chapter, quotations and recollections from Thorsten are from this interview.

3. Betty Goldiamond, phone interview with author, June 2012. Unless otherwise noted, all Betty Goldiamond quotations and recollections in this chapter are from this interview.

4. These references to Schindler and Goldberg were an important part of Charis and Thorsten's memories. Their mother paid attention to architecture and knew the names of architects, admired Chicago's Frank Lloyd Wright homes, and pointed these things out to her children.

5. Scott Bates, who was the director of the HFS board in the 1960s, told me that he heard Myles talk about Zilphia only once, after a few cocktails, when he mused that he wished he had treated her better and appreciated her more.

CHAPTER SEVENTEEN: CONTEMPT AND JOHNS ISLAND

1. Glen, *Highlander*, 175.

2. Frank Adams, *Unearthing Seeds of Fire: The Idea of Highlander* (Arcadia, WI: Blair, 1975), 194. Adams wrote, "As could be expected, Horton clashed with the government during the McCarthy era, specifically with Senator James Eastland of Mississippi. Just as Joseph McCarthy saw a Red behind every government door, Eastland, in Horton's view, saw a Red behind every black."

3. Myles Horton, "Family," undated essay, Myles Horton Papers, 1851–1990, Box 1, Division of Library, Archives, and Museum Collections, Wisconsin Historical Society, Madison.

4. "An Interview with Myles Horton: Radical Hillbilly—A Wisdom Teacher for Activism and Civic Engagement," June 5 and June 11, 1981, *Bill Moyers' Journal*, PBS, youtube.com/watch?v=qSwWozc-QBQ.

5. Adams, *Unearthing Seeds of Fire*, 198–199.

6. Hearings before Subcommittee on Internal Security of the Senate Judiciary Committee, New Orleans, Louisiana, March 18, 1954 ("Statement of Myles Horton, Highlander Folk School, Monteagle Tenn," 3–4), Myles Horton Papers, 1851–1990, Box 3, Division of Library, Archives, and Museum Collections, Wisconsin Historical Society, Madison.

7. Adams, *Unearthing Seeds of Fire*, 198–199.

8. Ibid., 199.

9. Myles Horton, "Family," undated essay, Myles Horton Papers, 1851–1990, Box 1, Division of Library, Archives, and Museum Collections, Wisconsin Historical Society, Madison.

10. "Zilphia Horton's participation in Camp Laquemac August 13–23 1954" report, and accompanying program from the Laquemac Festival, Zilphia Horton Folk Music Collection, 1935–1956, Tennessee State Library and Archives, Nashville.

11. *Brown v. Board of Education of Topeka*, Implementation Decree, May 31, 1955, Records of the Supreme Court of the United States, Record Group 267, National Archives.

12. John Glen also refers to Zilphia's visit, albeit in passing in *Highlander*, 190: "Impressed by Jenkins's initiative and by Zilphia Horton's report of her visit to Johns Island in November 1954, HFS staff members made a series of trips during 1954 and 1955 to explore the possibility of starting a leadership training program on the island."

13. Glen, *Highlander*, 188–189.

14. HFS records, quoted in Horton, *The Highlander Folk School*, 218: "'Zilphia Horton represented the staff and was invited to the Jenkins home where she got acquainted with the family and neighbors. Sang at church and school.' From the point of view of island neighbors and others who saw the white woman or even heard about her visit, the process of moving away from isolation had begun."

15. Ibid. "December 1954, a leadership conference for local political, school and church leaders on Johns Island and other parts of Charleston County, South Carolina; February 1955, a conference with Charleston County community leaders; March 1955, a so-called 'Charleston County Conference on Leadership Training' and by May 1955, individual and group conferences with community leaders and an 'all day community meeting on Johns Island.'"

16. Candie Carawan, phone interview with author, August 2018.

17. Various sources disagree on the exact year the Gullah arrived in the sea islands of South Carolina, but Wilbur Ross, in his ethnographic study of Gullah culture, notes, "The Gullah people are the descendants of African ethnic groups who arrived in America as early as the late 17th century and were forced to work on plantations in South Carolina and later Georgia." Wilbur Cross, *Gullah Culture in America* (Arcadia, WI: Blair, 2012), 18.

18. Clark, *Ready from Within*, 42–43: "It took about nine hours to travel the fifteen miles from Charleston to Johns Island. You had to ride a gasoline launch through miles of creeks and swamps that were drained and filled by the tides. So the people had been very isolated for a long time."

19. Unless otherwise noted, Gullah culture notes extrapolated from 2012 and August 2018 interviews with Candie Carawan and from Wilber Cross, *Gullah Culture in America*.

20. "Esau Jenkins Gathering with Kids," Esau Jenkins Papers, 1963–2003, Low Country Digital Library, Avery Research Center, College of Charleston.

21. Esau Jenkins, "Ain't You Got a Right to the Tree of Life," Esau Jenkins Papers, 1963–2003, Low Country Digital Library, Avery Research Center, College of Charleston.

22. Charis Horton in-person interview with author, September 2018.

23. Horton, *The Long Haul*, 101.

CHAPTER EIGHTEEN: SUSTAINABILITY

1. Zilphia Horton, "ZH at Camp Laquemac," undated journal entry, Zilphia Horton Papers, Myles Horton Papers, 1851–1990, Box 15, Division of Library, Archives, and Museum Collections, Wisconsin Historical Society, Madison.

CHAPTER NINETEEN: ROSA PARKS AND THE END OF THE LINE

1. Rosa Parks biographical information extrapolated from Jeanne Theoharis, *The Rebellious Life of Mrs. Rosa Parks* (Boston: Beacon Press, 2013), 35–91.

2. Ibid., 18.

3. Notes from Advisory and Executive Meeting, Highlander Folk School, March 3–4, 1956, Highlander Research and Education Center Records, 1917–2005, Wisconsin Historical Society, Madison. Answering Myles Horton's question as to whether she had been asked to move before, Parks responded, "Well, I hadn't in quite a long while. It had happened in the past I did obey somewhat reluctantly the times that I had to move back. I think a person in the back, a colored woman, gave me a seat."

4. Theoharis, *The Rebellious Life*, 39.

5. Rosa Parks, *My Story* (New York: Puffin Books, 1999), 124.

6. Horton, *The Long Haul*, 149.

7. Clark, *Ready from Within*, 33–34.

8. Theoharis, *The Rebellious Life of Mrs. Rosa Parks*, 37: "Parks tried to get her husband to go to Highlander with her, but he refused. According to Brinkley, Raymond was 'irate' about Rosa going because he considered the school suspect. This may have stemmed from his work with Communists and former Communists on the Scottsboro case."

9. David J. Garrow, "The Origins of the Montgomery Bus Boycott," *Journal of the Southern Regional Council* (1985): 24.

10. Notes from Advisory and Executive Meeting, Highlander Folk School, March 3–4, 1956, Highlander Research and Education Center Records, 1917–2005, Wisconsin Historical Society, Madison.

11. Letter from Rosa Parks to Anne Lockwood, December 23, 1955, Highlander Folk School File, Division of Library, Archives, and Museum Collections, Wisconsin Historical Society, Madison.

CHAPTER TWENTY: A SUDDEN, SHOCKING ACCIDENT

1. Zilphia Horton speech recorded at Montana Farmers' Union School, February 16, 1956, Zilphia Horton Folk Music Collection, 1935–1956, Tennessee State Library and Archives, Nashville.

2. Thorsten Horton, in-person interview with the author, June 2013. Un-

less otherwise noted in this chapter, quotations and recollections from Thorsten are from this interview.

3. In September 2019, the High Point was still open and serving high-end cuisine in Monteagle. A Facebook page and website (highpointrestaurant. net) attest to its history and Capone's ownership.

4. Charis Horton communications with author, 2017–2018. Unless otherwise noted in this chapter, quotations and recollections from Charis are from these communications.

5. Charis and Anne both remembered this trip to the Opry with great clarity, as though they had discussed it and shared memories about it several times throughout their lives.

6. Anne Lockwood Romasco, interviews and correspondence with author, 2012–2015. Also, Lawrence MacDonald, "The Remarkable Life of Anne Lockwood Romasco, 1933–2017," *Medium*, medium.com/@LMacDonaldDC /the-remarkable-life-of-anne-lockwood-romasco-1933-2017-53ea2f1f006d.

7. Anne Lockwood Romasco indicated that there was a man who had Zilphia's emotions astir during this time, and Charis had a guess as to who it was but didn't remember his name. She recalled a man who had worked on the house after the tornado, whom all the women liked and who perhaps had a relationship with Zilphia—or wanted one. Thorsten, meanwhile, cautioned against the gossipy nature of this narrative, as it doesn't really matter whether she was thinking about a crush she had or not.

8. This account of what happened when Zilphia drank the carbon tetrachloride was provided by Anne Lockwood Romasco, the only other person present at the time, during an in-person interview at her home, July 2012. Lockwood Romasco spoke of the end of her friend's life with much raw emotion, regret, and sadness still sixty years later.

9. National Kidney Foundation, kidney.org/about/history.

10. Myles Horton, personal essay, undated, Myles Horton Papers, Box 1, Division of Library, Archives, and Museum Collections, Wisconsin Historical Society, Madison.

11. Willimetz, *Gringo*, 432.

12. Myles Horton, personal essay, undated, Myles Horton Papers, Box 1, Division of Library, Archives, and Museum Collections, Wisconsin Historical Society, Madison. Charis and Thorsten dispute Myles's memory of this. "Myles didn't stay with Elsie Pearl that night," Thorsten said and Charis added, "Myles told Thorsten about Zilphia's death when he came down to Murfreesboro the next day." Thorsten Horton and Charis Horton, phone interviews with the author, October 2018.

13. Myles Horton, personal essay, undated, Myles Horton Papers, Box 1, Division of Library, Archives, and Museum Collections, Wisconsin Historical Society, Madison.

14. Thorsten Horton and Butchie Grant, eds., "Highlander News," April 15, 1956, courtesy of Thorsten Horton's personal collection.

15. Letter from Zilphia to Myles, undated, Zilphia Horton Papers, Myles Horton Papers, 1851–1990, Box 15, Division of Library, Archives, and Museum Collections, Wisconsin Historical Society, Madison.

16. Aleine Austin interview with Sue Thrasher, August 19, 1982, 50th Anniversary Files, Highlander Research and Education Center Library and Archive, New Market, Tennessee.

17. Letters of mourning collected in the Zilphia Horton Folk Music Collection, 1935–1956, Tennessee State Library and Archives, Nashville.

18. *Highlander Reports*, July 1956, Highlander Research and Education Center Library and Archive, New Market, Tennessee.

19. Letter from John Thompson to Myles Horton, Zilphia Horton Papers, Myles Horton Papers, 1851–1990, Box 15, Division of Library, Archives, and Museum Collections, Wisconsin Historical Society, Madison.

20. Program from Zilphia Horton memorial service, Zilphia Horton Files, Highlander Research and Education Center, New Market, Tennessee.

EPILOGUE

1. Ermon Fay Johnson Duschenes quoted in Candie Carawan, "Zilphia Horton: A Profile," Guy and Candie Carawan Collection #20008, Wilson Special Collections Library, University of North Carolina at Chapel Hill.

2. Shelby Flint, phone interview with author, October 2012.

3. Pete Seeger, quoted in Willimetz, *Gringo*, 436.

4. Notes from Lanie Melamud interview with Candie Carawan, undated, Guy and Candie Carawan Collection #20008, Southern Folklife Collection, Wilson Library, University of North Carolina, Chapel Hill.

5. "An Interview with Myles Horton: Radical Hillbilly—A Wisdom Teacher for Activism and Civic Engagement," June 5 and June 11, 1981, *Bill Moyers' Journal*, PBS, youtube.com/watch?v=qSwWozc-QBQ.

Adams, Frank. *Unearthing Seeds of Fire: The Idea of Highlander.* Arcadia, WI: Blair, 1975.

Adams, Frank T. *James A. Dombrowski: An American Heretic, 1897–1983.* Knoxville: University of Tennessee Press, 1992.

The Big Red Songbook. Oakland, CA: PM Press, 2016.

Clark, Septima. *Ready from Within: A First Person Narrative.* Lawrenceville, NJ: Africa World Press, 1990.

Cross, Wilbur. *Gullah Culture in America.* Arcadia, WI: Blair, 2012.

Egan, Timothy. *The Worst Hard Time: The Untold Story of Those Who Survived the Great American Dust Bowl.* New York: Mariner Books, 2006.

Gilmore, Glenda. *Defying Dixie: The Radical Roots of Civil Rights, 1919–1950.* New York: W. W. Norton & Company, 2008.

Glen, John. *Highlander: No Ordinary School, 1932–1962.* Lexington: University Press of Kentucky, 1988.

Glendon, Mary Ann. *A World Made New: Eleanor Roosevelt and the Universal Declaration of Human Rights.* New York: Random House, 2001.

Hawes, Bess Lomax. *Sing It Pretty: A Memoir.* Urbana: University of Illinois Press, 2008.

Horton, Aimee Isgrig. *The Highlander Folk School: A History of Its Major Programs, 1932–1961.* Philadelphia: Carlson Publishing, 1989.

Horton, Myles. *The Long Haul: An Autobiography.* New York: Columbia University Press, 1990.

Horton, Myles, and Paolo Freire. *We Make the Road by Walking: Conversations on Education and Social Change,* ed. Brenda Bell, John Gaventa, and John Peters. Philadelphia: Temple University Press, 1990.

Klein, Joe. *Woody Guthrie: A Life.* New York: Delta Books, 1999.

The Little Red Songbook. Oakland, CA: PM Press, 2014.

Niebuhr, Reinhold. *The Irony of American History.* Chicago: University of Chicago Press, 2008.

Rosemont, Franklin. *Joe Hill: The IWW & the Making of a Revolutionary Workingclass Counterculture.* Chicago: Charles H. Kerr Co., 2003.

Roy, William G. *Reds, Whites, and Blues: Social Movements, Folk Music, and Race in the United States.* Princeton, NJ: Princeton University Press, 2010.

Stotts, Stuart. *We Shall Overcome: A Song That Changed the World.* New York: Clarion Books/Houghton Mifflin Harcourt, 2010.

Theoharis, Jeanne. *The Rebellious Life of Mrs. Rosa Parks.* Boston: Beacon Press, 2014, 35–91.

Walker, Alan. *Franz Liszt: The Virtuoso Years 1811–1847*, vol. 1. Ithaca, NY: Cornell University Press, 1988.

Whitman, Walt, and Edward Weston, *Edward Weston: Leaves of Grass*. London: Paddington Press, 1941, reissued 1976.

Willimetz, Emil. *Gringo: The Making of a Rebel*. Portsmouth, NH: Peter E. Randall Publisher, 2003.

Wilson, Charis, and Wendy Madar. *Through Another Lens: My Years with Edward Weston*. New York: North Point Press, 1998.